T0331079

Dramatic Storytelling and Narrative Design

This book provides an industry professional's first-hand perspective on narrative design's practical usage, day-to-day roles and responsibilities, and keys to breaking in and succeeding. The book delves into the foundations of compelling storytelling through structural analysis and character archetype breakdowns.

The understanding of game narrative is widened to include examples from other media. The author breaks down the structure of popular games and shows how the structural elements are applied in practice. In addition to discussing industry trends, the author illustrates how the leveraging of transmedia can make a video game franchise endure over time. This updated new edition contains brand new chapters on *Conflict* and *The Future of Interactive Storytelling*, as well as deepened coverage on *Character and World* and *Roles and Responsibilities*. The author adds new discussion to the *Analysis of Narrative in Contemporary Games* through an examination of the HBO television adaption of *The Last of Us*.

This book will be of great interest to all those interested in the craft of storytelling, narrative design, and game writing.

Dramatic Storytelling and Narrative Design

A Writer's Guide to Video Games and Transmedia

2nd Edition

Ross Berger

CRC Press
Taylor & Francis Group
Boca Raton London New York

CRC Press is an imprint of the
Taylor & Francis Group, an **informa** business

Second edition published 2025
by CRC Press
2385 NW Executive Center Drive, Suite 320, Boca Raton FL 33431

and by CRC Press
4 Park Square, Milton Park, Abingdon, Oxon, OX14 4RN

CRC Press is an imprint of Taylor & Francis Group, LLC

© 2025 Ross Berger

First edition published by CRC Press 2019

ISBN: 9781032571621 (hbk)
ISBN: 9781032571614 (pbk)
ISBN: 9781003438113 (ebk)

DOI: 10.1201/9781003438113

Typeset in Minion
by Newgen Publishing UK

To Liat

Contents

Preface

SINCE THE FIRST EDITION of this book came out in the fall of 2019, so much has happened in the world and, consequently, in my work. I never expected to enter academia and teach the craft of game writing and narrative design. But the doors opened to me on separate occasions – some temporary, some ongoing – starting in the fall of 2021. Since then, I've imparted wisdom from this book to future generations of game writers at ArtCenter College of Design, Rensselaer Polytechnic Institute, and the University of Southern California's School of Cinematic Arts. These are some of the best schools in the world for game development, and I am honored and humbled to have been part of their prestigious faculties as an adjunct.

In the classroom, I surprised myself in knowing more about the subject than I expected, particularly when it came to character and conflict. As a result, I added a new chapter entitled, simply, "Conflict" and greatly amplified the one on "Character and World." I find that these elements of story deserve their own books and classes, so I did my best to distill the insight of these subjects into their most critical parts. Chapter 13 – now entitled "The Future of Interactive Storytelling" – goes into greater detail in this edition than it did in the first one (formerly Chapter 12), as I tackle disruptive technologies that have changed not just the media landscape but people's perception and expectations of story. The chapter comprises vastly more content than before and virtually embodies a new focus.

The *Last of Us* video game reignited its fanbase seven years after its launch with a 2020 sequel and then with a 2022 remake of the original. The IP, however, expanded beyond its fandom roots to widespread acclaim with the launch of a mini-series adaptation on HBO in January 2023. I have spoken about the mini-series during several lectures and speaking engagements and failed to contain my excitement each time. I therefore felt a need to add a section about it at the end of Chapter 10. In it, I discuss the mini-series' secret to success and how it differed from the source material. I still hold that The *Last of Us* is one of, if not the best, video game story, and feel equally as strong about Season 1 of the mini-series as one of the best of its format. It proves to me that great stories can transcend its original medium and can thrive in any incarnation.

In this edition, I also needed to address newly disruptive forces to game narrative, including artificial intelligence (AI), TikTok, and cozy gaming. I write about them in Chapters 7 ("Structure") and 13 ("The Future of Interactive Storytelling"). Their impact on not only game narrative but also the media industry as a whole is considerable and will likely trigger new ways in which stories will be told, in content and through process.

Other chapters have received updates, tweaks, redefinitions, modest deletions, and immodest additions, but the majority of the book remains intact and just as relevant today as it did in 2019. I made new allies when writing this edition. A big thank you to Will Bateman, Cat Sze, Maurice Suckling (once again!), Ben Chang, Joshua Garberg, Shamayita Dey, Mitch Reed, Noah Jampol, Christophe Gomez, Danny Bilson, David Isaacs, and A.J. Feuerman.

And, of course, to my students at ArtCenter, RPI, and USC: Not a day goes by where I am not grateful for your kind spirit and unbridled enthusiasm for video games. When in your presence, never do I forget why I do what I do. Whatever field in game development you ultimately choose, I hope my words have sparked an interest in story, either to create it or to champion it. So, when the big day comes for the launch of your first game, take pride in all the hard work it took to get there and don't forget what I told you in class ...

"Send me a free copy."

—*Ross Berger*
July 2024

Acknowledgments

HOW FAR I'VE COME from being a penniless playwright in New York. Never in my wildest dreams did I think I would leave that city to do anything else. But when you need to eat, you'll go just about anywhere to earn a living in your craft. That adventure took me to Hollywood in 2006. Under my belt, I had one co-writing television credit, another paid but unproduced (and therefore useless) TV writing credit, and a bunch of plays that no one wanted to read. Certainly not the recipe for success, but I thought with my "New York edge," I'd have the cachet to get in the door at a television production company somewhere. Alas, no one would even take a meeting with me. The best I could do were lunches with assistants to junior executives ... where I'd pick up the tab, despite my dwindling funds. Prospects were grim. Not to mention there was an impending Writers Guild of America strike the following year, so no one was hiring anyone that wasn't already in the Hollywood system ... or wasn't related to someone who was.

I had to wait till 2007 to find work as a writer. It wasn't for TV; it was for digital content for YouTube. The pay was dirt (when there was pay) and the prestige was nil. Yet, it was popular. And it was the future. So I hopped on board. The shows I worked won Webby awards and got airtime on cable news networks. Again, it was the future. Video games followed later that year. Luckily, they paid more. And they were fun. I pushed forward on all fronts, writing for whatever new, disruptive technology was changing the way stories were being told. I figured if I wasn't going to get staffed as a writer on a TV show, I wanted to be part of the emerging media technology revolution.

I've been lucky to work up and down the West Coast, creating content for new platforms as soon as (or before) they hit the marketplace – YouTube, iPhone, Xbox One, Oculus Rift, Google Daydream, and others that I can't reveal due to non-disclosure agreement (NDA). I'm therefore grateful to those who gave me a chance (and the chops) to be a part of the revolution: Richard, Michael, Eduardo, Keith, Kelly, Mesh, Miles, Greg, Ben, Eric, Dana, Robert, Tony, Rich, Jeff, Tom, Geoffrey, Jenna, David, Sean, Bay, Josh, Katie, Brandon, Brian, Jonathan, Niels, Andy, Matthew, Brittany, Marshall, Perrin, TJ, Yuri, Daniel, Ryan, and Sterling.

A special shout-out to Maurice Suckling whose work I've admired for a long time. Without his encouragement, this book would never have become a reality. Rick Adams and Jessica Vega of Taylor & Francis – thank you for your patience and your belief in the first edition of this book. You helped make a lifelong dream come true.

To my family and friends – Avram, Allison, Joely, Peyton, Rhoda, Vivek, Adam, Jeff, Barry, Damon, Yitzi, Boris, Sandy, Rhoda, Eric, Jody, Lawrence, Mark, Laura, Zachary. Thank you for reminding me that the difficult path I've chosen is worth it. And to my LA family – Leora, Oded, Yfat, Nadine, Joey, Molly, Mari, and my beloved Juka and Lacey. You were in the trenches with me, and I couldn't have made it to the end without your love and support.

Most importantly, I send my love to Liat, my motek, to whom this book is dedicated.

—*Ross Berger*
August 2019

Author Biography

Ross Berger started his writing career as a playwright in New York, where he received the Cherry Lane Mentorship Fellowship, the Dramatists Guild Playwriting Fellowship, and the Ensemble Studio Theatre's Next-Step Fellowship. In 2004, he co-wrote the Emmy-submitted Sweeps Week episode "Gov Love" for NBC's *Law & Order*.

Since 2007, his career has been part Hollywood and part Silicon Valley. Ross bridges the gap between the two by designing, writing, and producing story experiences across traditional and new media platforms. Credits include the Webby award-winning *lonelygirl15* (2007–2008), the *Obama Girl* franchise (2007–2008), and Go90's highest-rated show *The Runner* (2016). In the video game industry, Ross was the senior narrative designer for Microsoft Studios and Electronic Arts for such titles as *Quantum Break* (2016), *Sunset Overdrive* (2014), and the *NBA Live* franchise (2017–2018). Ross' first console title was *CSI: Deadly Intent* (2009), where he learned video game storytelling from the former masters of game narrative, Telltale Games. Other titles include *Shadows of the Damned* (2011) and Niantic Lab's *Peridot* (2023).

Ross has also worked extensively in AI-enabled chatbots and robots as a conversation designer and in virtual reality as a writer for Meta's Oculus Rift launch title *Farlands* (2016) and for the award-winning *Eclipse: Edge of Light* (2017).

In addition to writing the first edition of *Dramatic Storytelling & Narrative Design: A Writer's Guide to Video Games and Transmedia* (CRC Press, 2020), he is the editor/contributor of *Storytelling for New Technologies & Platforms: A Writer's Guide to Theme Parks, Virtual Reality, Board Games, Virtual Assistants, and More* (CRC Press, 2022) and is the author of several short stories including "Football with Leatherman," "Evie A.I.," and "Kleiner in the Woods."

A graduate of Brandeis (BA, Philosophy) and Columbia (MFA, Playwriting) universities, Ross has been an adjunct professor at the University of Southern California's School of Cinematic Arts (Interactive Media & Games), ArtCenter College of Design, and Rensselaer Polytechnic Institute.

Introduction

MOST, IF NOT ALL, of the game titles I mention in this book are published by mainstream publishers who have high budgets for development. Due to their financial resources, longer development cycles, and expansive gaming experiences, their games are classified as AAA titles. I omit any discussion of indie games, not because the quality of their narrative isn't up to par. Quite the contrary. Games like *Journey* (2012), *Papers, Please* (2013), and *Braid* (2008) have made considerable impacts on the video game art form and are among the best games in their respective genres. Nevertheless, the thrust of this book is to educate fledgling game writers and narrative designers on what it means to break into this field, apply their craft effectively, and assure themselves consistent employment as a result. Indie games do not have the budgets to support a dedicated writing staff. Many times, the creator of an indie game will write the game herself. Or, she will hire a writer to perform a series of short-term writing deliverables. Yes, there is more freedom to create what one wants for an indie title. And perhaps they will sharpen their writing skills along the way. While these creative environments are fun, they do not reflect the typical daily routine (or reality) of an AAA publisher or studio. Most of those companies have business interests that greatly influence the content of their portfolio of games. More microtransactions, more cooperative play, more download-able content (DLC), more live events – all of these put tremendous pressure on a dev team. The goal is simply not just to sell enough copies to make a profit; rather, the goal is to sell as many copies to become a hit, not just once, but for cycle after cycle.

Indie games don't have this concern, as there is little-to-no expectation of turning a profit. An indie game's goal is to be an exemplar of the purity of the art form and to innovate without corporate pressure or influence. One can break the boundaries by offering bold storytelling and brilliantly designed features. An indie game does not have to cast a wide net to capture maximum fans; they just need a loyal following, even if that following is small.

In many ways, an indie game is a stepping stone for a dev studio to have their next game picked up by an AAA publisher. Or, have their current iOS game get repurposed for PlayStation Network or Xbox network. Or maybe have a console version of their game hit the market à la *Journey, Minecraft* (2011) or *A Way Out* (2018). But those are rare opportunities.

If a writer wants to earn a consistent living in games, they must understand how to tell stories for AAA games. Writing for this type of game is the focus of this book.

Glossary

THE FOLLOWING IS A list of terms I will use liberally throughout this book. Please take a moment to absorb these terms and acronyms, as they will allow for an easy shorthand between author and reader. They are also industry jargon and will be useful outside of the discussion of narrative design.

TERMS

Alpha – the second-to-last stage of the development production cycle where content is being added into the game (Beta being the final, but seldom does this involve narrative contributions). It should be the time before content is locked and everyone is testing the game and making slight corrections. In reality, new content is being added and everyone's working around the clock to keep up with the new additions. This is the most grueling time for a game developer, as endless hours, painstaking testing, and heavy revisions are par for the course.[1] This is the last moment to get things right, so one slight change to make the game better could have a downstream effect on other parts of the game. Everyone is working in lockstep to field these curveballs and optimize. Alpha is a pure grind.

Anchor property – the central medium from which all other connected media originate. The anchor property is where game studios (or movie studios) put the majority of their financial resources and labor into. It is the main attraction of a franchise for a specific time frame. The transmedia extensions of that property include the media that builds to its release and then follows it to renew interest during a high sales season (like Christmas). Also known as the "tentpole" project, an anchor property is one of the biggest and most expensive products of a single company's annual portfolio of games because it either initiates a new franchise or builds upon a pre-existing one, but represents a heightened standard within it. This term was, at one time, exclusive to the film and television industry, but now applies to video games as well. A tentpole or anchor property doesn't have to be the first product of a franchise; it could be a sequel as well. It just needs to be the focal point of the transmedia extensions during select phases of a franchise's life cycle.

Conflict – the main driver of a story. Without conflict, there is no story. Conflict is, in essence, an overarching challenge that requires the protagonist to solve it in a set amount of time, or else the repercussions will be devastating. An antagonist is usually at the helm of the conflict, either by causing it or perpetuating it. Upon the antagonist's defeat, the protagonist can resolve the conflict. Example: a chemistry teacher is indentured to make crystal meth for a drug lord, who keeps the teacher's life under constant threat (*Breaking Bad*, Season 4). A Pinkerton detective must tear down a utopian society hellbent on purging the world of people who are neither white nor Christian (*BioShock Infinite*). An advertising executive must take care of his young son after his wife suddenly abandons the family (*Kramer vs. Kramer*). The last example demonstrates that not all conflicts require physical danger. A conflict is about a massive dilemma that suddenly burdens the protagonist. The conflict might be small in the grand scheme of things, but to our hero, it is profound. If no action is taken, the conflict will be paralyzing and the consequences could change them detrimentally and irrevocably. Discussed at great length in Chapter 5.

Cut scene – an animated scene within the game that either instructs a player on gameplay mechanics or serves as a dramatic moment within the story of the game. Some will be interactive, as in you can select responses to questions that characters ask you or you can move around within the environment. A cut scene is also known as a cinematic.

Dev – short for developer. This can refer to anyone on a product team who applies their craft in the creation of a video game, be they engineers, producers, project managers, writers, audio engineers, animators, level designers, visual artists, user interface/user experience (UI/UX) designers, or other digital tradespeople. However, at some studios, a "dev" refers strictly to a software engineer. In the context of this book, I will use the former definition.

FPS – first-person shooter.

Game mechanics – the building blocks of gameplay, such as how the game is played and what are its rulesets. Some mechanics include resource management, shooting, victory and fail state conditions, and player movements like crouching, jumping, parkour, and hack-and-slash.

Gameplay – a series of interactive experiences that ties a player to a game. What makes a game fun? What makes it addictive? These answers lie within the quality of the gameplay.

Golden path – the central and ideal trajectory of the game's experience.

IP – intellectual property. This refers to any story, design, invention, or interactive experience that is owned by a company or individual. IP is used freely in the video game world as legalistic shorthand for the game itself. Oftentimes, it has broader implications and can refer to a franchise, that is, a game, movie, book, or TV show that lives beyond the medium itself and has an enduring shelf life, thanks to sequels, reboots, or other media incarnations (like comics, books, or animation).

Narrative mechanism – one of many parts within the narrative arsenal used to reveal or deliver fragments of the story. These "parts" can take the form of a medium or device. Examples include a cut scene or cinematic, a collectable item, in-game dialogue, user interface (UI) text on screen, a push notification through a companion app, voice-over during a loading screen, and interactive conversations with NPCs.

NPC – non-playable character.

Plot point – a single event, action, or moment that either escalates or progresses the protagonist's journey toward the resolution of the conflict. Not to be confused with story beats, which are story moments that trigger a change in tone or character intention.

Production – the stage of game development where everything is being built. Pre-production and the sprints before production are the blueprint phase with some foundational elements being built (like the vertical slice). Production is when the vast majority of the house is being constructed, fastened, painted, polished, inspected, stress-tested, repaired, inspected again, and varnished.

Replayability – when a completed gaming experience is played more than once. More specifically, when someone has played the game once through, they will play it again, either to experience the same fun or to explore different paths that were not explored during the first go-around. (Games do not have to be completed to encourage replayability. A completed objective that encourages a player to re-experience it also qualifies.) Replayability is the goal of every game designer. From an artistic standpoint, it allows the player to experience additional gameplay opportunities. From a business standpoint, replayability increases the opportunities for microtransactions or in-game purchases to enhance a player's experience.

Story milestone – a type of plot point that is grand in scale. It assumes that the hero has accomplished something significant or has experienced a major setback. Milestones include the following: Inciting Incident, Point of No Return, Low Point, Climax, Obligatory Scene, and more.

Vertical slice – a playable level that is built during the last phase of pre-production. The vertical slice should include one of the biggest gameplay moments in the game and should have the best representative contributions from all disciplines – art, audio, level design, narrative design, programming, etc. If the vertical slice is approved by high-level executives at a publisher or studio, the game is then ready for production. If it isn't, the dev team will work to improve it for another executive review. If it fails once again, the game is at risk for being cut.

DISTINCTIONS

Context vs. Story – one of the biggest challenges for a narrative designer is distinguishing context from story for non-writers. First and foremost, context is not story. It is, instead, basic descriptions about a level, a new environment, an objective, or an accomplishment of an objective that informs the player of their progress toward a "leveling up" milestone or a specific goal. Context is crucial information that provides clarity and purpose for the player. Context, however, is not a driver of a story. How one conveys this information is often through on-screen text or even short cut scenes or live action videos.

It is, therefore, easy to confuse words on the screen or information performed by an actor for narrative. But context isn't narrative. It's news. More specifically, it's news about you, the player.

Story, on the other hand, is the overriding journey upon which the player embarks. Along the way, the player (as the game's hero) learns more about themselves, those around them, and the responsibility of the role they've just assumed. Context often has no bearing on the story; it can be easily removed. A player can figure things out themself by moving forward and piecing clues together in their new environment. Story, however, cannot be omitted. Without the character's journey, there will be nothing at stake for a player to play for.

Nonetheless, writing these context moments falls squarely on the shoulders of narrative designers and game writers, mainly because our experience with words qualifies us to do so. Make no mistake about it: people will continuously confuse context for story. Therefore, always make sure to draw the distinction clearly and quickly before the rest of the development team sets expectations and detrimentally redefines story-telling for their game.[2]

Plot vs. Structure – plot is the series of events that moves the story forward. "What happens next" is the appropriate way to understand it. Consider plot (or plot points) as the street-level view of a story; in other words, the micro details of how one event leads to another. Structure, on the other hand, is the 30,000-foot view of the story. Structure includes the major events of the story (aka story milestones) in which the plot is interspersed. Structure is the organization of events designed to strategically escalate the story. Plot is the tactical. Structure is architecture. Plot is logistics. More about this in Chapter 7.

Publisher vs. Studio – a game publisher is the entity in the gaming industry that subsidizes the development of the game, provides development support in its production, and cultivates the relationships with the console makers (e.g., Sony or Microsoft) or platform distributors (e.g., Steam, Android). The publisher will provide safe passage of the game from its completion to its distribution. The studio actually makes the game; they own the creative experience. They will work with publishers to assure that the development is running smoothly and on time. Publishers will jump in and help if there's any glitch or potential slowdown of production. Studios though are the rock stars of the dev experience. The creative vision and its implementation begin and end with them. Many publishers have their own studios, for example, Microsoft and 343 Studios (makers of *Halo*) or Sony and Naughty Dog (makers of the *Uncharted* franchise). Microsoft and Sony also have their gaming hardware (Xbox vs. PlayStation) and distribution platforms (Xbox network vs. PlayStation Network). Most publishers who own studios (like Take-Two Interactive or Electronic Arts) have neither proprietary hardware nor their own distribution platform.

Story vs. Narrative – story is the protagonist's journey, inspired by a central conflict, where a series of escalating events forces them to achieve self-discovery. That awareness of self and purpose culminates once the protagonist accomplishes an overarching goal or prevails in a final confrontation. Narrative, on the other hand, is the fictional universe that comprises a multitude of stories featuring related worlds and characters. For the sake of a single game, the narrative often refers to a single story but leaves room for more stories to be told with the protagonist or different characters if (a) the game expands beyond its medium (to cinema, comics, alternate reality games, digital series, etc.); (b) it offers game sequels, prequels, or side stories; or (c) it is vast enough to continue with in-game side quests or via downloadable content.

Theme vs. Premise – please check out Chapter 3: Roles and Responsibilities under "Reinforce the Theme."

NOTES

1 Some studios call this "Crunch Mode." Typically, this will begin sometime during production, long before Alpha. Nevertheless, the high pressure and endless hours in a race toward content lock are generally called "Crunch."
2 For a deeper analysis, please review my article, "Game Writer's Dilemma: Context vs. Story" (2018) from the *Encyclopedia of Computer Graphics and Games* (Springer).

REFERENCE

Berger, Ross. (2018, February 2). "Game Writer's Dilemma: Context vs. Story." *Encyclopedia of Computer Graphics and Games.* Springer. Springer Link. https://link.springer.com/referenceworkentry/10.1007/978-3-319-08234-9_129-1

CHAPTER 1

Orientation

COMING OUT OF OBSCURITY

Narrative design has been living in the shadows of game development for close to two decades now. In fact, the profession was defined only in 2007 at a game publisher that no longer exists, that being THQ.[1] Before, there was always narrative, but it was under the category of "Game Writing," which still exists today. (This book will later differentiate between the two.)

Even then, the writing responsibilities were seldom assigned to professional writers. Game designers took on this role with varying degrees of success. And the results didn't improve much when outsiders – namely screenwriters with neither game development experience nor interest in the medium – were engaged by publishers and studios to write the narrative. In the case of the former example, the designer failed to understand the basics of storytelling and character development. In the latter, a screenwriter's ignorance of interactivity would make their work impossible to design around and would therefore be unusable.

The concept of narrative design is still being debated among developers today. *Why are they not just game writers*, as some might argue? *And why employ their services if story is often a disruption to the gaming experience?* Again, these are two significant topics I will address later on. But for the sake of this section, the dismissiveness by the majority of game developers is a primary reason why narrative design struggles for visibility.

Its adoption by game studios – and granted, adoption at a modest scale – is promising, albeit delayed. Big publishers like Microsoft (including Xbox and Activision-Blizzard) and Electronic Arts have been known to have their own narrative design departments or embed at least one role within a development team.

But story, as with any non-core game feature, is vulnerable to the appetite of the consumer. There are windfalls and there are droughts. But mostly, there are droughts. While no one can predict what a consumer will want, defining a unique, compelling intellectual property (IP) remains crucial. And cool gameplay moments are not enough. The competition will have cool gameplay moments as well. But story – that is, on a basic level: the world, the premise, the origin of the conflict, and multidimensional characters – is a massive differentiator for a product. So, it can be upsetting when story can define an IP, but those who create it are often not prioritized (or even included) in its development. Why narrative is not considered a critical role in a studio is, I hope, a momentary lapse of judgment. It will take writers and narrative designers to graduate to creative directors and executive producers to reverse it. In the meantime, the narrative designer continues to plow ahead with complex creative challenges that make the battle for visibility worth it.

Transmedia, which I will delve into in Chapter 14, has also struggled for acceptance or even basic understanding. The struggle is less of an issue of visibility – though that remains a serious issue – but more so one of legitimacy. Traditional Hollywood studios do not understand the importance of shared worlds and continued storylines outside of their anchor properties. Why spend financial resources to continue the storyline of, say, a supporting character? Any external media will be marketing and brand promotions.

Today, however, 30-second Pizza Hut commercials do not satisfy the appetite of consumers (no pun intended). Before 2019, for every *Star Wars* movie that was about to come out, you had millions of fans prepping for its release by watching *The Clone Wars*, playing *Battlefront*, and reading *The Screaming Citadel* comic series. The world of *Star Wars* continued to grow, thanks, in some part, to these other media. Today, through Disney+, original shows like *The Mandalorian* and *Andor* substitute the film launch for seasonal episodic dramas. Because Disney+ serves as a centralized media hub for all screen content related to *Star Wars*, the transmedia experience has become contained (as in localized to one destination) and almost predictable (new content, multiple shows, every year). It's arguably not as ambitious as it once was.

To be clear: other media extensions like comics, video games, and animation series aren't intended to be marketing for big budget films. They are, in themselves, their own significant contributions to the lore of the *Star Wars* universe. They extend its mythology by adding deep, rich stories about characters we love. To deem them as marketing for the next big film is to insult the franchise. And it's this attitude that is pervasive in traditional Hollywood. Games, comics, books, animation, live experiences, amusement parks, and virtual reality exhibitions – all of these are genuine, significant drivers of story. They expand parts of the world we already know or add new information that compels us to experience the other media in order to see how different parts of the mythology tie together. Why they don't get the respect of traditional Hollywood executives is because (a) the big-ticket items traditionally are the films and (b) executives don't experience these different media like the fans do, or even at all. Executives seldom play video games or read comics. Therefore, how would they ever know how compelling stories in these media can be?

Yes, it is Hollywood elitism that has prevented transmedia from hitting the bigger stage. But this is the old guard. And the old guard is dying. The beloved *Halo* franchise was recently a television series on Paramount+. *Halo* is owned by Microsoft. *The Last of Us* was a blockbuster game for Sony back in 2013. By 2024, as a mini-series adaptation for HBO, it won 8 Emmy awards out of its 24 nominations.

These forays into the entertainment space by technology and video game companies represent a massive sea change. These companies see the significance of the changing media landscape and wish to harness it as a way to drive consumers to their most profitable platforms. There is no elitism here in terms of what the content is. Every medium, no matter the budget, is another prime opportunity to attract customers.

There is a glaring exception to the close-minded Hollywood studio. Disney's efforts behind *Star Wars* and the Marvel Cinematic Universe franchises are paving the way for a new appreciation of transmedia. The franchise planning behind *The Avengers* films is nothing short of amazing. Character cameos at the end of the credits foreshadow potential alliances in future movies; this shows Disney's commitment to creating holistic, enduring story experiences.

Disney has radically transformed the blockbuster film into a multiyear, multimedia experience. *The connective tissue that ties these parts together is at the heart of transmedia.* To dismiss its importance is to deny the massive cultural and financial impact it brings to the table.

In today's rapidly and radically changing media landscape, studios can no longer afford to keep the connective tissue in the shadows.

WHO THIS BOOK IS FOR

Over the past seven years, I have been contacted by folks from various walks of life, who are seeking a way into the games industry as a storyteller. Initially, those who sought me out were looking for a temporary refuge away from unemployment of traditional screenwriting. Then later, the majority of the people I spoke to were hardcore gamers who grew up playing games and still hit the sticks several hours a night. While they watched film and television religiously, their primary love was video games.

The disparity between the two types of people who reached out to me is primarily generational. Gen X folks grew up with shorter games, both in the arcade and at home, but still considered movies as the central entertainment medium. Kids of the '80s grew up with 8-bit to 16-bit to the early days of 32-bit games. Those who stuck around for 64-bit games were fewer in numbers. But the kids who grew up on 64-bit games, also known as the fifth generation of video game consoles, witnessed colossal advancements in game technology from 1993 to 2006.[2] CD-ROM game storage, now capable of 650 MB, was much vaster than before, and graphics now comprised 3D polygon graphics with texture mapping and 24-bit true color depth.[3] But this was only a primer for the real gaming revolution: the sixth generation of consoles, which introduced to the world the PlayStation 2 and the Xbox. Such classics like *God of War*, *Grand Theft Auto III*, *Half-Life 2*, *Metroid Prime*, and *Halo: Combat Evolved* were not only blockbuster sellers but were also highly rated games on Metacritic, the primary aggregator of all relevant game reviews in the marketplace.[4]

A new standard of gaming was introduced, and kids who grew up on these titles developed a kinship with gaming that had never been seen before. Those kids are now working professionals in their early 20s to mid-30s. Their appreciation for gaming does not come from a place of just wanting to earn money or to work temporarily in the field until a TV writing gig pops up. These people are passionate about games and want to make a meaningful, lasting, and profound impact on the industry. It's great talking with these folks. There's no hard sell nor is there a moment to justify why one prefers games over another medium. These individuals are sold even before the conversation begins.

I quickly discovered in my discussions with them that the most critical guidance I could provide centered on the realities of the job. Because, while games are fun to play, making them is a different story.

Generation X understands that challenge. Where they lack in passion, they make up for in sobering reality. They can easily detach themselves from the creative challenges ahead and deliver on corporate directives. But they too need to understand what's involved in the everyday grind before taking the plunge.

This book isn't just for one generation. It's not about age. It's about devotion to storytelling in an unconventional medium for stories. And those devotees, whether they want to write games or just understand them as a way to fine-tune their own skill set, fall under the following categories.

The Student

If you're in school studying video game development and want to pursue game narrative, then you will find that the basic requirements of storytelling delineated here are a good primer for your thesis project, internship, or first job. Or, if you're not interested in becoming a narrative designer, but are interested in all facets of game development, this book will give you a firsthand perspective of what writers need in order to succeed in the workplace. Perhaps you'll be well informed to empower your fellow scribes once you're in the trenches with them.

The Writer from Another Field

This professional writer is either looking to leave their current field of writing or trying to find a place in a related field that carries tremendous cultural impact. Many screenwriters of film and television have made successful inroads into game writing and narrative design. Some pursue it while simultaneously pursuing a lucrative television and film career. Others go into it temporarily to earn a living as they try to sell a screenplay or get staffed on a TV show. Some see games as an avenue to earn decent money while still actively keeping their options open. Typically, these kinds of writers are willing to write the content but not willing to learn how to make that content interactive. For that writer, they will quickly discover that, in games, there is no quick payday. The work is too hard, as it's governed by strict boundaries in software development. They will also face the constant demand for making alternate content for the same story beats as a way to prevent staleness in replayability.

There is no phoning it in. And there is no working in isolation. A writer's work will have to go through a strict software pipeline – from writer to implementer to engineer, or from writer to actor to sound engineer to implementer – that will prove whether or not the writing works. If not, it has to be revised until it does. Constant iteration is the name of the game, and you cannot expect the work to improve through visual spectacle or an actor's performance.

Then there are screenwriters who are genuinely interested in the medium. They want to transition into games in order to pursue their craft and avoid the vicissitudes of Hollywood. If you love storytelling and don't care about the medium just as long as you can tell a great story, then this book will help you get started in the field.

The Entertainment Executive

For nearly two decades, video game revenues have eclipsed those of film.[5] [6] [7] The monstrous demand is impossible to ignore. If you're a parent of a teenager, you can relate, maybe thanks to *Fortnite*.[8]

Blockbuster films often had video games released soon after its premiere. The games were either loose adaptations of the films or side stories of one of the characters. Seldom were these games ever any good, mainly because they were strict marketing ploys. As mentioned earlier regarding Disney, games are opportunities to continue the story of the world of the film (and *vice versa*).

A blockbuster IP can no longer afford to be expressed through one medium. Along with books, comics, board games, and amusement park attractions, games are the perfect next stop in the transmedia journey for a film or TV show. Games capture a consumer's attention for hours on end, many days a week, several weeks a month. Games are the perfect opportunity to expand the world of an anchor property and secure fan loyalty.

Executives are constantly on the hunt for the next movie blockbuster. If they wish to create a franchise – that is, a film that expands to sequels or has a life that extends to television – then they must learn to understand the impact of games and how a blockbuster film can expand the power of its franchise potential as an interactive medium.

Game Designer

For those who are already in the games industry, this book will dive into the elements of what makes a good story and an enduring IP. Game designers – those who design levels, systems, front-end experiences, or gameplay – are often the closest collaborators with narrative designers. They must figure out how to balance the narrative within their features.

Game designers will often serve as points of contact for freelance writers who are working off-site. In this context, the game designer is intimately familiar with the details of their feature that, by the time they are collaborating with the writer, the task at hand is coverage. That is, game designers will know which moments in the game require dialogue, on-screen text, or environmental elements that communicate information.

Many times, they will write the narrative themselves and not engage the services of a professional writer. If that happens (and it is something I recommend against), then this book's chapters on conflict (Chapter 5), character and world (Chapter 6), and structure (Chapter 7) will be instructive.

Also critical: the chapters devoted to what the role of a narrative designer and game writer is (Chapters 2 and 3). These should set proper role expectations before collaboration begins.

Game Producer

Understanding the narrative designer's role, as well as the scope of work, will help game producers figure out how to budget for: (a) story development time, (b) freelance resources, and (c) narrative pipeline dependencies such as audio recording, motion capture, film production of live action content, and more.

With this understanding, producers can map out the scope of work into deliverables that correspond to major development milestones. These deliverables should align with the duties of other developers to help determine when and how the narrative content can merge with other elements of the game.

Producers aren't always familiar with story development, so a deep dive into the elements of character, structure, and world building ought to provide strong baseline knowledge. Story development and resources are often on the chopping block when games get re-scoped. Gaining a full grasp of what story entails and how critical it is to the game's identity, as this book aims to do, will empower producers to make smart decisions on narrative deliverables.

Technologist in Media

Giants like Meta, Alphabet, Amazon, Apple, and Microsoft aren't only tech leaders; they're content leaders as well. Meta's Facebook and Alphabet's

YouTube, while they have their own original content initiatives, are mostly avenues for a consumer's original creative output or for user-generated content. The individual can post a live stream on Facebook Live or write a post about the most random things and gain instant audiences through their friends. YouTube is home to billions of videos filmed and/or edited by users looking to gain optimum views. Apple took the plunge into Hollywood several years ago and, as Apple TV+, has been developing award-winning original screen content (like *For All Mankind* (2019) and *Ted Lasso* (2020–2023)) for its devices. Microsoft, on the other hand, has had a longer tenure than the other entities due to the Xbox and its proprietary content like *Halo* and *Minecraft*.

Technologists today are mindful of the need for content. In many ways, narrative can highlight features of the platforms they are building. Thus, understanding what makes a great story will arm them with the tools they need to optimize their platform.

Content Designer for Artificial Intelligence

If you design voice technologies like Siri or Alexa, consumer-facing software outside of games, or even chatbots, then you'll find lots of synergies with narrative design. Chapter 9 focuses on meaningful choice and branching narrative, which are also key pillars when designing experiences that help consumers find solutions to routine problems. Whether it's checking on the weather or seeking the status of a stock trade, automated services through artificial intelligence (AI) are becoming a popular alternative to the human employee. Predicting what consumers will ask and then providing them with customized responses involve the same problem-solving skill set of a narrative designer. We are always deepening the layers of player interaction by writing, in advance, answers to the questions of the minutest detail. With every pivot of a conversation, we have already mapped out a series of responses.

Warning for Career Changers

Make sure your decision is well measured and reassessed continuously. Upon first blush, game development might seem like the perfect next step. Who can argue with growing sales, gainful employment, expanded annual reach, or increased cultural significance? Plus, it seems like fun!

Once again, playing games is vastly different from making them. The hours can be brutal and the demands can often seem ludicrous. Everything you've learned about good storytelling (or have been validated for if you're a writer from another medium) can be greatly compromised during the development of the game.

Games are software. Software is dictated by software engineers. Creative is often held hostage to the demands of code. And story – being a subset of design and creative direction – is often held hostage to the whims of gameplay. In other words, if something is fun to play, the story can be butchered or stretched to impossible lengths to accommodate the fun.

But the fun is why people buy games. So, if you want to be a story expert in this medium, *learn to be adaptive.* The key to doing so isn't just about applying your craft; it's also about having the right attitude. Be nimble, be open minded, be respectfully forceful, and most importantly, be empathetic to your consumers. Adopting their mindset will dictate the majority of your team's creative decisions. If you're not on board, you might be working on the wrong game or in the wrong field.

Finally, my advice to anyone who wants to break into games is the following: *don't go into games unless you love games.* If that isn't possible, don't go into games unless you play games. If that still is not possible, then please – for the love of God – don't go into games unless you *respect* games. If you cannot satisfy this basic minimum requirement, there's no way you'll get hired. Developers can smell the holier-than-thou attitude a mile away. No one – *I mean no one* – wants to share the foxhole with either an arrogant tourist or an indifferent zombie.

But if you're the type of person that, at bare minimum, respects games, then pull up your sleeves and get ready to do some extremely hard work. Keep the consumer in your focus. And remember: if what you're doing does not enhance their enjoyment, then you're doing something wrong.

WHAT THIS BOOK IS NOT

This book is a practical guide to narrative design as a craft and as a profession. This is not a book that is heavy on theory. Nor is it a book that provides an academic perspective of this type of storytelling. Instead, I will provide key insight into professional expectations and basic how-to's to tackle challenges in the field. The goal is to properly equip storytelling professionals with the tools they need to succeed.

But, once again, this book isn't written just for gamers or professionals already in the field. It's for *all* storytellers. In the chapters ahead, readers will find a solid balance of references between games, movies, TV shows, books, digital series, and plays.

If you're someone who just got out of school or are transitioning from a related field to games, then I hope you will find that this book provides you with an honest depiction of a growing yet challenging field. Bear in mind: challenges ought not to dissuade you from pursuing it; they should, instead, galvanize you. In the midst of your narrative design journey, you will find that those challenges will make your job infinitely more gratifying.

Writing is an intensely challenging, often thankless endeavor. Getting paid for it, on the other hand, is a privilege. By the end of this book, I hope you'll have learned how to make the most out of that privilege once it presents itself.

NOTES

1 Despain, "Narrative Design for Company of Heroes" 2007.
2 Wikipedia, "Fifth Generation of Video Game Consoles" n.d.
3 Ibid.
4 Wikipedia, "Sixth Generation of Video Game Consoles" n.d.
5 Chatfield, "Video Games Now Outperform Hollywood Movies" 2009.
6 Shieber, "Video Game Revenue Tops $43 Billion" 2019.
7 Entertainment Software Association, "U.S. Consumer Video Game Spending" 2023.
8 Shanley, "'Fortnite' Earned $2.4 Billion in 2018" 2019.

REFERENCES

Chatfield, Tom. (2009, September 27). "Videogames Now Outperform Hollywood Movies." Retrieved on February 9, 2024 from www.theguardian.com/technology/gamesblog/2009/sep/27/videogames-hollywood

Despain, Wendy. (2007, August 3). "Narrative Design for Company of Heroes: Stephen Dinehart on Writing for Games." *Game Developer.com*. Retrieved on February 9, 2024 from www.gamedeveloper.com/design/narrative-design-for-i-company-of-heroes-i-stephen-dinehart-on-writing-for-games

Entertainment Software Association. (2023, January 17). "U.S. Consumer Video Game Spending Totaled $56.6 Billion in 2022." Retrieved on February 9, 2024 from www.theesa.com/news/u-s-consumer-video-game-spending-totaled-56-6-billion-in-2022/

Shanley, Patrick. (2019, January 16). "'Fortnite' Earned $2.4 Billion in 2018." Retrieved on February 9, 2024 from www.hollywoodreporter.com/heat-vision/fortnite-earned-24-billion-2018-1176660

Shieber, Jonathan. (2019, January). "Video Game Revenue Tops $43 Billion in 2018, an 18% Jump from 2017." Retrieved on February 9, 2024 from https://techcrunch.com/2019/01/22/video-game-revenue-tops-43-billion-in-2018-an-18-jump-from-2017/

Wikipedia. "Fifth Generation of Video Game Consoles." (n.d.) Retrieved on February 15, 2024 from https://en.wikipedia.org/wiki/Fifth_generation_of_video_game_consoles

Wikipedia. "Sixth Generation of Video Game Consoles." (n.d.) Retrieved on February 15, 2024 from https://en.wikipedia.org/wiki/Sixth_generation_of_video_game_consoles

CHAPTER 2

Definitions and Distinctions

WHAT IS NARRATIVE DESIGN?

Based on the discipline's first word, you probably can gather that narrative design might have something to do with storytelling or, at the very least, writing content for a game. You're not wrong in that assumption. However, if it involved strictly writing content with no purpose other than to fill a screen, then the proper term would be "content writing." Or, if that content is strictly fiction, then the term would be "game fiction writing." (Alas, "game writing" is the currently accepted term when no design is required.) Narrative design is as much a strategic role as it is a creative one. And while the field does require the traditional duties of a fiction writer (which we will dive into in subsequent chapters), the "design" within "narrative design" calls for distinction.

Based on the various games I've worked on with different studios for different genres, I have found that narrative design can be summed up accordingly:

> *It's creating a pathway for story, to be revealed one bit at a time, once conditions have been met, within or in between gameplay moments.*

Let's unpack this:

> *It's creating a pathway for story …*

This is the "What" of the profession. Narrative designers must carve out a trajectory of the story. In this architecture phase, a narrative designer

 DOI: 10.1201/9781003438113-2

must identify the types of moments where the narrative is intertwined with gameplay; what are the various mechanisms that reveal the story (e.g., a cut scene, collectable, in-game dialogue, etc.); and what are the rulesets for those story mechanisms (i.e., how do these mechanisms work, what do they look like, what are the criteria by which they are unleashed, what part of the narrative will I be playing inside this mechanism at this given moment in the game?).

… to be revealed one bit at a time …

This is the "When." Narrative designers must rely on proper story structure and dramatic escalation as a guide to parceling out narrative moments throughout the game experience. Then, the narrative designer will assign or implement those milestones to particular gameplay moments. Escalation of the story is dictated by the escalation of the gameplay moments on the golden path.

… once conditions have been met …

"How." The narrative is not going to be unleashed willy-nilly. A player will have to (a) reach checkpoints or objective completions; (b) achieve certain rewards over time; or (c) collect items that are natural to the environment. The result of these criteria is the unlocking of a fragment of story. What makes game narrative different from passive media like film or TV is that there is an *exchange between player and games creator*: a player must accomplish a task in order to receive the next part of their journey. Narrative is like a reward in the sense that a player must actively progress within game by using their skills on the controller in order to be rewarded with the next installation of media, be it new gameplay moments, narrative, or XP (aka experience points).

…within or in between gameplay moments.

Obviously, this is the "Where." Narrative should never be a separate entity within the gaming experience. It needs to be embedded within those moments where players are hitting the sticks (i.e., buttoning on their controllers) and having fun. And players will do this for hours on end. So, the question is "how is the narrative properly distributed within those fun moments on the sticks in a way that doesn't take them away from the fun for too long?" This is a never-ending challenge, and that's why narrative design is very much a strategic role in game development.

The "Why" is the story itself. I will dive into this in great lengths later on. Lastly, the "Who" are the characters of the narrative, mainly the protagonist and non-playable characters (NPCs) through which the player experiences the story.

WRITING FOR GAMES VS. TRADITIONAL MEDIA: WHAT'S THE DIFFERENCE?

One of the hardest lessons I learned during my first console game-writing experience was surrendering control to the player. Writers play God in traditional writing efforts such as books, film, or TV. They create the world and characters, and then they thrust those characters onto a journey filled with scenarios wrought from the writer's imagination.

Games can be the complete opposite. Players set the course for their own journey, that is, within the confines of game design. They turn left when they want to; they can enter different buildings upon their leisure; they can listen to another character or not. Games are all about player agency, which requires game makers to encourage player freedom while still offering those players a stunning spectacle, intense gameplay, and incentives (like rewards or bonus points).

Many games are "on rails," meaning they give little to no choice for the player and instead offer a proscribed, sequential experience with no variation. This is also known as a *linear storytelling experience.*

But other games relish player choice and provide alternative storylines and gameplay moments based on player decisions. In turn, these create alternative story paths and varied content. So, if a player walks into Door A, she will get a unique set of scenarios and gameplay moments. But if she chooses Door B, she will get a different set of scenarios and gameplay moments (and hopefully as compelling as those in the Door A path). Not surprisingly, this is known as *non-linear storytelling* or *branching narrative.* Non-linear storytelling also refers to open world or sandbox games where players can participate in any aspect of the interactive experience at their own speed or whim. They can ignore missions or story arcs altogether or can experience them in an order that was not intended by the game designers.

Some games will "gate" or prevent a player from pursuing an alternative path or certain locations in order to direct them back to the original path. For example, a player opens Door B. It leads them to a deep, dark chasm where the player immediately falls to her death. Yes, Door B was a different choice, but it was a false choice because it did not provide a tantamount alternative to Door A and instead provided a frustrating fail state for the player. Players crave variation and freedom of exploration. And both have to be meaningful. In other words, *not* a "Door B" approach.

In a sandbox experience, a writer's biggest challenge will be enticing a player to experience narrative when they are given absolute, boundless freedom to walk around, however long they choose. Specific objectives are key to incentivizing the player to keep moving forward. Within the pursuit of these objectives, bits of narrative can be conveyed. But if the narrative is revealed through in-game dialogue from an NPC that does not force a cut scene, the player can easily evade the NPC and continue to meander. That NPC most likely had critical information that reveals more about the narrative. When a player ignores that opportunity, it is likely that the player was never a big fan of narrative to begin with. And if given the opportunity to sit back and watch a cut scene, the player would most likely skip it.

Writers and narrative designers cannot control which players will absorb the narrative. (Absorb as in "to accept or welcome," not "comprehend.") Games are about gameplay first. Narrative is often subservient to it.

That is the other fundamental difference between writing for games vs. other media: *players are not buying the product for your words.* Sure, the same thing could be said about a blockbuster movie with great special effects or a famous movie star. The difference there, however, is that the blockbuster film has a screenplay that dictates when the special effects go off and what the famous movie star says. In games, gameplay is the primary focus and everything else is built around it. Keeping the gamers' fingers moving is paramount. Games often survive without words to make that happen.

Prime Objective: Addiction

There's one thing you should know about this industry before you move forward: games are an addictive medium. Perhaps too addictive. But, in this day and age, they are not alone. Social media is also an addictive medium. "Likes," "retweets," and post replies from friends tap into our brain's reward center. Addiction to these media has spurred the establishment of Digital Detox rehabilitation centers, where people learn to manage their addiction through yoga, meditation, and mindfulness practices.

The science behind addiction focuses on a chemical in the brain known as dopamine, which is released when we react to reward-motivated stimuli such as gambling, eating, or thrill-seeking adventures. It's all about feeling pleasure, for which dopamine is responsible. And naturally, we want to feel as much pleasure in our life as possible. When we trigger dopamine's release at an excessive level, addiction sets in. It is hard to break the cycle because the desire for more dopamine increases steadily. When we eventually break it, withdrawal sets in. Negative behavior follows. We realize it is much more gratifying to pursue our addictive activities than not, so we continue where we left off with that behavior.

Games are addictive because they are designed to be addictive. Developers know what fun is and we create the mechanics to prolong that fun as much as possible. Slashing a series of beasts, punching a mixed martial arts fighter, or shooting an M50 submachine gun in 1940s Normandy gets the fingers in a near endless cycle of hitting buttons on the controller. There is tremendous validation when that enemy dies, as if to say your efforts led to something tangible. Moreover, you are a tough and worthy hero. The power of someone's life is in your hands. The more you destroy, the more rewarding it is (and the more rewarded you are). This reward-motivated behavior triggers more dopamine in your system. There is no stopping this behavior until the game ends. (And even then, one can look forward to downloadable content – aka "DLC" – and title updates.)

This is a lot to compete with for a writer or narrative designer. However, the mindset should not be how to craft narrative around addictive moments (aka gameplay), but rather *how to craft narrative that enhances these addictive moments.* As I will discuss later, the majority of consumers today want as frictionless a narrative as possible. If the story has no direct impact on the gameplay, it is often viewed as a waste of time. Therefore, the key is creating a reactive and proactive storyline that affects gameplay (proactive) and is affected by gameplay (reactive).

The term "addiction" is seldom mentioned in any meeting room at a publisher or studio. Not because we developers don't believe in it; rather, we just accept it for what it is: a by-product of fun. And the more fun our games are, the more our players will play it.

In game development, it's all about enhancing the fun for as long as you can, for as many times as you can. Balancing the narrative within those parameters is not an easy task. Again, it's about minimizing the friction.

NARRATIVE DESIGNER VS. GAME WRITER: WHAT'S THE DIFFERENCE?

This is a controversial topic for us story people. The designer title holds a lot of weight in the industry, and many studios are loath to dispense it freely. Some feel that story people are just typing words and not crafting design documents that shape gameplay. That is a very naïve perspective of what we do.

In most cases, a narrative designer is the one who writes the fictional content that goes into the game, be they scripts for cut scenes, interactive dialogue trees, and/or environmental storytelling cues. Narrative designers often assist other creative artists in development to create specificity for a game's characters and worlds. Accordingly, narrative designers will work closely with artists and audio engineers by providing extensive character and world biographies that, to granular detail, give the other artists enough information to create three-dimensional characters and vibrant worlds.

Game writers can take on these responsibilities as well, and, for some studios, these roles are interchangeable. But for most cases, the narrative designer has greater specialization. In addition to the aforementioned responsibilities, they create the story architecture, identify the vehicles that deliver story, design the rulesets for when these vehicles are triggered in game, identify and itemize the types of lines that need to be written (barks, ambient dialogue, unique NPC dialogue, and dialogue that changes based on conditions of environment), or write and curate the story bible, plan and itemize the numerous story variations influenced by player choice, lead voice-over sessions, and lead localization efforts. (Chapter 3 will dive deep into what these responsibilities and others entail.)

The narrative designer's role is strategic, whereas the game writer's role is tactical. Game writers are often hired after the architecture and the various categories of content have been cemented. They will work off a spreadsheet, designed by a narrative designer, and fill it in with the necessary content. These can be scripts for scenes, on-screen text, and in-game dialogue.

Barks

The latter is the most common task a game writer will undertake. It's a thankless, arduous effort if it requires redundant dialogue or chatter. This type of dialogue writing is known as "bark" writing. "Barks" give the game freshness to moments that seem repetitive when replayed or that take a long time to progress though. Consider, for example, the endless stream of dialogue when running through a battlefield and getting orders from a commanding officer to take cover. These dialogue variations don't move the story forward, but they add tonal authenticity to the moment.

This is often the lion's share of work for game writers and requires pure mental grinding. Typically, a game writer will be tasked to write ten different ways of saying "Hello."

- "How are you?"
- "Welcome."
- "Good to see you."
- "Hey, there you are!"
- "Well, look who's here! When did you get in?"
- "I don't believe my eyes! Is that you?"
- "SO Good To See You! How've you been?"
- "Well, I'll be a monkey's uncle. Get over here and shake my hand!"
- "Is that … no, it can't be … wow, it's been too long!"
- "Hi."
- "Hiya."

Each of those can be performed in numerous ways based on the mental or physical state of a character and can therefore count as a separate line. For example, an ironically lifeless "How are you?" will sound different from a speaker that is meeting a new corporal for the first time, after just witnessing an explosion of an enemy's jeep vs. a curmudgeonly "How are you?" from that same speaker, who is meeting that same corporal for the first time and has to tolerate yet another torrential rain in an otherwise uneventful day. It's the narrative designer's job to identify all of the possible conditions that could affect these greetings and where in the game they will be triggered. They will then assign the game writer to write lines to those conditions.

Mental fatigue sets in quite fast when writing barks. That's why the smartest strategy here is to break up the monotony by doing a set amount for one hour, then moving on to another category. Mixing it up, so to speak, definitely helps.

Narrative designers can write barks as well. But it is often the case that they will be overseeing other parts of the story development process instead.

What's in a Name?

In the past several years, titles such as "Narrative Writer" have emerged to usurp "Narrative Designer" from literary professionals. Some studios reserve "Narrative Designer" for technical designers only, those with scripting language proficiencies to integrate the narrative content in the game engine. From my experience, such roles took on titles like "Narrative Technical Designer", "Narrative Implementer", "Narrative Systems Designer", or even "Game Designer (Narrative)." For the purposes of this book, "Narrative Designer" refers to a creative professional whose primary goal is to craft the game story experience through literary prowess and content savvy, without the expectation of programming or technical design skills. As Chapter 3 will describe, literary prowess and content savvy are not buzzwords, but actual high-level categories of expertise that require a slew of complex responsibilities.

Roles and Responsibilities

WHEN A TEAM HIRES a narrative designer, they are bringing on someone who fulfills the following roles: screenwriter, UI/UX writer, producer, director, content planner, game designer, implementer, localization expert, and editor (as in words, not film). They will help programmers, artists, level designers, creative directors, marketing specialists, actors, audio directors, producers, and project managers in their roles and responsibilities. When they are not wearing their creative hats, narrative designers will determine the scope of what needs to get written, acted, and filmed.

These skills are used primarily in the following categories.

ID THE IP

When creating a new video game property, the creative team (led by the creative director) should gather all the data from competitors, determine what's missing in the marketplace, and set a vision for the game on the basis of what kind of intellectual property (IP) the team should make. Is it ripe for sequels? Is there franchise potential beyond games (like film, TV, merchandising, etc.)? What age group is it for? What demographic is it for? What's the genre? Who are the brandable characters? What are the brandable moments (that marketing can leverage to promote the game)?

Creative directors oftentimes go at this alone, but a narrative designer ideally should be there in the beginning, mainly because the questions a creative director is asking themselves are the questions that a storyteller has

DOI: 10.1201/9781003438113-3

come across before. At this stage of development, a fully fleshed out story is not the end goal. Rather, one should strive to acquire the main ingredients of a successful franchise. These ingredients include the world of the game, tone of the experience, major characters, important brandable "totems" or tools (like weapons or vehicles) of those characters, backstory of the characters and the world, and big-event moments.

The latter is key. These are selling points that a marketing department can leverage when promoting the game. Additionally, they are the north star for software engineers, artists, and designers. The larger the expanse of these moments, the more parts of these moments can be re-skinned or repurposed for other parts of the game or for future sequels. Big, dynamic gameplay moments are usually where you start because they are the most memorable and hardest to pull off.

Above all else, it is important to distill the IP into a single elevator pitch, that is, a brief but vivid description of the IP in one sentence, no more than 50 words. Consider the examples from these Sony classics (which I have altered slightly):

God of War (2018 reboot)

> His vengeance against the gods of Olympus far behind him, Kratos now lives as a man in the lands of Norse Gods and monsters. It is in this harsh, unforgiving world that he must fight to survive… and teach his son to do the same.[1]

The Last of Us (2013)

> After a pandemic causes infected humans to destroy the rest of civilization, a survivor is hired to smuggle a young teenage girl out of an oppressive military quarantine. Their brutal journey across the country forces each of them to redefine their relationship to the world and to each other.[2]

Shadow of the Colossus (2018 remastered version)

> A hero must walk among the Colossal beasts of a fantastical land in order to obtain their power. Only then will he be able to bring his loved one back to life.[3]

Succinct, accurate, vivid. The goal is to give just enough info to provide a hint of the tone, the world, and the subject matter while also providing differentiation from the competition.

It is imperative that the idea must be communicated in the simplest and briefest of terms; otherwise, the creative vision is susceptible to becoming obscured and convoluted. Game developers have a tendency to want to pack a lot into a game – not just features, but ideas as well. Successful games adopt the "less is more" dictum and let their succinct, but compelling creative pillars trickle down to every other part of the game. But if the creative cannot answer "What this game is about" in clear terms, the development will struggle.

Most importantly – and I cannot stress on this enough – the elevator pitch should not be a stale list of features. *You are creating a game, not a smartphone.* Think about character and world first before you think about modes. Allow the description to transport a potential consumer into the middle of your world. A list of features *will not* do the job.

HELP DESIGN THE GOLDEN PATH

Creative directors or lead designers often exclude a narrative designer in this process. But here's why that's a mistake: the golden path is based on a logical, ideal sequence of events that, by their very nature, are narrative in spirit. This isn't to say that a player should expect a cut scene to be triggered any time you visit a new locale.

Rather, a new locale will have an inherent logic attached to it. Why am I going to this locale right now and what am I to expect when I get there? Gameplay moments will be the main attraction to those locales, but the context to justify why they are where they are falls squarely on the shoulders of narrative designers.

Thus, the narrative designer's value in the co-design of the golden path is providing the logic, context, ideal experience, and escalating dramatic action that furthers a player's progress. The escalating dramatic action – for example, the capture of a loved one, the decimation of a base, the death of a friend or partner, the seizure of a city, etc. – will intensify the journey on the golden path and should coincide with escalating gameplay moments. If not, the game will miss out on achieving optimum entertainment value.

ESTABLISH STRUCTURE

A narrative designer will have to figure out the end-to-end journey of the protagonist within the confines of the golden path. This entails infusing coherent and compelling story beats into the journey that will need to be closely hewn to certain moments on the golden path, including big events that highlight the gameplay. These are usually visually spectacular moments that are often part of the marketing of the game. They draw in players through either trailers, game review videos, or online screenshots shared on social media.

It is the narrative designer's role to make sense out of the big event moments, even if there doesn't seem to be any on face value. However, because these moments carry so much weight, they cannot be ignored in the narrative. They must be elegantly (or, at least, coherently) justified through previously seeded story beats.

Later on, I will delve into this subject more comprehensively, as structure is the most critical part of game narrative. Brandable characters and compelling worlds are perhaps the most memorable elements, but without a sturdy foundation upon which character, action, and stakes are built, there is nothing but unharnessed noise.

ESTABLISH CHARACTERS AND WORLDS

This responsibility goes hand-in-hand with the aforementioned topic of "ID the IP." The identity of the IP can often be distilled into who are the heroes, the villains, the weapons they use, the vehicles they ride, and the environment in which they reside. I'll dive deeper into this in Chapter 6.

IDENTIFY STORY MECHANISMS AND DEVISE THEIR RULESETS

How the story is revealed is just as important as what that story is. But you will lose the attention of players with an egregious force-feeding of narrative through the traditional route (i.e., cut scenes). There are savvier ways to provide plot points and context without getting in the way of a player's "lean forward" experience. This type of entertainment requires the consumer to interact with the medium by actioning on the user interface (UI) of the product. Video games, board games, software, interactive learning modules, interactive videos, and participatory live events qualify as active, lean forward experiences.[4] "Lean back" or passive entertainment experiences, on the other hand, require nothing more of the viewer than to sit back and watch. Film, television, theater, and digital content are examples of these.[5]

I've briefly mentioned dialogue trees and collectables that happen inside the game and, later, I will discuss second-screen experiences and independent media that are triggered outside of it. Whatever a narrative designer decides to employ to tell the story, they must establish the ruleset that triggers these mechanisms.

Take, for example, a hypothetical first-person shooter. It's a war game that takes place in the near future. You, the player, are armed with a series of futuristic assault rifles to mow down enemy combatants. You're wearing a smartwatch, which indicates how much progress you're making and how far away you are from reaching your next objective. The watch also provides you with directional information of the landscape as well as messages from fellow soldiers who are watching you through satellite.

In order to reach the next objective, you need to find an abductee and bring her to a safe haven – a newly claimed hospital by your military. If you kill an innocent bystander, it's a mulligan – you can continue on and maintain your rank. If you kill two innocent bystanders, you will lose your current rank, but still be able to advance in the mission. If you die along the way, you get resurrected and can continue where you left off. If the abductee dies along the way in either of the first two scenarios, you will not be able to advance. You must replay the mission.

Let's look at the two different results here if you survive. If you provide safe passage for the abductee and have not killed any innocent civilians, you will embark upon a new mission with your current rank … or maybe higher, depending on whether there's a level up at the end of the mission. This scenario would involve customized content. At minimum, it's a change of title in how you are addressed – for example, "Thank you, Captain." vs. "Thanks, Sarge." At most, it could provide different, more exciting missions.

If you provide safe passage, but kill up to two or more innocent bystanders, you'll experience a suboptimal customized experience. At the very least, how you are addressed will change – for example, "Thank you, Private." vs. "Thanks, Sarge." And it's likely you'll be set on a course to accomplish the same missions as the ones just mentioned, but the visuals might be different, less exciting. Or you have to engage in lower-quality missions because your rank is lower.

The ruleset that allows the player to move forward is a system that requires different criteria to (a) allow or deny the player to move forward, (b) recognize their achievements (or lack thereof), and (c) unlock awards (or penalties) and a customized path for that player.

How this narrative mechanism is triggered is part software engineering and part design. It also involves different voice-over, art, and sounds to provide the customized paths going forward. A pure designer will then coordinate how these different disciplines work together and integrate the non-narrative mission progression criteria within the narrative mechanism.

Now let's take a look at the smartwatch. The information that's provided to the player is made possible by a pure narrative design system. The communication stream – that is, the text that keeps filling the screen of the watch, including plot points and information that guide the player forward – is written and designed by the narrative designer. Design, in this sense, is establishing the criteria for triggering different information within that communication stream. A good way of thinking of it is given in Table 3.1.

Table 3.1 implies a certain order through which the player experiences the narrative content. Without a strong narrative design, the text will trigger randomly and haphazardly, mainly brought on by movement of the player character in the environment. That's why the triggers are so important to identify before the writing begins. A pure designer might just infuse the scene with narrative and ignore the importance of the order and frequency of the information. It's the identification of these triggers and their activation criteria that puts the "design" in "narrative design."

A narrative system, at its most basic form, is the underlying triggering criteria for a story mechanism. It requires the skills of (1) a pure designer to establish the in-game, non-narrative criteria (e.g., achievements, unlocks, collections, progression in the environment) for the triggering; (2) a writer or narrative designer to segment which part of the story to reveal at a given time and to write the content per each segment; and (3) a software engineer

TABLE 3.1   Narrative Mechanism Ruleset – Collectable

Text on a Watch	Is Triggered When
Watch out for the swamp. Serpents will come out of nowhere and bite you.	Player comes within 12 meters of the Gregarian Swamp.
You are running out of ammo! Find the nearest recon shelter to refill.	Ammunition is at or has dipped below 15% capacity.
This must be the abandoned warehouse where the Killian files are. Look inside and see what you can find.	Player has traversed past the swamp and has approached a dilapidated building.
The Killian files will give us what we need to prepare ourselves for the impending war with the Etakians.	Player has entered the second floor of the dilapidated building.
Quick! Take out your syringe. The files have been laced with a bio-agent.	Player has opened the files. After reading the files for a beat, the player becomes exposed to a puff of dust.

to create the programming logic to actualize the triggers and content in game. Art, animation, and audio are important contributions after the system is built and ready for implementation.

Other delivery mechanisms of narrative include the following:

- Cut scenes – These are mini cinematics that are sometimes interactive, but mostly not. They can possess the same animation style of the game (known as machinima). Or, they can take on a different visual style, pre-rendered as computer-generated imagery (CGI) or live action content. These are known as full-motion video (FMV), which I will discuss later in this chapter.

- Environmental storytelling – These are visual details in the game's environment that: signal major events, the tone of the world, and status of the environment (e.g., a decimated world with abandoned buildings, flipped-over vehicles, and dead bodies sprawled all over); communicate through words on surfaces or items that reveal time period, entities in the world, player thoughts, or status of the inhabitants (e.g., a journal for the player to record evidence and clues, newspaper headlines, spray-painted walls, or cave dwellings with hieroglyphics); and leverage visual spectacle (as in something that is out of the ordinary or inherently too stunning to ignore) to induce player curiosity or exploration that could lead to landmark events of the past or current disruptions to the status quo (e.g., a spacecraft embedded into a cave, a train wreck, a volcano spewing out lava from afar). Environmental storytelling also involves sonic cues, such as gunshots, music (not score, but a diegetic performance from someone or something within the fiction of the game), or murmurs from large crowds. Like visual environmental storytelling, sonic environmental storytelling can provide personality to characters or even lure players to certain locations where one can discover fragments of the lore of the world.

- Voiced non-playable characters (NPC) dialogue – When characters communicate with the player through voice-over, there is ample opportunity to reveal information about the world, relevant characters, and conflict. NPC dialogue allows the player to traverse through the world and pick up critical narrative information without stopping the gameplay. Cut scenes do the opposite.

- Dialogue Trees – When NPC dialogue triggers different protagonist responses for the player to choose from, a dialogue box on the screen can motivate players to move the story forward based on their preferences. Dialogue choices can reflect different attitudes of the hero (as revealed through tone or topics in the options). They can also convey traces of current narrative, player backstory, or world lore. The mechanic of offering different dialogue choices is known as a dialogue tree (or conversation tree). The complexity begins if any of these choices triggers different plot points or NPC dialogue later in the game. If so, the narrative designer or game writer will take on the infuriating, but gratifying task of architecting a branching narrative (which we will discuss in Chapter 9). Many times, varied choices in a dialogue box are contained strictly to the moment in which they are offered. In this case, they affect just several exchanges within the same conversation and do not impact future story beats or subsequent NPC dialogue. These varied choices, nonetheless, provide replayability opportunities for players, especially if choosing ideal options in the dialogue box leads to unique rewards, reveals, or paths.

- Diegetic off-screen voice – Diegetic refers to anything that is in the world of the game. NPCs that talk to the player, therefore, are diegetic. But there are moments where the hero encounters or enacts an off-screen diegetic experience. A protagonist could have an inner monologue that helps them pieces clues or memories together (e.g., *What Remains of Edith Finch* (2017)). The protagonist could communicate through a headset or walkie-talkie with a character in a different locale (e.g., *Spider-Man 2* (2023)). Or, the protagonist could hear a voice from a radio that delivers creepy war updates (e.g., *Spec Ops: The Line* (2012)).

- On-screen text – These are words that are imposed on-screen either during an in-game scene (like a chyron) or on a loading screen. On-screen text is a very simple way to communicate location, time period, tutorial or how-to information, mission context, summaries of lore fragments or past events (on loading screens primarily), and descriptions of locales, collectables, and weapons. While this kind of on-screen text explains the parts of the world, they themselves are not part of the world (i.e., they are non-diegetic). They are written to provide clarity through the point of view (POV) of the developers of the game. On-screen text can also be used in dialogue boxes for NPCs and the playable character to communicate with one another without voice-over. This type of on-screen text, because it is written in the voices of the characters, qualifies as diegetic.

- Companion Apps – Apps or second-screen experiences that can sync with the game can provide navigational guidance and occasional narrative information but are seldom used these days.

- Out-of-game narrative – Players can migrate to the game's online hub to read short stories or watch animation shorts to get a deeper narrative experience of beloved characters that the game can't integrate seamlessly within the interactive experience. More about this in Chapter 8.

PLAN AND MANAGE THE CONTENT

Finding out what needs to get written is a crucial step before the writing begins. While this may seem like an easy task, it's not. There are so many dependencies that dictate what story mechanisms can be built. Budget and talent resources are the two most common ones.

The first step for a narrative designer is to draft a blueprint to explain what the story is. This could be in the form of a story bible (explained later on) or an addition to the game design document (GDD). Second, you'll need to draft a visual representation of the overall narrative, potential variation moments, and the different vehicles (cut scenes, collectables, in-game dialogue, etc.) that will deliver segments of the narrative. The final blueprint should explain how those vehicles will deliver specific segments of a story. This is crucial as it should dive into its mechanics and the rulesets by which the story segments are triggered. This blueprint is not something you will need to do alone. There's a lot of software engineering that will take place. In fact, anything that is designed on your behalf will be scrutinized by a programmer for *technological viability*. Afterward, narrative designers will create prototypes of story mechanisms to prove *creative viability*. Successful outcomes will impact the prioritization of writing deliverables. The narrative designer will then determine estimates of how much content needs to be written per each story mechanism, how many employees will be dedicated, and what kinds of external talent will be needed (for voice or film). This process will inform the development pipeline and expectations of delivery (i.e., deadlines, number of employees to staff, technology costs, etc.). All of this will feed into the game's production schedule.

Additionally, there are many tech, art, and audio dependencies within a single piece of narrative. Figuring out the schedule, to which those other disciplines will need to contribute, will fall squarely on the shoulders of a writer or narrative designer. You will also need to "own" the narrative's full content delivery. This means you will manage and oversee the various stages of the writing's creation; its enhancement by audio, art, and others; and its proper implementation and triggering in the game.

For example, imagine you are tasked to write a series of letters that gets peppered throughout the gaming experience and collected by the player. (This assumes that the ruleset for the letter mechanic has already been designed and coded.)

A narrative designer will need to:

- Write the content of those letters.

- Work with level designers to implement where in the game (as in environment and progression) the individual letters are disseminated and collected.

- Work with user interface designers to figure out what is the best visual representation of the letter on-screen.

- Assure the letters' proper triggering for collection by collaborating with a pure designer and programmer.

- Identify if there is music or voice-over associated with the letters, in which case a series of other requirements will follow, including casting the talent and directing said talent to voice the letter.

- Assist in the proper localization of the text of the letter (and/or voice-over, if necessary).

Again, not an easy task. Narrative designers don't just write the content and forget about it. There is a rigorous and collaborative process, where one must manage the content to assure its thorough creation and implementation. And if something isn't working after testing those letters in game with the help of quality assurance (QA), the narrative designer has to put on the hat of a supply chain manager, figure out where in the assembly line of content creation did that letter fail to trigger, and work with others to solve the issue.

REINFORCE THE THEME

So much of writing the story hinges upon the overall message you want to convey. It could be political or social. It could be about achieving goals that go beyond what we think we can do as players (and as characters in the fiction).

In games, the theme is a result of the creative vision. The story, therefore, must reinforce that theme through subtle means, such as escalation in the story beats, visual reinforcement through environmental storytelling, and context descriptions before missions.

A theme should speak to a higher ambition about the human condition. It's a driving moral statement or message. For instance:

- Honor, country, and self-sacrifice.
- Pushing yourself to the limits to surpass the expectations of those who don't believe in you.
- Becoming something greater than yourself by helping others.
- Learning to be a hero in a world where there are very few.
- The path to self-redemption for yourself and for your community.
- Family over everything else.
- Love conquers all.

Now, some of these might seem cliché. In fact, they are. Then again, there is little that is unique about theme. There are only a handful of general messages about the human condition as is. Theme is a guiding principle, not a series of plot points or character nuances.

One more thing …

Do not confuse theme with premise. As we'll tackle later on in the "Elevator Pitch" section of Chapter 12, premise is a basic description of what the story is about. Theme, on the other hand, is the overall general moral message that guides your hero's journey. A breakdown is given in Table 3.2.

TABLE 3.2 Premise vs. Theme

Game	Premise	Theme
Call of Duty: World War II	It's the Battle of Normandy, and a squad from the 1st Division Infantry will do whatever it takes to thwart Nazi aggression in World War II's most decisive moment.	Honor and country above everything else.
God of War (reboot)	A warrior and his son set forth on a journey to honor the boy's dead mother only to incur the wrath of Norse Gods.	One can never escape their fate.
Shadow of the Colossus	A young hero enters a forbidden land of giants to rescue the love of his life.	Love conquers all.

WRITE, REVISE, AND POLISH THE CONTENT

The writing of the game's content is the primary reason why a narrative designer is hired. In many ways, this is the easiest part of the job. Once the story mechanisms are designed and the content plan is secured, it's time to write.

And you'll be writing different types of content based on the narrative mechanisms you designed. These could include mini-screenplays for cut scenes; prose writing in the voice of the game's characters for collectables; mission descriptions presented on-screen; casual dialogue that is uttered randomly by minor characters as you travel through an environment; marketing copy to help explain or sell the game internally and externally; and instructional copy for manuals and/or on-screen tutorials.

The latter two won't be something the narrative designer is responsible for "designing." Nonetheless, team members might request help in these areas and you'll need to add them to an already-overloaded queue of work.

It's impossible to assess how much content needs to be written. This number is in constant flux, just like the game itself. Not surprisingly, it's also impossible to commit to a specific line count, due to numerous variations for a single sentiment (e.g., "Get down!" or "Hello"). For a typical console game, the amount of written content is often greater than a 120-page screenplay. That's not set in stone. But it is common. So, if you're a film or TV writer, be prepared to write a lot more than what you're used to.

As with all games, so much of the second-to-last part of the development cycle (aka "Alpha." "Beta" being the last, but somewhat "hands off" to writers as it is tech-centric.) is seeing how everything looks and feels in game and then making the necessary adjustments. Some of these adjustments could include wholesale changes on what is written inside an already-secured narrative mechanism. Take, for example, the aforementioned letter collectable. The individual letters and their placement in the game will be scrutinized *ad nauseum*. If the change recommendations are merely cosmetic, you're in luck. (Example: change the word "haunting" to "foreboding.") But, if the letters tested poorly with focus groups due to lack of coherence, then a narrative designer must provide deep writing revisions and (if need be) work with a pure designer to re-implement them in different points in the game. However, such changes are only permitted if the narrative mechanism that needs fixing is not already carved in stone or is too expensive to change at the last minute. Cut scenes, for instance, are too expensive and rigid. But collectables or dialogue trees – since they do not require heavy animations, voice-over, or motion capture (aka MOCAP) – are the most vulnerable and easiest to change.

As Ernest Hemingway once wrote, "The only kind of writing is rewriting." Yes, you will be busy revising. But so will everyone else. Polishing features, re-tuning the frequency of certain character appearances, fixing bugs in code – all of these and more are compounded during the seemingly never-ending but ever-fatiguing production phase of game development known as "Crunch Time," "Crunch Mode," or just plain "Crunch." This is game development. Expect nothing less than an all-hands-on-deck approach to perfecting the product until content is locked.

ASSIST IN THE LOCALIZATION OF THE WRITTEN AND SPOKEN CONTENT

The video game industry is massive in part because it is a global industry. More and more people have access to technology than ever before and often have more than one device through which they play games. Phones, tablets, consoles, computers, virtual reality headsets – games are omnipresent. Game companies realize that, to spread consumer goodwill across the world, it is a *must* to translate voice-over subtitles and on-screen text into numerous languages.

There are whole departments in video game companies devoted to translation of this content. This process is known as localization and it requires not just the straight word-for-word translation from one language to the next but an actual cultural translation as well. For instance, an off-handed insult in English about one's lack of Americanism ("You red-diaper, Commie bastard!") will need to be translated into one of the many Chinese languages that does not offend the country's political or familial sensibilities. A more appropriate translation could be, for example, "You disrespectful, treasonous simpleton."

Narrative designers are key to the localization process. While they will not translate the materials, they will instead prepare all of the materials that need to get translated. Additionally, they will input the content into a translation tool, monitor the changes that affect the translations, and make the proper revisions and updates so that the localization team is aware of what new content they need to translate.

Localization is a very time-consuming process that occurs near the end of the development of a game. The work is often thankless, but it is critical. It is, really, the final step in making sure that a writer's words truly reach a large audience.

DIRECT VOICE-OVER SESSIONS AND FILMED CONTENT

Voice-Over

Voice-over is a common component to games. Even if there is no story *per se*, actors are often used to provide ambient dialogue to a scene in order to add authenticity. In a sports game, for instance, broadcasters react to any and all moves that the player conducts on the court, field, or ring. That extra layer of authenticity gives players a deeper connection to the game.

Outside of the sports arena, ambient dialogue again provides that extra layer of believability. Even if the game is sci-fi, hearing a nearby soldier kill a Lekgolo will force you to follow him into the next spaceship, which enhances the intensity and suspense of the moment.

Voice-over without narrative can also provide essential context to features in the game. A voice from an off-screen character that guides you through tutorials and character customization or provides descriptions of modes or features before you play them gives the player the necessary information on how to proceed. Without that voice-over, the player would have to fend for themself. And, if there's one thing game developers do not want to do, it is to frustrate or slow down a player in experiencing fun.

But, most importantly, voice-over actors provide the performances that enhance and communicate the narrative. Their performances are often the voice of in-game characters that are either motion captured or just purely animated. Sometimes, there is no on-screen character that they are voicing. Instead, an off-screen Voice of God character (diegetic, once again) is a common motif for games, especially for those with a limited character-animation budget. These characters will guide the player through the experience, not just as a provider of context but as a person who watches over the player. These Voice of God characters typically serve as a parental figure, friend, or mentor.[6]

No matter the role, the narrative designer must have a strong command of the characters' intentions, roles, and other details that can be used to inform the actor's performance. When the actors are in the sound booth, you must be hyper-aware of their performance. Is it providing the right intention? Is it true to the character you created? You'll need to adopt basic directorial responsibilities to assure the high quality of the performance.

If there is already a director assigned to the voice-over sessions, then the narrative designer's role includes the following: (1) making sure the lines are properly performed and influenced by the sequence of events in the game; (2) maintaining the integrity of the script if there are ad-libs from the actor that could compromise the accuracy of the story; (3) rewriting lines if the actors are having a hard time with the direction or with what's written; (4) assuring everything is delivered within a certain time constraint per line, if such a constraint exists (which it can); and (5) consulting with the director to assure high-quality performances without being intrusive. The latter seems like common sense, but you'd be surprised at how many writers and narrative designers ignore that rule. It's often the case that many of these writers have never worked with actors before, so they have yet to learn the rules of etiquette that govern the relationship between actor, director, sound engineer, and writer.

Voice-over sessions do not happen regularly; therefore, the time in the sound booth is precious. If a writer doesn't have their ducks in a row – as in, they do not have all of the content written that needs to be recorded or they want to add too much unnecessary content just for extra coverage – the actor's performance will deteriorate quickly. Voice-over sessions, ideally, should be about getting the best performance possible out of an actor. It should not be about figuring out stuff on the fly or adding more to the plate than is needed. Content that is "nice to have" can often ruin a voice-over session. Solidify those nice-to-haves at least a week before the recording and prioritize accordingly.

Filmed Content

Cut scenes, as referenced earlier, are animated scenes within the game that move the story forward and provide greater context to the world and characters. Gamers can find these moments disruptive if the cut scenes are not interactive (and most of the time they aren't). Cut scenes are skippable, and many gamers take advantage of that function to get to gameplay as quickly as possible. But for those who want to experience everything a game has to offer, cut scenes are a game's version of cinema.

The animation process involves the capturing of an actor's facial gestures and body structure. This is done through a process known as motion capture (MOCAP). Actors will wear a suit and facial markers that serve as a scanner of an actor's unique subtle movements and skeletal structure. The suit and markers are basically data receptors that are activated by a series of cameras spread throughout a stage or studio.[7] A single camera's positioning will differ from another, but its goal is to capture structural and skeletal pieces of data that a body and/or body part gives off. Since our bodies are so complex and filled with nuance, thanks to our 650+ muscles and 200+ bones, more cameras will capture more data of an actor's body and movement and map it to a 3D model.[8] The more the data, the greater the authenticity of the actor's representation in an animated form.[9]

Narrative designers and writers are not responsible for the process of MOCAP, but they will be responsible for writing the scenes that need to be performed and captured. Cut scenes are opportunities for actors to perform at their highest level. The subtleties of their facial expressions will need to be captured and done so thoroughly. Otherwise, an improper facial expression could undermine the tone and content of a sentence. Narrative designers and writers can direct or assist in the directing of these scenes. However, it is often the case – especially at big studios for big-budget games – that a director who specializes in MOCAP will take the reins. The writer will be a crucial contributor, not only to help communicate the intention of the scene but also to educate the actors on what the consequences of that scene will be in gameplay.

A false step from a performance will yield imperfect animation data. This will kill a cut scene. Scenes will have different takes that are recorded, so the creative team does have an opportunity to choose which data-driven shots work best for a scene. However, a writer cannot rely on too many takes. While MOCAP is expensive, it's even more so arduous and physically demanding. Actors are wearing suits that are not breathable. Facial markers are susceptible to falling off or breaking, thus preventing accurate data from being captured. Time is short, so make sure you know what to communicate to an actor before the MOCAP begins.

While animation is the predominant form of character representation, some games rely on traditional live action film to fuel the narrative. As mentioned before, these are known as FMVs, or full motion videos. FMVs' popularity peaked in the 1990s with game versions of such famous franchises as *The X-Files* and *Star Trek*. But they are used sparingly today and usually as a way to provide cameos of well-established personalities to add authenticity to the world of the game. Sports games are the perfect genre for this. Seeing a live action version of a superstar, sportscaster, or coach that talks about the player (as if the content was customized to them) can be an effective addition to the experience.

If FMV is part of the game, a writer will need to think of it as traditional film production. The actors' performances cannot be fixed through animation. Therefore, expect a degree of finality when working on a film set. If you lack film production experience, rely on those who do have it and make sure to be a watchdog for the story. If an ad lib or improper interpretation of a line could undermine the narrative or subsequent gameplay moments, be ready to provide instant feedback by working through the director.

OTHER

When a game is in crunch, new roles and responsibilities will be thrown at everyone. In fact, taking on more than what your job description entails is *de rigueur*. A narrative designer will be asked to help edit designer's tutorials or guidance content; they will work with the marketing department to write about certain features of the game for print and digital outlets; they will work with key stakeholders in drafting or updating game manuals (yes, they still exist, albeit digitally); they will work with a UI team to help reword on-screen content to fit the needs of an updated user interface; they will work with an art team to provide information on characters or locales to assist that team in getting a better visual picture of the task at hand; and they will work with engineers to write software notes for title updates.

For better or worse, a narrative designer is the editorial subject matter expert of a game development team and will field requests that have nothing to do with story. Proper mastery of grammar, vocabulary, semantics, and sentence structure is constantly in need. If a writer is soft in these areas, they will need to fine-tune that skill set posthaste.

NOTES

1 PlayStation, "God of War" 2018.
2 Metacritic, "The Last of Us" 2013.
3 Metacritic, "Shadow of the Colossus" 2018.
4 Katz, *The Media Handbook* 2010.
5 Ibid.
6 GlaDOS in the first *Portal* (2007) game is a perfect example … although when her true intentions are revealed, she is neither a parental figure, friend, nor mentor. She's just a cold AI seeking to end your existence. Still, her presence is mostly off-screen as a Voice of God character.
7 Wikipedia, "Motion Capture" n.d.
8 Ibid.
9 Ibid.

REFERENCES

Katz, Helen. (2010). *The Media Handbook: A Complete Guide to Advertising Media Selection, Planning, Research, and Buying* (4th edition). London: Routledge.

Metacritic. "The Last of Us." (2013, June 14). Retrieved on February 9, 2024 from www.metacritic.com/game/playstation-3/the-last-of-us

Metacritic. "Shadow of the Colossus." (2018, February 6). Retrieved on February 9, 2024 from www.metacritic.com/game/playstation-4/shadow-of-the-colossus

PlayStation. "God of War." (2018, April). Retrieved on February 9, 2024 from www.playstation.com/en-us/games/god-of-war-ps4/

Wikipedia. "Motion Capture." (n.d.). Retrieved on February 9, 2024 from https://en.wikipedia.org/wiki/Motion_capture

CHAPTER 4

Game Writing at the Ground Level

THERE's A LOT OF prep work during the early stages of game development. Character bios, world bios, sample dialogue, sample scenes, a vertical slice script, and more are written in a standard doc form *a la* Microsoft Word or Google Docs. They are great pre-production tools and allow the writer to write unencumbered. An empty canvas to be filled with your words is extremely empowering. However, once the game is in production, writers will have to make huge compromises on their process.

EXAMPLE SPREADSHEET FOR NARRATIVE CONTENT

The heavy demands of production require a game writer or narrative designer to work almost exclusively in a spreadsheet. The transference of data – and yes, at this stage, narrative content, such as dialogue, is data – will go through several different hands from several different specialists, including designers, audio engineers, localization specialists, and quality assurance analysts.

It's imperative that the information in these spreadsheets provides the most comprehensive, up-to-date data so that the above stakeholders won't miss anything once applying their trade. Missing data or misinformed data can create bugs with serious downstream effects that can slow down production.

Figure 4.1 is a bare-bones example of a spreadsheet that a writer would typically contribute to. Let me describe in detail what each column means.

 DOI: 10.1201/9781003438113-4

Asset ID	Category	Character	Line	Character Count	Notes
Library_Hero_001a_Male	Murder Investigation in Library	Smith	Hello -- may I bend your ear for a sec?	39	Informal path. Not sure we can pay off. Check out latest update to character bible.
Library_Hero_001b_Male	Murder Investigation in Library	Smith	Hey, were you here during last night's murder?	46	
Library_Hero_001c_Male	Murder Investigation in Library	Smith	I need to ask you some questions.	33	
Library_Hero_001a_Female	Murder Investigation in Library	Smith	Hi there -- do you have a moment?	33	
Library_Hero_001b_Female	Murder Investigation in Library	Smith	Sorry to bother. Just need to ask you some questions about last night's murder.	79	
Library_Hero_001c_Female	Murder Investigation in Library	Smith	Excuse me. I need a moment of your time. Right now.	51	
Library_Librarian_001_Male	Murder Investigation in Library	Chen	Of course. How can I help you?	30	
Library_Librarian_001_Female	Murder Investigation in Library	Chen	Of course. How can I help you?	30	

Figure 4.1 Spreadsheet for writing game content. (See full-scale version of this graph at www.routledge.com/9781032571614.)

ASSET ID

Under Column A, the data refer to an asset identifier. If this line is either voiced or represented through in-game text, the narrative designer will affix this asset ID to the asset type (in this case, in-game text), so that a pure designer knows what asset they are implementing into the game. If it's an asset that is voice-over, audio engineers will use the asset ID as a way to track progress of their polishing and implementing of that voiced line.

Once it's out of the hands of a pure designer or audio team, the localization team can then translate that asset into various languages and provide the subsequent subtitles for it.

The quality assurance team can also refer to the asset ID in case the exact representation of the asset ID pops up as a string instead of the in-game text. In other words, what pops up on screen is "Library_Hero_001a_Male" instead of "Hello – may I bend your ear for a sec?" Then they can report a bug to the designer to see what went wrong in the implementation process.

Let's break down the data in the asset ID itself. Going back to the first line: "Library_Hero_001a_Male." There's a lot there in just a few characters. Ideal nomenclature for the identifier should provide the location in the game environment that the line is stated in ("Library_"); the person who is uttering the line ("_Hero_"); which line in the series of lines in that scene that the same character is uttering ("_001"); the version of that line, in case variations are written ("a"); and the gender of the speaker of that line in case, once again, there are different versions of that same character ("_Male").

Each team has different rules under which the nomenclature of the asset ID is written, but the goal is to clarify whom the line came from, where it took place, and what the numeric or alphabetic distinctions are if there are variations of that same line. And the last challenge is to make the asset ID as economical as you can. The tools that allow for the implementation usually display an enormous list of IDs that need to get put in game. Oftentimes, reading a huge list of these can strain the eyes and increase the chance of human error. Longer nomenclature will compound that likelihood.

This can be hard to adjust to at first but will make sense eventually once you're charged with adding several variations for a single line. The artificial intelligence (AI) of the game could trigger any one of these three lines (_001a, _001b, or _001c) if you are the Male Hero Smith as an introduction to the conversation, so make sure the appropriate variant corresponds with the appropriate asset ID.

If you are the Female Hero Smith, the AI will launch one of the three – Library_Hero_001a_Female, Library_Hero_001b_Female, or Library_Hero_001c_Female – for the same introduction that involved the Male Hero Smith.

Now these lines of dialogue could be the same – and that is likely the case when a writer or narrative designer writes this scene. Nonetheless, the lines will need to have separate asset IDs (mainly influenced by gender), so that they are properly translated once these IDs are in the hands of localization.

CATEGORY

Here, the type of scene needs to be communicated, so that the writer understands when, in the game, this part of the narrative is delivered. The near equivalent of this in a typical screenplay would be stage directions.

The category column also refers to the type of moment that gets triggered that is independent of the story. Barks, as mentioned earlier, are the perfect candidates for this. Their criteria could be as simple as 27 different ways of saying "Hello." But a different ruleset, event, or environment could dictate how, where, or when these barks are triggered and (sometimes) performed. For example, you collected an item. If the collection mechanic is common, but as common as a greeting like "Hello," you will need to account for *all the variations* (including degrees of variations!) of that type of line under the "Category" column. This allows such variations as "Oh, look a red stone!" vs. "Oh, look a green stone!" vs. "Oh, look a dark red stone!" to be easily accounted for.

CHARACTER

This is pretty straightforward and sometimes redundant if the name of the character is already embedded in the asset ID. However, it's most useful in the aggregation of the lines for a specific character. If a wholesale rewrite is needed (for instance, Chen is no longer a librarian, but a construction worker) or if the lines need to be grouped for a voice-over session, a simple function on the spreadsheet can easily organize the data in the "Character" field.

LINE

Another straightforward column. But it is here where writers and narrative designers will do most of their work, either through the creation of the lines or the editing of them. Pure designers will import the spreadsheet into a database that will then be imported into the game's engine in order for the new dialogue to be present in the game. Again, designers might have a different setup of the spreadsheet to make the transference as seamless as possible.

The same method applies when importing this information into a database for localization.

CHARACTER COUNT

One of the biggest challenges for a writer in video games is writing under the constraints of a character count. Character count refers not to a fictional entity but to the symbols and spaces that visually represent dialogue. For example, the sentence *I love pastries!* comprises 16 characters from the first letter to the final punctuation mark – specifically, two spaces that separate three words and 13 letters that make up those three words ("I" = one, "love" = four, and "pastries" = eight) and one character for the exclamation point.

It's important to understand character count because it can pose constraints on how dialogue (through subtitles) or on-screen text is represented in the user interface (UI) of the game. These constraints aren't necessarily bad, especially when players don't want to be bogged down with long blocks of text. That's why it's critical that the dialogue remains taut while still revealing character psychology and crucial information.

But there's a flip side to character count constraints. Games can over-index on economy of dialogue. Again, players want a frictionless narrative; the least amount, the better. But too little dialogue can lead to overly cryptic messaging, leaving a player confused as to what is happening. Ideally, UI and art teams will need to impose realistic character counts without sacrificing clarity and sophistication, no matter if the dialogue is voiced and subtitled; as part of an on-screen dialogue tree or dialogue box; or as an environmental storytelling vehicle like newspaper headlines. There is precious real estate on the screen, and every UI element has to have its own specifications so as not to distract or disrupt the others.

Games are embracing character counts more and more, so it's crucial to write with brevity. Establishing visual restrictions in a spreadsheet can help. For example, in Figure 4.1, I imposed a rule to shade any cells if the character count went over 70 (cell E6).

NOTES

Here, you can flag any questions you have about the line, asset ID, or category. Or if there's a mistake or an update, this column allows for the proper annotation of issues in the development cycle. Information in this column allows the other discipline specialists to be on the same page in terms of how to execute. Providing links to other documents within a drive shared by the team will allow others to click and determine how best to advise or take action.

Notes are also an opportunity to add suggestions for the creative that have yet to be explored, especially if the dialogue is going to be performed. Casting suggestions, tone recommendations for the actor, potential alternative line rewrites, etc. help the writer see what steps need to be addressed in the recording of the talent.

PIPELINE

Typically, the narrative designer will create the spreadsheet and fill it with data, such as asset IDs, character count, and the lines (yes, once again, dialogue is data).

As touched upon earlier, once the writing is complete, the spreadsheet will be handed off to a pure designer who will input the lines and asset IDs into game. (Alternately, an audio engineer will do the same if the lines are voiced, but only after they've cleaned or "sweetened" the data by removing unnecessary, yet subtle background noise or adding slight vocal enhancements.)

Concurrently, the designer will import the data into a database for localization. That team will provide translations of the on-screen text or voice-over into several languages in subtitle form (if the dialogue is voiced) or as substitute on-screen text in a different language.

The quality assurance (QA) team will then play the game and see if there are any bugs in the narrative to assure proper implementation and/or coherence of the writing. If a line is improperly triggered, the QA team can refer to the original spreadsheet to see what needed to be launched in its place. Thereafter, the team notifies the relevant parties – pure design, audio, and/or narrative design – on what needs to be fixed.

Additionally, if the writing was properly launched, but the content itself is deficient – either through lack of coherence, typos, or lines from characters that are off-tone – the QA team will report these bugs for the narrative designer or writer to revise.

This process will continue until content is locked for the entire game, wherein there are no more opportunities to optimize. (Exceptions being title updates, but those are often specific to a new feature being launched or intended for colossal bugs that have huge downstream effects.)

The pipeline of narrative creation and implementation is a tight one. The process is very specific to the games industry. It is one that a writer and a narrative designer are required to adopt or else they will struggle to be an asset to the team.

CHAPTER 5

Conflict

Cᴏɴꜰʟɪᴄᴛ ɪꜱ ᴛʜᴇ ʟɪɴᴄʜᴘɪɴ of storytelling. Without it, there is no story. There is no purpose of the hero. In games, conflict is tied to the main objective. Save the princess from the dragon. Purge the village from goblins. Prevent a nuclear bomb from landing in Gotham City. The various acts that lead to the resolution of this conflict is an ongoing, painstaking effort undertaken by the protagonist for the vast majority of the story. In narrative and design terms, this effort comprises plot points and gameplay moments.

THE ENGINE OF A STORY

Conflict arises when the hero of the story (protagonist) has certain goals and values that clash with an individual who possesses rigidly held opposing goals and values (antagonist). When the protagonist and the antagonist fail to reach a compromise, the conflict propels forth and pits the protagonist against the antagonist, whereby resolution is achieved when one must triumph over the other.[1] For happy stories, the hero defeats the antagonist and status quo is restored. For unhappy stories, the antagonist defeats the hero and the status quo of the hero's world is permanently disrupted and likely transformed into a new world that conforms to the vision of the antagonist. In bittersweet stories, the protagonist defeats the antagonist and status quo is restored, but the hero loses something dear to them – either a loved one, a sacred object or home, wealth, land, or even their own life.

Conflict, as the nucleus of story, propels our hero onto a journey that helps them evolve as a person. Their emotional growth engenders a player's emotional attachment and investment. Without conflict, not only is there no story, but there isn't a compelling or aspirational hero to latch onto. Conflict is a test. It challenges the resolve of a hero, how they rise under pressure, how they treat others when the odds are against them, and how their skills burgeon when the proverbial noose tightens around their neck. Conflict either makes a hero or makes a coward. The latter is not why people buy video games. Yet, while there is an expectation that a game hero will rise to the challenge, there is never an expectation that the hero will always succeed. Dying valorously marks the end of a valorous hero, and valor is the primary desirable trait of a hero, no matter the medium or genre. Of course, valor doesn't mean using a sword to hack and slash away at goblins and ghosts. It could also mean: asserting oneself when silence or obedience is expected; advocating for others; or putting oneself in an uncomfortable situation for the greater good. Surviving outside of one's comfort zone is an underrated heroic trait, yet it is where most heroes grow from.

Conflict in the Home World

Conflict presents itself as an imminent problem to solve because it disrupts the status quo of the hero's home world. As the story requires the hero to resolve the conflict, there are three possible outcomes:

- With the defeat of the antagonist, status quo is restored in the hero's world. (Light prevails.)
- With the defeat of the protagonist, status quo is destroyed and the world morphs into a new world with values that reflect the antagonist's. (Darkness prevails.)
- With a pyrrhic victory over the antagonist, status quo cannot be restored to the world. Its people must rebuild it and redefine status quo. (Light and darkness prevail.)

These examples assume that the hero is in conflict with an intruder who trespassed upon the hero's home world. The hero, thus, is in a constant defensive position, either to stave off the destruction or sinister influence of the antagonist on the hero's turf; or the hero must leave their world temporarily to stop the antagonist on their enemy's turf. In either case, the hero's primary objective is to thwart the antagonist and restore the status quo of the home world.

Conflict in the New World

Now let's assume that the hero enters a new world before the conflict begins. The hero is a stranger in this world. And to some people, the hero might pose a threat to its status quo. Conflict then centers on the hero's struggles of conforming in a new world where conforming might be an impossibility for them. These stories are typically *fish-out-of-water* scenarios. They make for great comedies ... and for some disturbing dramas and horror films as well. This fish-out-of-water character has the potential of being a change agent in their new world, which threatens those who don't like change or who thrive in the environment and do not want their success to be affected in any way. Of course, those who are bothered most by the presence of the change agent naturally assume the role of the antagonist (or an abettor thereof). The hero will encounter numerous tests that challenge their professional competence, mental tenacity, compassion and love for others, and ability to identify what's most precious to them. If, for instance, the hero comes to New York from Indiana to climb the corporate ladder in advertising and falls in love with the CEO's daughter, there is a strong likelihood that career decisions will interfere with their courtship, and rivals will stop at nothing from destroying the country bumpkin with the heart of gold. The bumpkin will either get revenge, get the girl, get the promotion, or – if this were a 1980s Michael J. Fox or Andrew McCarthy movie – all of the above. But such an overly optimistic story fails to be relevant these days. There are more realistic and sometimes more cynical resolutions to conflict for the fish-out-of-water story:

- Hero enters the new world, struggles to fit in, overcomes those who stand in their way, and stays in this new world as a changed person who now reflects its values.
- Hero enters the new world, struggles to fit in, fails to overcome those who stand in their way, leaves the new world, and returns to where they came from.
- Hero enters the new world, struggles to fit in, fails to overcome those who stand in their way, and destroys the world and those responsible for the hero's misery.
- Hero enters the new world, struggles to fit in, fails to overcome those who stand in their way, leaves the world, but those left behind change themselves to conform to the hero's values.

- Hero enters the new world, struggles to fit in, defeats those who stand in their way, and changes the new world and its people to conform to the hero's values.

- Hero comes to the new world, struggles to fit in, fails to overcome those who stand in their way, but the hero cannot leave, so they destroy themself instead.

As one can see, a hero entering a new world offers more variety in conflict than it does for a hero in the home world. The new world conflict pushes the hero into uncharted waters, where survival is all about conformity and adaptation. The new world, however, doesn't always have to be a new physical locale for the hero. It could also mean a new set of rules or a new order that pervades the home world due to a redefining event of considerable magnitude, such as a parents' divorce, a sibling going off to college, a new boss taking charge, or physical changes that greatly alter the hero (either for good or bad) and how the world reacts to them. This version of a new world, thus, is a wholesale change of the status quo where the hero is well past the point of restoration of their original home world, but understands that new rules of the old world is a new world unto itself. The hero does not question it and takes it on subconsciously as a step toward personal evolution and as a natural progression in life.

The hero, as a fish out of water, is a pretender who must gauge their level of conformity depending on their values and priorities. A loner will have little tolerance for conformity, whereas a social butterfly will have a high tolerance for it. In many ways, a fish-out-of-water conflict measures a hero's range of social tolerance from subversive to loner to well-intended misfit to social butterfly to social monarch.

- **The subversive** does not have the capacity to conform, due to either a lack of desire or an inherent inability. They often don't understand social cues or are so cynical toward the way the new world operates that they do not want to be a part of it. But when the world forces them to participate and conform (often through acts of cruelty, dehumanization, or erasure of their past), the hero will lash out and either tear down the world or destroy those responsible for the cruelty. Bear in mind, this hero will not escape from this new world. Anger and a rigid sense of what's right will drive them to excise the social cancer or destroy the body in which the cancer is found. Examples: Travis

Bickle (*Taxi Driver*, 1976); John Rambo (*First Blood*, 1982); Joker (*Joker*, 2019).

- **The loner** is thrust into the new world that doesn't understand them. The loner is similar to the subversive, except the loner is not an extremist. They would rather escape the new world or make a devil's bargain to get out of a bad situation than destroy everything around them. The loner just wants to be left alone and do their own thing. A typical, benign example of this is a shy student moves to a new town, attends a new school, and is instantly made fun of for being different. This student finds a small social circle of their own (often outcasts) and thrives by creating a new world of their own. This hero engenders respect at the end because they refuse to change amid the pressure from more popular kids. The hero's strength is measured by how they stand by their individuality, forcing the antagonist to realize they have no power over the hero. A more popular example of the loner is Han Solo in *Star Wars: Episode IV – A New Hope* (1977), who reluctantly joins Luke Skywalker to rescue Leia from the Dark Side. Developing a kinship with Luke and Leia is a by-product of his mercenary role to help them. He'd rather fly the Millennium Falcon with Chewbacca than get involved in any cause. Yet, he softens up to them and opens his heart to morally just causes and still maintains his independent streak as his new friends (which are small in number) allow him to do what he wants to do. Example: Kratos (*God of War* franchise).

- **The social misfit** is often a lovable, goofy, misunderstood protagonist who wants to "fit in" but can't. They are clumsy, desperate, and eager to please. They find acceptance either by shedding some bad habits that they always wanted to shed or they realize that they must stay true to who they are and, therefore, others (and the new world) must conform to them. Example: Scott Carlin (*The King of Staten Island*, 2020).

- **The social butterfly** is one who climbs the social hierarchy not only for acceptance but for primacy as well. A threat to their world takes the form of someone of the same social clout who wants to maintain the same primacy, but there is only one or a few "slots" for such a privilege (aka an "Equal Competitor"); or undermine the protagonist's credibility because they represent a threat to the antagonist's reign (aka an "Incumbent"). Example: Cady Heron (*Mean Girls*, 2004 original film and 2024 musical version).

- **The social monarch** is someone who does everything in their power to achieve adulation by others and to be viewed as the leader or main attraction of the new world. Like the subversive, this hero is single-minded and unable to compromise. If their goal is achieved, it's likely because this protagonist shed a part of themselves, often their compassion. At what cost was this position in the new world worth it? This is a question for the audience. The hero, at this point, does not even consider such a question. They are ruthless and, eventually, controlling. Examples: Michael Corleone (*Godfather I* (1972) and *II* (1974)); Nikolai Luzhin (*Eastern Promises*, 2007).

Conflict vs. Evil Atmosphere

One can easily mistake bad events or a corrupt and evil environment as conflict. Neither is necessarily true. For example, a protagonist doesn't have to be a law-abiding, good person. They could be a convict who escapes from prison, triggering a pursuer (typically a US Marshal or another law enforcement professional) to be on their tail. The conflict is clear: the convict values freedom, whereas the US Marshal values putting a dangerous convict back in prison. The hero's objective is also clear: escape prison and find a safe haven without getting caught. A successful resolution to the conflict, therefore, is the convict's eluding of the US Marshal by the end of the story.

A corrupt environment captured the attention of millions during *Breaking Bad's* time on the air (2008–2013). Walter White isn't a convict, but a high school chemist. As discussed earlier, after season 1 when his attachment to his family lessens, Walter cooks crystal meth in order to become a powerful drug lord in New Mexico. Neither the aforementioned escaped convict nor Walter White is a virtuous person, and their worlds are dark and evil. But darkness alone is not conflict. An effective way to create a compelling conflict is establishing the hero's goal, identifying the person who wants to get in their way, and determining why that person wants to get in the hero's way. The "why" will lengthen the conflict (as in delay its resolution) because a mission-driven antagonist is the hardest one to defeat.

As I will discuss in Chapter 6 regarding the Hannibal Lecter character, the presence of evil is not a requirement of an antagonist. All that is required for conflict is a clash of goals and values between the hero and the antagonist. Look to the Latin: "pro" means forward; "ant" (or "anti") means against. If the hero and the person standing in their way had to be purely good ("eu" in Latin) and purely evil ("mal" in Latin), they would then be referred to as, respectively, "eutagonist" and "maltagonist." Thankfully, the established nomenclature invites more complexity into our storytelling.

Conflict and Tragic Mistake

So far, the provided scenarios of conflict assume that the hero is a victim of an aggressor, a controller, a pursuer, an invader, or just a rotten circumstance. But there are situations where the hero caused a disruption to their world's status quo and must pay the consequences. If the hero lived in a forgiving world, this disruption would be ignored by the community and the story would stop right there. But, for characters looking for a reason to exact harm or are justifiably shaken by the hero's action, then an antagonist's reaction (as an act of reprisal or restoration of safety to the status quo) will set a conflict in motion. A tragic mistake, as best defined by Aristotle,[2] is the action a hero makes without understanding its magnitude that sets forth a conflict that typically leads to a tragic ending. *Oedipus the King* (429 BC) is the primary example of this. Had Oedipus not sought the blind prophet Tiresias for advice on solving the plague that has been assaulting the citizens of Thebes, he would never have come across Tiresias's cryptic prophecy, "I say that you are the murderer whom you seek."[3] Oedipus' curiosity to find out what that means, despite its being irrelevant to the Theban plague, drives him to insanity and ultimately to the horrible truth: that while he killed the previous king of Thebes, Laius, and married his widow Jocasta, he did not know that they were actually his parents who abandoned him at birth. With this knowledge (now tinged with incestuous depravity), Oedipus stabs himself in the eyes and, as revealed in the follow-up *Oedipus at Colonus*, loses the throne of Thebes only to live a life of misery and penury.

Tragic mistakes are often confused with tragic flaws. A tragic mistake is an actual plot point (often a singular action conducted by the protagonist) and often the impetus of conflict (and sometimes the inciting incident, which I will discuss in Chapter 7). A tragic flaw, on the other hand, is a psychological shortcoming of a hero. Tragic flaws typically lead a hero to make bad decisions, exacerbating the conflict. So much of their journey is learning how to manage that flaw or purge it altogether.

Tragic mistakes nowadays don't have to lead to tragic endings. However, it is worth noting that tragic mistakes play upon the concept of fate. To what extent are heroes in control of their own destiny? If a hero is responsible for an invasion into their home world, how do they not only fend off the antagonist but how do they heal the emotional wounds of those in the community? If the hero is responsible for engendering enmity from an antagonist in a new world, how does the protagonist achieve stability when they possibly destroyed the status quo of the new world? Tragic mistakes involve a redemptive path from our hero. It is not enough to save the day; one must also rebuild trust and credibility from the innocent people who surround the protagonist or were impacted by the hero's mistake. The tragic mistake implies that the hero is not all that innocent in the rise of the conflict; in fact, its resolution is not sufficient even if the bad guys die. Hearts have to be mended in an overcompensated manner. Whatever the next adventure, the hero must have greater community support in tackling the new conflict than they did in their first adventure.

The Lurking Menace

There's nothing like an unseen threat that adds tension to a story. A legendary beast that strikes at night; an imminent war between two villages; an anticipated natural catastrophe that will devastate a city ... the sheer mention of an unseen threat complicates a hero's resolution to the conflict either by diverting the hero's attention onto a newly imminent disaster or by adjoining the primary conflict (as in the antagonist exploits the threat to slow down or even destroy the protagonist). This "Lurking Menace" feeds off of a player's curiosity or, when appropriate, paranoia when the aforementioned menace is presented or mentioned early on in the story. This sets an expectation that the Lurking Menace will eventually strike – when or how remains a mystery and adds to a player's uncertainty.

The film *Key Largo* (1948), based on the 1939 play by Maxwell Anderson, exemplifies an elegant usage of the Lurking Menace. World War II veteran, Frank McCloud, visits the family of a fallen war buddy, George Temple. McCloud immediately sees that the Temple family and their hotel in Key Largo are everything George raved about before his death. When a hurricane gradually develops, McCloud finds himself trapped in the hotel. Besides Temple's widow and her father-in-law, a few guests are also trapped with McCloud – unfortunately, they're of the "unsavory" variety: a Mafia boss named Johnny Rocco, his alcoholic girlfriend, Gaye Dawn, and several of his gunsels, each of whom is traveling under an alias. Eventually, they hold the Temples and McCloud hostage. It's discovered that Rocco, excommunicated to Cuba years back, has returned to the US to undertake a counterfeit money deal. After the deal goes through, Rocco strong-arms McCloud into piloting a small boat to Cuba. The veteran cannot say no – his life hangs in the balance. Once they make their way onto the boat, the hurricane continues to rampage. But it's McCloud's resolve, not the storm, that proves too much for Rocco and his men. Hours later, McCloud, with a gun that Gaye Dawn slyly handed to him before he left, shoots each one of them down in cold blood.

The hurricane as a Lurking Menace serves as a danger to both the protagonist and antagonist and provides uncertainty and tension for the filmgoer who could never predict whether the hero would ever escape harm's way. The Lurking Menace is typically an overwhelming force that is greater than a single person (or people). It doesn't have to be a hurricane, like in *Key Largo*. It doesn't have to be a beast that hides in the woods. It could be an impending: divorce or breakup within a tension-filled relationship; fall in the economy; illness that slowly strikes those in a small community; dreaded decision that a boss has to make, or; (even) failure to graduate from high school. The Lurking Menace is primarily an emotional force that wreaks havoc, breaking the safety and sanity of the world of the hero by sheer suggestion first and then in its actuality. Its danger is not only in its power and reach but also in its unpredictability. No one knows when the Lurking Menace will strike, nor will they know how much damage it will inflict. It's the unknowable that makes the Lurking Menace an effective storytelling device that enhances and accelerates tension.

The Lurking Menace is similar to the "Chekhov's Gun"[4] trope in theater, where a prop that invites danger (historically, a gun) is made visible to an audience early on in the drama, even highlighted in conversation or action or as visual spectacle. Its potential is either innately understood as dangerous or is referred to as such. But then, as the drama progresses and audience's attention is on the relationships between characters, the gun surprises everyone with a reappearance, usually at the end of a play, when another character uses it to the detriment of others (e.g., death or injury). Chekhov's Gun is an example of a setup and a payoff, where an object, character, or piece of information appears initially as innocuous or irrelevant to the plot (setup) but later turns out to have tremendous impact upon it (payoff). Audiences have grown accustomed to Chekhov's Gun-like story devices, but storytellers remain a step ahead by offering red hearings to derail audiences from making predictions of the story's outcome. Nonetheless, exposure to these "Chekhovian Guns" trains an audience into thinking, "Whatever sticks out must be important later on."

IN CONCLUSION

A writer must identify the conflict of their story in the early stages of the writing. One might argue to start with the conflict before figuring out who the protagonist is. Identifying both concurrently, if possible, is the ideal solution. It's the pursuit of the resolution of the conflict where the hero is tested. Each hardship within that test ought to escalate and align with plot points of the story. More importantly though is tracking the emotional journey of the hero (to be discussed in Chapter 6). While slaying dragons or blowing up military targets is all fun and good, if those activities don't lead to something significant in how the hero grows as a person, then the conflict is anemic at best. Bear in mind that emotional growth is not about mastering a skill or weapon; it's about managing one's emotional deficits. Coming to terms with the past, growing from a trauma, making amends with a past confidante – all of these emotional hardships (and more!) outweigh a hero's mastering a spell or rare sword. Yes, mastering spells or a rare sword can be intertwined with past emotional hardships (or serve as a symbol for emotional growth). However, if a writer conceives of the mastery of a skill absent of any corresponding emotional needs, the story devolves into a checklist of tasks or an empty journey of a forgettable hero.

NOTES

1 Egri (1960: 123).
2 Aristotle (1996).
3 Sophocles (1982: Line 144).
4 The famous Russian playwright, Anton Chekhov, discussed the power of this trope in his letters with Sergei Shcukin. "If you say in the first act that there is a rifle hanging on the wall, in the second or third act it absolutely must go off. It it's not going to be fired, it should be hanging there."

REFERENCES

Aristotle. (1996). *Aristotle's Poetics* (M. Heath, Trans.). London: Penguin Books Ltd.

Chekhov, Anton and Sergei Shcukin. (n.d.). Personal letters.

Egri, Lajos. (1960). *The Art of Dramatic Writing.* New York: Touchstone, p. 123.

Sophocles. (1982). *Three Theban Plays: Antigone; Oedipus the King; Oedipus at Colonus* (R. Fagles, Trans.). London: Penguin Books Ltd.

CHAPTER 6

Character and World

G REAT STORIES COMPRISE GREAT characters. Charisma, honor, intelligence, quirkiness, and eccentricities are psychological building blocks of characters we love. Our emotional investment would not be possible without, first, a compelling central character.

THE PROTAGONIST

Players, readers, and audience members experience story through the lens of the protagonist. Also known as a hero, the protagonist is the center of all drama. They either create events that affect its plot or are subject to these events that also affect the plot. Without a protagonist, there is no journey or point of view. There is just a series of events with no cohesion or justification of plot escalation.

The protagonist is the magnet of the author's imagination. And whatever additions or subtractions the author makes to the story, they will affect the protagonist more than the other characters. The hero is the cornerstone of a story's theme, conflict, premise, and structure; how they pursue their journey and how they change at the end govern all of the above.

The protagonist doesn't have to be likeable or even honorable in a traditional sense. They just have to have their own code and be loyal to it. The lengths they go to maintain it make them compelling. Walter White from *Breaking Bad* is a morally repugnant human being. However, his sick obsession with always being right and being the smartest person in the room (as evidenced by his making the best Meth in the marketplace) compels audiences to obsess over his every move. We root for him because

 DOI: 10.1201/9781003438113-6

we cannot believe he continues to get away with murder – both literally and figuratively. Audiences are captivated by his sense of purpose.

We are also captivated by the underdog. Walter White led a disappointing life as an overqualified school teacher with a PhD, who works a second job at a car wash to provide for his pregnant wife and disabled son. Diagnosed with inoperable lung cancer, Walter dedicates himself to applying his education as a chemist through the making and selling of enough crystal meth to provide for his family after his death. However, the fact that he created the most addictive drug in the market validated his sense of worth. Finally, his life as a chemist is paying off. And his skills, while underappreciated before, are beloved by countless addicts because they keep buying his drug. This is sick and twisted. But it makes sense based on how poorly his life was led up to now. All of us can relate to being an underdog in some part of our lives – at school, at work, in relationships, in business. Walter's journey is wish fulfillment to some degree. His ability to gain wealth and validation in such a short time is something we all crave. How he got there is reprehensible; nonetheless, in fiction, audiences, players, and readers constantly yearn to escape from everyday life, even for a brief moment. We live vicariously through characters we can relate to, or – in regards to Walter White – who help us imagine how we can beat the odds like they do.

Change is also a factor in how compelling a protagonist can be. If a character does not learn from mistakes, does not adapt to challenges, or does not evolve from static situations, they become stale and one-dimensional very quickly. The genius behind *Breaking Bad* lies behind Walter White's refusal to become good. His singular focus on being the greatest meth maker in the Southwest only added more complexity to his depravity. His ability to outwit drug lords was some of the most entertaining television in the history of the medium. Walter White changed not from being bad to good, but from being bad to worse. A compelling character change does not require that they abandon who they are in order to be whom the world wants them to be. It is more compelling, in fact, if they hold true to who they are and expand on it. In the world of a story, a great character does not bend to the world; the world bends to them.

This isn't to say that you can't have a character turn from bad to good (or good to bad). A character's transformation to their polar opposite has to be seeded throughout the story and must escalate organically with every challenge the hero faces. How do they learn about themselves with every new challenge? How can they see that what they did in the past will no longer work in the future? If there are new people in their life, how do they respond to situations that feel familiar? Above all, how are they changing?

MAKING A PROTAGONIST WHOM PEOPLE WANT TO PLAY AS

When crafting a compelling protagonist for games, one must think about how much time a player will be spending with them. A player doesn't want to be stuck with a lifeless dud with stale capabilities.

If, however, the protagonist is fun to play, a risk emerges; game developers can get away with making that character flat. Heroes with neither an emotional growth nor a psychological albatross to overcome elude devs whose focus is just on exciting gameplay. These aren't memorable characters that engender emotional investment from the player. If their capabilities are dynamic, then the hero is nothing more than an empty vessel, a showcase for those capabilities. In that case, it's the capabilities that are memorable, not the hero.

It is in the best interest of a corporation or studio to make characters both fun to play and emotionally interesting, simply because the competition is already doing that. Kratos from the blockbuster *God of War* reboot (2018) is a vastly different character than Kratos from the original *God of War* series (2005–2013). Why? Because the moment we meet Kratos in the reboot, he is not an adrenaline-fueled killing machine like he was in the original series. He has transformed into a cerebral, contemplative hero who must care for his son, Atreus, in the wake of the death of Kratos's wife, Faye. For Kratos, care is mentoring and teaching the ways of survival in the cold, harsh Asgardian world they find themselves in. Teaching Atreus is not only about what it means to be a warrior but also to be a considerate and responsible person who can survive on his own. The new Kratos has more humanity, more accountability, is more so a father and grieving widower than a ruthless slayer of mortals and gods. The new Kratos is now relatable, and relatability is a major criterion of making a memorable, compelling hero.

Professional Goal vs. Personal Goal

Making hard decisions, even if the decisions are wrong or immoral, is another important criterion in crafting a compelling hero. This doesn't mean having a player choose between a sword and a battle-axe to kill a villain. Rather, it is the pitting of two global forces that motivate a character, and then dramatizing how the character responds when one force challenges the other. This shows that the hero is continually conflicted on which force to prioritize. In games and most screen media, these forces comprise a hero's professional goal and personal goal. The professional goal is typically the main mission of the game or film. Save the kidnapped princess from the evil dragon. Stop an evil scientist from destroying the city. Reunite a lost orca with his family, etc.

These are familiar goals that share a very critical element to great storytelling: high stakes. Without a sense of urgency from a challenging conflict, the story is inert and unimportant. All playable heroes need a mission that is all encompassing, with life-or-death consequences (if not physical endangerment, then catastrophic impact upon reputation, love, career, or community acceptance), to be pursued with the greatest of skills, under the constant threat of loss (again, either their life, the lives of others, reputation, community acceptance, love, etc.). The professional goal of a story provides the urgency behind every plot point, gives credence to the playability of the story, and infuses clarity and forward momentum in the pursuit of the game's main objective.

But the urgency of a professional goal will not suffice. A hero's main personal goal ought to heighten the stakes even further. A personal goal involves the psychological makeup of a character, what they value, what they fear, what they desire, how they want to be known or validated by, what they are triggered by, what traumas they've encountered in the past, and what emotional absences affected their past and present. The personal goal requires a journey of emotional growth through the addressing and resolving of the story's main conflict. Accordingly, the tasks that derive from the professional goal will challenge the hero psychologically and emotionally. It's not just about mastering a skill or a weapon but about mastering one's tenacity and clarity of purpose when challenged. Emotionally broken heroes will struggle with these tasks; in some instances, the personal goal isn't to solve emotional problems but to manage them. For those who are sound psychologically, the emotional struggle is a solvable one, often caused by a misunderstanding or a lack of confidence or lack of belief in one's capabilities or new role. The psychologically sound character comprises most popular heroes in media. Consumers, typically, don't want to be saddled with the emotional heaviness of darkness. They play a game or go to the movies to be entertained. Writers need to prepare for that.

But there can be an appetite for the emotionally darker hero, and not just in art house movies. Batman, for instance, is an emotionally broken hero. The murder of his parents remains at the forefront of his mind and serves as the reason why he protects Gotham City. But to what end? We have never seen Batman as anything but a suspicious person, never healthy enough to sustain a long-term romantic relationship. He has, at times, polarized his closest allies in the Justice League of America (e.g., "Tower of Babel" *JLA* story arc July–October 2000) and even with the various people who have assumed the sidekick of Robin (Dick Grayson, Jason Todd, Tim Drake, etc.). It is likely his enemies know more about him than his allies do; arguably, he might be defined by them. It is safe to conclude that Batman suffers from post-traumatic stress disorder (PTSD) and anhedonia (inability to experience joy). Thus, living in the darkness is not just an opportunity for him to be at his most menacing; it also reflects his outlook on life.

Despite this darkness, Batman has been a seminal figure in pop culture for over 80 years in comics, movie serials, animated TV series, video games, toys, other branded merchandise, and billion-dollar blockbuster movies. Why has he endured? Why do we love him?

For starters, he's good at his job. He's single-minded in his goals and values, which are well understood and never compromised. He's creative. He never backs down. He's well branded and makes his presence known through identifiable signals, weapons, vehicles, and – of course – his costume. We can tolerate the darkness for these reasons (and also because he's great at hand-to-hand combat!). But more importantly, audiences tolerate his darkness for the same reason they celebrate his greatness: he's dependable and effective. Whenever there's an evildoer in Gotham, we can rely on Batman from stopping them. He absorbs the hits of corruption and violence so that audiences don't have to. Wherever there is chaos in Gotham City, Batman always restores stability. His efforts are comforting. They appeal to the basic human needs of order, clarity, and routine. His enemies, especially the Joker, represent the opposite, and while audiences may go for the roller coaster ride of whatever havoc these villains bring to Gotham City, audiences find relief – even if vicariously through Batman – once the chaos is over. But Batman is not like Superman or Wonder Woman. Nor is he like his Marvel counterparts Captain America, Spiderman, or Iron Man. These heroes, while not without their emotional flaws (especially the occasional dipsomaniacal Iron Man), are optimistic at heart. Batman is not. He fights darkness with his own darkness and eventually wins.

What makes the *Batman* movies so compelling (particularly the Christopher Nolan ones) is their immersive power. Moviegoers might live through (or aspire to be) Batman periodically, but the majority of their time is spent on being proxy citizens of Gotham City. When Batman fights, he's fighting for the audience. It might be wishful thinking on behalf of the viewer – "With all the hardship in the world, a superhero is in grave need," one might think. Yet, masked heroes with fancy gadgets or superhuman strength do not exist in real life. Consumers attend *Batman* movies for that sense of vicarious relief. The relatability for a multi-decade blockbuster hero isn't only about that hero's background; it's what audiences imagine that hero doing for them. Saving them, sticking up for them, helping them, protecting them, making them feel better about themselves – Batman is both savior and parent.

All of this is to say that when one crafts personal goals for a hero, one must think large. What is it about a hero's background that makes them unusual, makes them imperfect? When the moment of evil strikes, the hero not only heeds the call, they not only fight for themselves and their community, but the hero should also instill within the player a simple sense of relief: "They are fighting for me."

Once that moment is satisfied, players can digitally cosplay as superheroes all day long, but the goals expand beyond the player to a vicarious protection of others. The powers to save innocent lives, to kill bad guys, to make drastic change in a world gone awry are extremely powerful motivators for a player. The protagonist becomes not only aspirational but larger than life. Relatable, yet extraordinary.

Personal Priorities

A protagonist ceases to be generic when the conflict challenges their priorities. Such priorities ought to be personal, unique, and all-consuming. In the permanent absence of these priorities, the hero will become spiritually and emotionally destroyed. Consider a hero's:

- Loss of family
- Loss of a loved one
- Loss of friends
- Loss of credibility
- Loss of trust/respect within a community

- Loss of sanity
- Loss of belief in oneself (or loss of courage)
- Loss of money or resources
- Loss of a loved one's credibility, sanity, or resources (which can be more painful for a protagonist if living for others is their true nature)

One's personal goals, therefore, must intertwine with values that define their essence and pose as the most brittle of possessions in their treasure trove of identity. The story's main conflict will either focus on these personal values or challenge them. A successful resolution of the conflict will either restore these values or strengthen them (e.g., the hero loves the princess so much that he will betroth her; the hero believes in himself so much so that he will take on a new mission; the hero has gained the adulation and devotion of his community that they now want him to be their leader; etc.).

Avoiding Swappable Protagonists

As mentioned earlier, there is a risk of creating characters with tremendous capability, but with a vacant emotional interior. Many games center on an omnipotent hero with lofty goals and skills, but with no personal emotional weakness. It is also true that these characters are swappable with any other character with the same powers and, thus, they fail to be unique. In games, powers are features, not story. Character emotional traits are story, but not features. It is not hard to infuse unique psychological traits within a character, but this process must be a thoughtful one or else the protagonist's backstory can run stale. Revenge plots, for instance, tire easily. How many protagonists need to avenge the death of a loved one? This isn't to say that a revenge plot isn't worthy. It is. But the generic, superficial desire to pursue revenge for honor is a flimsy personal goal for a hero. If, however, revenge is all the hero knows and they have lived a life of sadism, even to avenge those who exercised the simplest of infractions, then the writer is dealing with a character with serious emotional issues and potentially triggers a compelling story. Does the hero struggle to keep these rageful impulses in check? Has the hero ever seen their rage in action before the revenge plot begins? Therefore, should an audience fear him? Or, was the rage bottled up for a long while and now the need for blood and destruction brings out the darkest impulses of the hero who is, ultimately, a butcher?

These are extreme impulses and not likely to be leveraged for a teen-rated game. The point is these dark secrets put the player at odds with what audiences perceive as typically heroic. A writer surprises a player with these dark secrets, and it is these types of surprises that keep the player guessing in terms of where the story is going. Surprises are good, just as long as they are organic to the world and credible in terms of the protagonist's background. Too many surprises or unfounded surprises can come across as contrived or desperate. Adding overcomplexity for the sake of being different is transparent and attenuates the impact of a single, elegant resolution of a conflict. For example, the excessive twists and overreliance upon exposition (via lengthy voice-over) that beset the ending of the Steven Spielberg film *A.I.* (2001) rendered an otherwise simple story about a robot boy trying to find familial belonging into a preachy, sloppy misfire. Yet, many games have been guilty of the same.

"Going against type" is another way to avoid the "swappability" of characters. Usually in reference to actors who play roles outside of their typical genre or brand, going against type can positively surprise an audience. When Adam Sandler and Jim Carrey, respectively, played serious roles in *Uncut Gems* (2019) and *Eternal Sunshine of the Spotless Mind* (2004), each actor received acclaim, defying expectations by going outside of their comfort zone of comedy.

Writers can do the same when crafting a hero. Establish a character's external perception, then defy it with a life-defining secret. Here are some examples:

- A macho Mafia boss sees a psychiatrist to deal with crippling neuroses (Tony Soprano from *The Sopranos* (1999–2007)).

- A slovenly, impoverished drunk publishes beautiful works of fiction (Henry Chinaski in *Barfly* (1987)).

- A chemistry teacher sells crystal meth to provide for his family after he is diagnosed with terminal lung cancer (Walter White from *Breaking Bad* (2008–2013)).

- A mild-mannered owner of a small-town diner must face his gangster past after killing two thieves who terrorized his customers in a failed robbery (Tom Stall from *A History of Violence* (2005)).

- A decorated Naval Officer stuck in the middle of a sex scandal turns out to be Russian spy (Tom Farrell from *No Way Out* (1987)).

These characters don't suffer from Jekyll and Hyde syndrome. They either have a secret from their past that comes out due to circumstances beyond their control and must now reckon with it, or there is a new disruptive event that compels the hero to change with it and restore a past self. Some, like in Henry Chinaski's case, are born that way, that is, with visible contradictions. In fact, opposing behaviors are nothing but incongruities that every human has. Fiction will magnify these incongruities for greater entertainment value. Just a warning though: excessive use of contradictions or overamplification of them runs the risk of rendering a character into a cartoon.

One might look at these incongruities of behavior as triggers for plot twists. Yes, some can be only twists in plot (especially the *No Way Out* ending revelation that Farrell is a Russian spy); however, most should be emotional twists foremost. Plot twists should come organically and not be imposed so as to come off as a contrivance. Unlike plot twists, emotional twists are not one-offs but are emotional challenges that constantly test the protagonist's resolve. Tony Soprano's crippling neuroses eventually affect his leadership decisions, his relationship with his family, and his ability to maintain authority from those within his own social and professional coteries. But these challenges instill within us interest, curiosity (albeit morbid), and investment for our emotionally conflicted heroes.

Who a character is behind closed doors is truly who they are. There are no social pressures to behave a certain way. There is no one around the corner to judge them by what they say, by how they groan when they take off their shoes, by what TV shows they watch. Alone, one is uncensored and unencumbered. But some heroes may not know they have a dark side until a life-changing event disrupts their status quo, often in the beginning of a story or series. The character then must either adapt to the change, restore the status quo, or perish from the inability to achieve either. The pursuit of adapting, restoring, or failing to achieve either is the hero's **professional goal**. How that character reacts and evolves (or devolves) from the disruption of status is the hero's **personal goal**. Whichever prevails – personal goal vs. professional goal – typically defines the hero. If the two goals are pursued together and result in balance, then the hero is an equal mixture of both or that the personal goal was uniquely inextricably linked to the mission of the story. Let's break this down further with the following examples:

- In *Superman II* (1981), after falling in love with Lois Lane, Superman sheds his superhuman abilities and immortality to fully connect with/relate to her. While their romance blossoms, General Zod and his cohorts, as vengeful exiles of Superman's father Jor-El, overtake Metropolis and bring it to its knees. Mortal Superman witnesses the downfall of his adopted home and becomes immortal again, forgoing his relationship with Lois Lane in order to save Metropolis from destruction. Superman's professional goal is to save Metropolis from General Zod, whereas his personal goal is to become human and fall in love with Lois Lane. In this case, the professional goal wins out and defines Superman as a servant of the people, bereft of self-serving needs.

- In *The Dark Knight Rises* (2012), a withdrawn Bruce Wayne slowly reacclimates himself to Gotham City right as a new villain, Bane, terrorizes the city and eventually bankrupts Wayne Enterprises. Wayne (as Batman) tries to stop Bane but suffers a broken back at the hands of his new enemy and is relegated to a harsh, underground prison in the Middle East. There, Wayne, now dispirited, must overcome the demons from his past to renew his faith in himself as a hero, as well as his loyalty to the people of Gotham City. When he successfully confronts his personal demons and scales the treacherous cavernous walls of the prison toward freedom, Wayne returns to Gotham City and, as Batman once again, takes down Bane and the person who planned the entire takeover to begin with, slain rival Ra's al Ghul's daughter Talia (posing as Miranda Tate). Wayne/Batman's professional goal is to save Gotham City from the clutches of Bane and Talia. His personal goal is to renew his sense of purpose and heroism. In this case, the personal and professional goals are symbiotic and equal. Batman is both a steward of Gotham City and his own spiritual wellness. If Batman is broken, Gotham City is broken. If Gotham City is broken, Batman is too. In other words, Batman is Gotham City.[1]

- In *Breaking Bad* (2008–2013), Walter White, a once reputed chemist for Gray Matter Technologies, finds himself in financial desperation as a public-school teacher in Albuquerque, NM, with a disabled teenager and a baby on the way. Because he and his wife Skyler struggle to make ends meet, Walter works as a cashier part-time at a car wash. A persistent cough drives him to see a doctor, who discovers that Walter has terminal lung cancer, a secret Walter then keeps from his family. After joining his brother-in-law Hank, a DEA agent, on a drug bust drive-along, Walter finds a former student of his, Jesse Pinkman, escaping from the scene of the crime. Walter later confronts Jesse and offers his services as a chemist to "cook" and sell crystal meth until, thinking to himself, he has enough money (nearly a million dollars) to provide for his family long after his death. Jesse agrees. So, caring for his family after his death is Walter's original personal goal. Selling crystal meth is the professional one, but all in service to the personal goal. Within a short time, Walter's crystal meth is the most popular drug on the streets. Eventually, he surpasses his original financial goals. For the first time ever, his work as a chemist is validated (regardless of the moral implications). The addiction of the product sways Walter to continue cooking meth, even when that puts him in the crosshairs of some very dangerous drug dealers. As warped as this is, the validation of his chemistry is the validation of his intellect and identity as a chemist. Achieving this validation is Walter's new personal goal. Beyond the first season, Walter's need for power surpasses his need to care for his family. How he amasses power in the drug trade is Walter's evolving professional goal. But that intellectual validation, now deeply rooted in power, remains as the new personal goal. All secrets will eventually be revealed to his wife, who eventually enables his enterprise through bookkeeping and safe storing of his cash. By then, Skyler and Walter are business partners, and familial obligations seldom register on his radar. Many seasons later, he will be responsible (or partly responsible) for the death of Hank, which permanently severs Walter from his family.

What should we make of Walter? His new personal goal, once again, is to seek intellectual validation from his work as a chemist, which consequently alters his professional goal to amass power through his superior product and intellect. His former professional goal is noble at first (once again, to raise enough money from selling crystal meth to care for his family after his death). But that professional goal changes once the personal goal of caring/providing for his family is met. These evolving goals eventually render Walter White a self-serving narcissist with little to no regard for neither his family nor the people hurt by the drug culture he contributes to. His success in the drug trade compounds his personal goal of rapacious intellectual validation, also a self-serving impulse. By the second season, the moral landscape of *Breaking Bad* is lost. The audience is now rooting for a bad guy and booing the people who stand in Walter's way, even if those people are pursing the moral good. A complex character, indeed.

Collision of Priorities

Professional and personal goals are not the only criteria in creating a great hero. They can, however, provide a collision of priorities that deepen the hero's emotional complexity. If the personal and professional goals align, then the latter is often a test of the former. In games, developers often over-index on the hero's professional goal. That goal, typically, is the catalyst for the gaming experience. However, the marketplace today favors heroes with more at stake than a typical objective completion. It, therefore, behooves game publishers and studios to develop heroes with greater complexity. Identifying their personal and professional goals and how those challenge the moral and mental fortitude of a hero is a great first step in developing that complexity.

PROTAGONIST SURVEY

When creating your main hero, you have to think about what makes them compelling and memorable. You also have to think of your player. Will they want to play your game through the lens of your hero?

You, therefore, have to ask yourself what strengths does this hero possess? What are their weaknesses? Is there something from their backstory that they are burdened by? Have they adopted a specific purpose or mission as a result of something from their past? Do they have people close to them? If so, who are they? How did they get to where they are by the start of the game?

Once those basic questions are answered, I recommend diving deeper through a Protagonist Survey. The results lead to a rich dataset that informs how to write dialogue for a hero (or any character, for that matter) and what actions they will take in response to a story beat. Below is a sample survey. You can modify it anyway you like. What's important is identifying granular, psychological details as a foundation for rich, memorable characters (Table 6.1).

This survey allows a writer to home in on what kind of hero they want to create. It also defines the character psychologically and tests whether the hero's personality is compelling enough to be heroic. Of course, a writer

TABLE 6.1   Protagonist Survey

Which Character?	Dolly
What is their role?	Dolly is the main hero/protagonist
What makes them noble?	Dolly grew up as a peasant but fought in a war that saved her village from destruction. Warriors looked up to her as their new leader
What makes them vulnerable?	Dolly has no family of her own; she was born an orphan and was left for the villagers to take care of her. She finds herself often seized by moments of great isolation, even when surrounded by others; she's reluctant to trust people, until they have proven themselves. She is rigid in her views of dignity, morality, and etiquette almost to a point where she is often prematurely intolerant or quick to judge
What purpose do they have that is greater than themselves?	With no family of her own, Dolly views each citizen of her village as her family. She lives for them and will fight for them even if it leads to her own death
What is a unique strength of this character?	She can summon the dead with spells; with an amulet she found in battle, she can increase her strength tenfold; she has the courage and savvy of ten men
Why are they chosen? What makes them uniquely suited for this journey?	Upon the savage death of the village's elder statesman, Dolly will seek revenge upon those who murdered this man, her father-figure

will never truly know how compelling the character is until the game, book, TV episode, or film is in the marketplace. To optimize for success, a writer must continue to ask themselves a flood of questions so that the specificity gets deeper and richer. If possible, test the traits with a focus group a few times in pre-production. The data will help indicate or solidify what makes your hero compelling.

THE ANTAGONIST

One must never forget that every good hero has to have a good villain. When defining the villain, the same initial questions have to be asked: What strengths does this villain possess? What are their weaknesses? Is there something from their backstory that they are burdened by? Have they adopted a specific purpose or mission as a result of something from their past? Do they have people close to them? If so, who are they? How did they get to where they are by the start of the game?

And most importantly, how did they become "evil?" Granted, not all antagonists are evil. They are, in their most basic sense, hindrances to the protagonist. It is the level of their being a hindrance that determines their depth of evil. Repurpose the aforementioned survey (Table 6.1) to make your villain compelling.

But first, get to the root of who your antagonist is at a high level. There are four kinds:

- *The evil sadist.* This character is born evil (or with the seeds of it) and just wants to wreak havoc because, simply put, that's who they are. There is no higher purpose. They are driven instead by an inexplicable thirst for causing harm. He could be a lone wolf psychopath, a criminal mastermind, or a chaos maker. He usually has no regard for his own safety; however, he has an impenetrable focus and usually achieves what he aims for. Anton Chigurh from Cormac McCarthy's 2005 novel *No Country for Old Men* (also adapted to an Academy Award-winning film by the Coen Brothers in 2007) is a perfect example. The Joker from the *Batman* franchise (film, TV, comics, games, etc.) is another.

- *The obstacle.* This is someone who feels infiltrated by the protagonist and will do everything in their power to stymie the protagonist's progress. The Obstacle Villain could be either:
  - Sympathetic – they are virtuous or driven to protect what they have and feel threatened by someone whose success could remove, reduce, or erode what the antagonist has. (A good example is Batman in the 2000 "Tower of Babel" story arc in the *JLA* comic series.)
  - Indifferent or oblivious – This villain is extremely myopic in their focus in life. The hero will find it difficult to engage with them because the villain is not concerned with anything but themselves. The personality traits range from narcissistic to cold to even good-natured. What ties these traits together is *action of omission*. In other words, what they are not doing or not being mindful of is just as harmful as an antagonist who is aggressively trying to subvert

the hero (*act of commission*). The indifferent or oblivious antagonist will cause harm as a result of:

- Accidentally being in the protagonist's way.
- Not seeing life in the same way as the protagonist does.
- Not having the same priorities, values, manners, or decency.

Del Griffith, played by John Candy in the 1987 John Hughes' comedy *Planes, Trains, and Automobiles,* is the perfect example of the oblivious antagonist. Neal Page (played by Steve Martin) is desperate to fly home and be with this family on the Tuesday before Thanksgiving, but a snowstorm forces his flight to land hundreds of miles away from his home in suburban Chicago. From there, he inadvertently "teams up" with Del – a shower curtain ring salesman – on a reckless journey across the Midwest through various modes of transportation, each of which ultimately breaks down, making Neal's return home an increasingly unlikely prospect. Del, as it turns out, is the unwitting catalyst for nearly every single breakdown of transportation and erosion of accommodation – from stealing Neal's cab to the airport in rush hour traffic to flicking a lit cigarette in their rental car that sets it on fire to leaving his enlarged underwear in a hotel sink, with which Neal inadvertently washes his face. Del is a good-natured, kind man who can't get out of his own way. It's this obliviousness that makes him the obstacle to Neal, a tight-assed, intolerant, quintessential '80s yuppie. While Neal's frustration seems to have no limits with Del, Neal creates a bond with him as a result of Del's good nature and eventually learns that kindness and patience are two indelible traits of being a decent human being.

- *The competitor.* This type of antagonist is common in sports movies. They are not necessarily a bad person, but are often arrogant and maybe even better at the craft than the protagonist is. This antagonist wants to achieve the same goal as the hero does, but only one of them can obtain it. This type of character could easily be the protagonist of their own story if the POV were flipped. Therefore, one must look at this type of antagonist as having the same nobility as the protagonist; they are just a vehicle to test the protagonist to see how far they can push themselves to become the best. Examples: Iceman (*Top Gun*), Apollo Creed (*Rocky I & II*).

- *The controller.* This antagonist has a rapacious thirst for money and/or power. His goal is to amass as much of it as possible, manipulate people to help him achieve this end, and destroy those who get in his way. He could be a thief, a dictator, a greedy capitalist, a bully who uses people, a dark lord, or a cult leader. He is often charismatic and social and is a leader or persuader of people. His darkness is often the great motivator of others; while they may love him, it is their fear of him that drives their loyalty. Examples include Zachary Hale Comstock (*BioShock Infinite*), Lord Voldemort (*Harry Potter* series), Darth Vader (*Star Wars* original trilogy), and Loki (*Thor* franchise).

Unity of Opposites

No matter the type of villain you create, they must be fundamentally opposed to the hero in order to bring on a meaningful "unity of opposites."[2] This is a term coined by Lajos Egri in *The Art of Dramatic Writing* (original publication: 1946). The unity of opposites assures that the sustained conflict, upon which all compelling stories are driven, is a result of deep-rooted differences between the protagonist and the antagonist whereby "compromise is impossible."[3] What this means is if the conflict is resolved quickly, then there is no animus between the two characters that merits a story. There has to be a vast gulf in morality or perspective of the world that drives the hero and the villain to vanquish the other. Without that intense need, there is no story, there is no interesting hero, and there is no villain worth fighting.

A Note about Hannibal Lecter

After reviewing the breakdown of villain types, one might ask, "Where's Hannibal Lecter? Sure, he might not run the Galactic Empire or attempt to relegate a mystic into an eternal dark dimension, but he tears the faces off of police officers and eats people." While those acts are repugnant and sick, Hannibal Lecter was the antagonist for neither *Red Dragon* (book: 1991; film: 2002) nor *The Silence of Lambs* (book: 1981; movie: 1991). In fact, he was never the antagonist in any of the books, movies, or for most of the *Hannibal* TV series (2013–2015). In *Hannibal Rising* (book: 2006; movie: 2007), in fact, he is clearly the protagonist … albeit a demented one.

Originally, Hannibal was a supporting character in the aforementioned books and movie adaptations. Imprisoned for life for multiple cannibalistic homicides, he served as a twisted mentor and guide to FBI profiler Will

Graham and later to FBI cadet Clarice Starling, each of whom was on the hunt for a different serial killer that could strike at any moment. Hannibal's past as a psychiatrist and (let's face it) psychopath helped Graham and Starling develop the critical thinking they needed to catch their killer before another victim was murdered. Hannibal might've slightly interfered in their investigations but never did he derail them. Therefore, he was never a direct or meaningful obstacle to these protagonists.[4]

That is the key here. Even if there is a character in your story who is sick, demented, and violent, they pose no direct threat to your protagonist if there isn't a fundamental obstacle that cannot be corrected through compromise. Another way of looking at it is if that psychopathic character is not the main driver of the conflict of your story, they are not the antagonist.

ARCHETYPES AND STOCK CHARACTERS

In addition to the villain, the supporting characters will play a major part in the fiction of the game. Many times, authors rely on character archetypes to help determine who surrounds the protagonist. Archetypes are established figures that have endured for thousands of years in storytelling and are visible in movies, games, and TV shows even to this day. A foundation was set – at least in the identification of archetypes – by famed Swiss psychologist Carl Jung in the early 1900s.[5] Some examples and comparable contemporary characters are shown in Table 6.2.

Jung codified these characters in his dissection of the collective unconscious, a somewhat cognitive repository of ancestral information. He believed there are figures in our dreams that are engraved in our psyche the moment we are born and represent years, if not centuries, of inherited knowledge. These characters as archetypes, due to their familiarity, have

TABLE 6.2 Jungian Archetypes

Archetype	Role	Example(s) in Media
Wise Old Man	The person who provides knowledge and guidance to the protagonist and helps them transform into a hero.	Yoda (*Star Wars* franchise) and Obi-Wan Kenobi (*Star Wars* franchise)
The Trickster	A figure who is seemingly a friend or ally but is mischievous and untrustworthy and is responsible for an event that puts the protagonist in harm's way.	Lando Calrissian (*The Empire Strikes Back*) and Little Finger (*Game of Thrones*)

TABLE 6.2 (Continued)

Archetype	Role	Example(s) in Media
The Fair Maiden	A character that represents purity and virtue; often a love interest for the protagonist; often comes from regal stock; a common target for villains as a way to hurt the protagonist. (Note: While this character's previous place in literature is culturally insensitive in this day and age, the role is no longer designated to young women only. Men too have assumed this role, though the numbers are still small.)	Princess Leia (*Star Wars* franchise) and Kevin (*Ghostbusters* reboot in 2016)
The Nixie	A seductress or seducer who lures people (often the protagonist or a close ally) into their lair and "sucks the life out of them."[6]	Sirens (*The Odyssey*), Zora and Lora (*God of War II*), and Queen of Pain (*Dota 2*)
The Mother	A figure that is helpful, loving, and wise. Or, negatively, a figure that is secretive and dark. She devours and poisons those around her.[7] This character could have both positive and negative attributes. (The controlling, manipulative mother who is overly loving to her son and nasty to others is an overused archetype but derives from these traits.)	**Positive Connotation**: Mrs. Gump (*Forrest Gump*), Tala (*Moana*), and Ramonda (*Black Panther*). **Negative Connotation:** Cersei Lannister (*Game of Thrones*), Norma Bates (*Psycho*), and Marie Barone (*Everybody Loves Raymond*)
The Child	A young character with a raw sense of emotion, almost a conduit to inexplicable, even magical or otherworldly events. He (or she) is "surrounded by unknown forces and must adjust himself to them as best as he can. Owing to this chronic state of his consciousness, it is often next to impossible to find out whether he merely dreamed something or whether he really experienced it."[8] The Child is often not believed by adults in their interactions with the magical or otherworldly. The Child will also separate from their family to explore what these forces are, either to adopt a new power or enhance the power they already have that enabled this connection in the first place. In some cases, the Child might be kidnapped by these forces.[9]	Will Byers (*Stranger Things*), Carol Anne Freeling (*Poltergeist*), Elliott (*E.T. the Extra-Terrestrial*), and Cole Sear (*The Sixth Sense*)

been cemented in myths and fairy tales from long ago and continue to endure as compelling characters in contemporary stories.

Many of these characters serve as the foundation to "stock characters," which are an expanded set of character types, each fulfilling a predictable role. Independent of Jung's findings, these characters have been collected from various different cultures over the years (some just in the past few decades and others in the last few centuries) and have made their way into the media of other cultures due to gradual demographic inclusion. Today, with a more discerning lens, we might dismiss many of these characters as caricatures (some offensively so), depending on the character's lack of depth and/or excessive adoption of cultural and gender stereotypes. However, there are some that have withstood the test of time and have evolved with public consciousness and good taste. To name a few:

- *The superhero* – the protagonist with extraordinary skills and strength, who faces challenges that are cataclysmic in nature and require athletic and physical abilities that go beyond the pale of the ordinary person. The superhero is often found in the adventure, sci-fi, and action genres. Yes, the typical superhero like Wonder Woman, Batman, Superman, and Spiderman is what one might instantly associate this stock character with. However, there are mere mortals that qualify as well: Indiana Jones, Lara Croft (*Tomb Raider* series), and Nathan Drake (*Uncharted* series) to name a few.

- *The supervillain* – the direct opposite of the superhero stock character, the supervillain is just as powerful, but with a heartless, diabolical obsession to their mission. They possess either superhuman abilities themselves or have access to exorbitant wealth, weapons, tools, and technology that can create profound devastation. They are the epitome of darkness. Examples: Lord Voldemort (*Harry Potter* franchise), Sheev Palpatine (*Star Wars* franchise), and Andrew Ryan (*BioShock)*.

- *Harlequin* – a lovable and loyal character, who often brings comic relief to the story, either through side cracks or clumsiness. Examples: Claptrap (*Borderlands* series), Darcy Lewis (*Thor* film series), and Snarf (*Thundercats*).

- *Loyal sidekick* – a compatriot of the protagonist; loyal, dogged protector or advocate. The most trustworthy of all those who surround the protagonist. Examples: Sancho Panza (*Don Quixote*), Chewbacca (*Star Wars* series), and Robin (*Batman* franchise).

Characters in games today are often a hybrid of traits taken from many archetypes and stock characters. Alternatively, some characters don't even have a specific archetype associated with them. There is no requirement to do so. Archetypes and stock characters are guides to creating a rich character universe, but they are by no means a requirement to do so.

The prime objective of creating great characters is specificity. *Are they specific enough in their personality DNA that when I close my eyes and hear them speak, I can distinguish their lines from the lines of others?* Other important questions to ask yourself: *If that character is missing, will I miss them? Or, if they are villainous, will I want to root for my protagonist more so in order to defeat them? In other words, do I care? Am I invested in this fiction?* Well-written characters are often the answer.

DIALOGUE

Of course, so much of the character's psychology is revealed not only through their actions but also through their words. Dialogue, be it performed by an actor or written on the screen, is the personality showcase of a character. *How* they express themselves is just as important as *what* they say to move the story forward.

Many books and courses on screenwriting and playwriting spend considerable time on dialogue. This is a tricky subject mainly because not all games can afford actors for voice-over or motion capture. Many times, "dialogue" appears as on-screen text and could either represent: the voice of the game (as in narration), a non-playable character (NPC), or the playable hero. Additionally, I have always found it nearly impossible to instruct people on what makes good dialogue when (a) audiences have become increasingly fractured and have different expectations that change as frequently as social media does and (b) verbal or linguistic eccentricities bring the charm of a character to the forefront while violating many of the traditional rules of tight dialogue writing. Case in point is when a skittish opera singer named Maggie is asked to mentor a rising star named Sonja, Maggie sheepishly says "Okay" and then rolls her eyes when her boss walks away. Maggie's politeness is clear – perhaps so too is her fear of saying no to her boss. The rolling of the eyes suggests she doesn't want to mentor a younger, rising star; the message is communicated succinctly. But today, you get more value with a character who stretches out the uncertainty by neither saying "no" nor saying "yes" quickly enough allowing her boss to make the decision for her.

Maggie: Well, um, you think I'm a good match for her? I dunno.
Boss: I think you'd be perfect. What do you say?
Maggie: I mean, well, I just, it's complicated. I'm kinda thinking I'm –
Boss: Excellent! I'll have her call you.

Why is this approach effective? It extends the humor, for starters. Second, it reflects how we communicate today. Very few of us, when approached with a request we don't want to do, answer resolutely. We typically hem and haw. What's also revealing is how Maggie's boss exerts his power. He just assumes that, by her inability to assert herself, he can get what he wants without waiting for her to answer definitively. This would not necessarily be conveyed if Maggie had responded "Okay" and rolled her eyes.

True, some characters might be resolute, even if they are in doubt. What that character sounds like, however, will take some creative exploration. A character's personality can be extremely arbitrary, so a writer must tailor a dialogue style to it. That said, there are some universal guidelines when writing good dialogue.

Authenticity is key to every character. How a character speaks (or writes) should reveal their psychology, behavior, background (racial, ethnic, gender), upbringing, social status, and backstory. If they are hardened due to a rough childhood, then consider the traits that need to be incorporated. Are they quiet around strangers? Are they cynical when they open their mouth? If they had a happy childhood, are they always positive in tone?

Less is more. This might be odd to bring this up in light of the example above. Nevertheless, the core idea here centers on *making sure you're not writing more than is necessary*. This isn't to say the dialogue should be a few words spoken each time (unless that's who the characters truly are). It just means there is no need to overwrite a character. Delete excess lines that express the same sentiment.

Lines need vitality. Dialogue can often be flat if there isn't an undercurrent of energy behind the character. When you write the lines, recite them out loud. Will the lines spark a good performance from the actor? Or, if just text on-screen, are the lines something players will want to recite out loud to themselves?

Lines need to be natural to the moment. Activities in games are often filled with ambient dialogue. Be it walking through an abandoned town, rowing a boat through a calm river, or web slinging from skyscraper to skyscraper, the character performing the activity is often accompanied by an NPC, either in person or via diegetic device (e.g., a walkie-talkie or cockpit radio). This NPC talks with the playable character very casually, often to provide context to the task at hand, the world, or the mission. But many times, these casual conversations cover subject matter outside the scope of the scene and can be unrealistic in the heat of the moment. Spider-Man in *Marvel's Spider-Man 2* (2023), for instance, slings from building to building and has – through a built-in communication system in his suit – calm, composed conversations with his girlfriend MJ and new hero Miles Morales about topics ranging from staying up too late and eating too much pizza with his best friend Harry to marveling about Harry's symbiote exo-suit that has mysteriously put into remission his recent illness. These lines can serve to reinforce past information or foreshadow events to come, but they are communicated in moments that a person in real life would not have the presence of mind to talk about because they are in the middle of an adrenaline-fueled act of parkour. Suspension of disbelief is, of course, the justification here, but with narrative information that is not directly tied to the current activity, it is a lot to ask of a player to remember such things, and it's likely they won't.

Distinction is necessary. Do not write universal dialogue, even if the lines crackle. Make sure each character has their own distinct voice. Make the lines alive by giving the characters a signature way of expressing themselves.

Power status has a profound impact on a character's psychology. This might seem obvious to most, but you'd be surprised to see how often power status has no impact on a character's dialogue in games. It clearly goes beyond the easy shorthand of ending or beginning the dialogue with the title of a character (e.g., "Yes, Sergeant."; "At your service, My Lord."). As Shakespeare taught us in *Macbeth*, the King might rule Scotland, but the Queen rules the King; thus, a title does not always equate power. What's more important is the *psychological power* one character has over another. *Interpersonal status is a massive influencer of dialogue.* For instance, is a father afraid of his daughter because she has run away from home before and the father wants to prevent a recurrence? If so, his dialogue will be obsequious, overly accommodating, maybe even timid. Is an assassin afraid of no one? If so, then her dialogue could be indifferent, almost without affect. Or perhaps she takes pride in her skill and her lack of attachments and is, therefore, overly brash when she talks to a new client. What about two mercenaries who are unwilling to cede control to one another and are equally stubborn in how to infiltrate a terrorist safe house? If so, then their dialogue will be contentious, maybe even playful at times. Power status may not necessarily be uniform from one character to the next. Perhaps one of those mercenaries is also the same father who is afraid of his daughter. Certainly, the mercenary will not talk to her as he does to his partner.

Before the writer identifies the power status among their characters, it's important they determine what drives the characters and what the potential emotional obstacles are. Otherwise, it will be hard to convey a power dynamic and could render the dialogue flat and uninteresting.

Understand subtext. Subtext is the unspoken dialogue between characters in a scene. In the example of Maggie the opera singer, the subtext on the most superficial level was her aversion to taking on an apprentice. But why? Is Maggie in the last years of her career and does not want to compete with someone who could take her job? Was she once a rising star and was traumatized by a previous mentor and, therefore, does not want to re-enact that? Why didn't she push back on her boss? Is it fear of losing her job? Is he in a bad place in his life and she couldn't bring herself to hurt his feelings? The various unrealized feelings of a character will influence not only what they say, but more importantly *what they don't say*. This creates a deep psychological foundation of our characters and, therefore, makes them more interesting.

In violating the subtext rule, there is little to discover about the characters we create. This brings to mind the necessary cliché: "show, not tell." Allow the behavior and actions of the characters to reveal what's happening in the plot and in their emotional journey. It's not interesting for Maggie to say to her boss, "I hate you." Dumping a laxative in his coffee and feigning interest in helping him find the bathroom are more revealing of Maggie's psychological makeup. They're also more entertaining.

Sometimes, it's unavoidable for a character to talk "on the nose" or just say what they're feeling outright, especially when we need to explain a specific gameplay mechanic, like for tutorials. These introductory gameplay "how to's" are almost always subtext-free because their purpose is to arm the player with key information on how to use the controller and play the game. In other circumstances, however, subtext is revealed when the dramatic moment is earned. Will Maggie reach her tipping point with her boss? After months of mentoring the young ingenue, Maggie is let go from the opera. Under those circumstances, Maggie's confronting of her boss is justified. It will allow her to unload on him and reveal past resentments in order to achieve closure to a frustrating relationship. (Aristotle referred to this as *catharsis*.) To get here, the character must go through a series of mental anguish and professional challenges, during which time the subtext of Maggie's dialogue becomes more multidimensional and complex.

Dialogue is elusive in the gaming world, mainly because casting is usually a last-minute addition. Writing for specific actors, therefore, is not recommended.[10] Dialogue is elusive also because performers aren't usually acting off of one another. They are isolated in a sound booth, reciting lines usually out of context. Also, because of their massive expanse, games don't always have a singular script. Lines can be recited as combat chatter or for ambient authenticity, or as an in-game dialogue moment to help move the gameplay along. These are often presented on-screen in a spreadsheet or as hard copies … of spreadsheets. Cut scenes are often the exception, but only in presentation. An actor will be presented with a script but will have no one to act off of except for the voice director … who is not in the recording booth with the actor.

Because of these challenges, a narrative designer or game writer will need to supplement the script with a bulletproof tone document and character bio to help inform the actor's performance. There will be off-the-cuff feedback during the recording sessions, so script changes will happen on the fly.

WORLD AS CHARACTER

Successful games have characters, worlds, and moments that are brandable and ownable. More specifically, a game's unique elements must be front and center and must be significant enough to differentiate it from the competition. Without these unique elements, the game will fail to capture consumers.

These differentiators are critical because they go beyond the game experience. In print ads and reviews, memorable images will capture cool-looking vehicles or a savage confrontation between two dynamic, vivid characters. These still images will also be on the front and back of the game package or as a thumbnail image in a digital store (via PlayStation Store, Xbox Games Store, Steam, App store, etc.). Gameplay clips also have their impact on creating ownable differentiation.

These images speak to something larger than a manipulation in marketing. It's about creating memorable, sticky characters and worlds that provide the game with the possibility of going beyond its original medium. Could I experience another journey of Aloy but in a *Horizon Zero Dawn* movie? I will delve into this further in the transmedia section of this book (Chapter 14), but it's important to bring up this topic up now because, as with structure, creating ownable worlds and characters is the most important part of a narrative designer's job. Gameplay can thrive on its own by tapping into a gamer's dopamine pleasure centers. But games are a competitive business. Without a vibrant world and memorable characters, they will buy the competitor's product over yours, plain and simple.

Narrative may not be the main selling point for most games. But games that do not offer narrative will struggle to differentiate themselves in the marketplace.

Think of world as character. Like a good character, a compelling world should have distinct, memorable features that invoke emotion in players – comfort, distrust, mystery, menace, resolve, etc. In asking yourself what makes a world distinct, you will wind up writing a backstory that is not unlike those of your characters. Set up a profile of this world, as you would a character. Here are some prompts to help you define the world you're trying to build (Table 6.3).

When describing the world, one cannot help but dig into its political nature. This is what makes world creation a fun endeavor. Worlds need to be filled by living entities. Each of those entities has an agenda. Entities will go at war when agendas clash.

TABLE 6.3   World-as-Character Survey

What's the Name of This World?	Piedmont
Where is it?	A town somewhere in New England, state unknown
How many people live there?	508. It's rural
What kind of people live there?	Sixty percent is made up of Army veterans; most are out of work and rely on the bottle to get through the day; 20% is Native American, as there's a reservation nearby and a casino not far away; the remaining 20% of Piedmont is a biker gang, who sells illegal firearms to subsidize the empire of their brotherhood

TABLE 6.3   (Continued)

What's the Name of This World?	Piedmont
Name an historical event that happened there in the past 20 years.	A senator was killed in a mysterious car accident that some have suggested was engineered by the biker gang out of revenge for his supporting new Federal funding to the Bureau of Alcohol, Tobacco, Firearms and Explosives (ATF)
What's the climate of this world?	Long winters. It snows starting in early October and ends in early May. The town experiences subzero temperatures during this time, along with heavy snowfall and limited hours of light. The summers are extremely humid. Moderate temperatures in May and September
What's the world look like?	Working-class town with high unemployment. Biggest employers are the casino 10 miles away and the ValleyMart, a huge discount department store. Lots of trailer parks. Houses have acres of space between one another. The woods are thick, filled with heavy streams but barren trees. Lots of RVs on abandoned streets. People do not pick up after themselves. It's a third world town inside of a first world country
How do the people in the neighboring worlds feel about it?	No respect for Piedmont. As far as others can tell, this is a barren wasteland. If you're not drowning your sorrows at the local saloon, you're tattooing your flesh to celebrate your gang
Who runs this world?	Derrick Ambrose, the leader of the Devil Spawn Biker gang. He is the most feared man in the state, but as long as you keep to yourself, you won't have any trouble
How is this world run?	Gangland rules. No snitches, no stiches. As long as you let the Devil Spawn Biker gang do as they please, you'll be fine. But if you cross them, your days are numbered
Are there any rivalries in this world?	Rival gangs occasionally drive through here, but at great risk. Recently, the Mafia set up shop in order to invest in the nearby casino
Are there any intruders or threats to this world?	The Mafia and undercover ATF agents, who track the activities of the gang
What's the most recent event that set the world into chaos?	The sister of an Army vet was killed at a local bar. Her boyfriend, a gang member of the Devil Spawn, fled the town
Is the status quo of this world being threatened? If so, how?	Yes. The Army vet is investigating what happened. Denied by the police because they don't want to cross the Devil Spawn, the Army vet has taken to arms to exact revenge on this gang, even joining forces with the Mafia to take the biker gang down

(Continued)

TABLE 6.3   (Continued)

What's the Name of This World?	Piedmont
Is there an event that the world is preparing for or responding to?	A massive snowstorm has cut off the power supply to the town. Everyone is living without electricity for the indefinite future. The roads are too dangerous to travel on
Will this world survive in five years?	No. It is on the verge of moral collapse if the gang cannot rise from the cover-up of the death of the Army vet's sister. Alternatively, the Mafia might take it over if they see a town in turmoil with crumbling leadership

Now, it's likely you will need to describe in detail the physical nature of the world, where the different inhabitants live, and its climactic elements. While I only touched upon these briefly, I find that physical descriptions are less about storytelling than they are about creating a blueprint from which artists and designers can build. Writers and narrative designers can spend too much time getting into the granular details of describing the visual nature of the world, as if they were a geologist writing down the various physical properties of a newly discovered rock. I do not find this to be a good use of a writer's time. While there is value in providing enough physical details to help artists do their job, the storyteller should look at world creation as an opportunity to inform compelling characters, introduce potential conflicts, and create a rich tapestry that influences how the lore of the intellectual property unfolds over time.

CHARACTER AND WORLD RULESETS

As discussed earlier, every character ought to have their own unique set of psychological traits and capabilities. A stoic character may have moments of greater talkativeness but not possess basic loquaciousness by default. In order to stay tonally consistent, that character ought to remain somewhat quiet or economic in their language whenever they appear. This personality trait is established upon the audience's first exposure to them and, consequently, sets expectations of their behavior for the remainder of the story. To violate those expectations is to diminish the quality of the character. Sure, there can be the occasional moment where the character is, say, drugged and suddenly talks a lot, but that state of mind is fabricated solely to add complication to a plot point and does not reflect the true nature of that character. And, sure, a character can grow or change, but the foundational elements of a character ought to remain the same. Great memorable characters possess rigid characteristics. Audiences rely on those characteristics to provide consistency in the conflict-driven world the character finds themself in. Too much chaos and too much rule-breaking reduce a story to incoherence or tonal flux. One cannot trust a story if it clumsily defies the rules of the characters that were established from the outset.

In this chapter, I brought up the notion of some complex protagonists as "going against type." It should be noted that capturing incongruity invites compelling storytelling. However, that incongruity should not come at the cost of a hero's basic immutable psychological traits and values. A disruptive event (such as Walter White's cancer diagnosis or Tony Soprano's visitation to a therapist) brought out their true selves and occurred in the first episode of those series. If Walter White was a mundane chemistry teacher for five seasons and, in season 6, decided to make crystal meth after a cancer diagnosis, Walter would come across as unbelievable because audiences got to know him a certain way for several years. Such a disruptive event as a cancer diagnosis in season 6 would spring forth a different reaction, such as recommitting himself to teaching or parenting. So, the disruptive event either brings out a character's true self (if it happens in the beginning of a story or series) or reinforces it (if it occurs anywhere in the story or series), but never does it extract a radically different set of psychological traits or values.

Consistent rulesets also apply to the world of a game. If it is a dark, cynical place, stories of Pollyannaish optimism will come across as out of place, as if they are appropriate for another fictional universe. If the world is horror, but the story centers on a gangster who is running cigarettes illegally across state borders, audiences will experience a genre disconnect, as there are certain expectations of tone and subject matter for horror films that are separate from gangster movies. And, yes, there are hybridizations or mashups of genres, but those work with just a few genres – sci-fi and Western, sci-fi and horror, and horror and noir. There are more examples, but not much more. Whatever genres one might hybridize, they must choose those that share tonal and subject matter synergies; otherwise, a disjointed story will follow.

Another way rulesets are important is through character powers and capabilities. In order for a special magical skill to make sense, how it works must be introduced and made clear in the beginning of the story or upon its first appearance or mention. Because humans are not endowed with magical or superhuman capabilities, we must be educated on what is unnatural to us. It is, therefore, a writer's responsibility to illustrate how a power works, when it's triggered, to what extent it has an impact, and to what extent it is vulnerable. Thus, when that capability shows itself in the third act leading to the climax of the story, there should be no surprises or *deus ex machina*. True, a power can evolve into something an audience hadn't seen before the climax. A proper illustration of its rulesets early on, however, "primes the pump" of its potential. But if nothing was explained before and the power suddenly exhibits a visually stunning, extraordinary capability, then it comes off as a cheat to resolve the conflict quickly or to "peacock" a hero. But such moments are contrivances,[11] and when contrivances hasten a story's completion, a hero never fulfills their personal journey. They are but an empty vessel of that power. The hero should always strive to master the power, not vice versa.

A few more words of advice:

Make characters unique, but not excessively specific. Beware of overcomplication. Special powers or eccentricities of a character's behavior should not be "Rube Goldberg" in nature. If the writer cannot communicate the rulesets simply and quickly through character dialogue in fewer than 40 words (i.e., "My sword turns red when the sun rises!") or through physical reactions to the environment (i.e., the player witnesses their sword turning red once the sun rises), then the writer has failed the playerbase. The writer might be struggling to make something memorable by being overly detailed or conditional. If it requires mental gymnastics to understand the circumstances upon which a power appears, then the story runs the risk of polarizing players.

Make characters complex, but not inaccessible. Characters that are too specific and idiosyncratic might be impossible to relate to. Never forget the basic humanity of a character, which means never forcing unnecessary traits upon them. Making social or political points, paying homage to an artist or writer of another work, or just trying to be different as a means to being bold – these impulses can ruin a character. The best way to render a character is by dramatizing them honestly, warts and all. Overloading them with too many disparate traits indicates that one should create multiple characters with few traits rather than a single character with exorbitant traits. Or, that same writer should write something separate (through a different experience or medium) to communicate that which is tertiary to the story's central conflict.

Be frugal, but not anemic. Finding the right balance of psychological traits for a single character is not easy. Infuse a character with **a few solid and meaningful traits** (such as *unique but relatable* values, behaviors, fears, and vulnerabilities – again, not skills or powers) so that the character can stand on their own. These traits should make the character feel like they belong to their community or coterie. However, do not make that process of belonging seamless. One of those traits ought to invite dissension or turbulence between the protagonist and a close ally or person of authority. Unrest at home always complicates things for the protagonist and lengthens their pursuit in resolving the conflict.

NOTES

1 Which is an interesting flipping of the Superman scenario in *Superman II*. The two are the most iconic heroes from the same DC Universe, often allies in crossovers of comics and cartoons (and a movie or two). The two are household names, staples of global pop culture for over 80 years. Yet, they couldn't be more different from one another. As mentioned, Batman is a cynical character in a bleak world. Superman is an optimistic character in a bright(er) world. But their differences are starkest when comparing these two movies. (Granted, the quality favors Nolan's, but the behaviors of each superhero are equally noteworthy.) Superman achieved complete happiness in the arms of Lois Lane while the city surrendered to Zod. Even when viewing the destruction of the city, Superman did not consider re-becoming immortal immediately. It wasn't until clashing with a roughneck in a Metropolis diner that Superman (as Clark Kent), upon seeing his own blood for the first time, understood the gravity of his new situation: that there is no bliss in being mortal. Batman, on the other hand, never wished to be anything else but a savior of his beloved Gotham City. In Bane's breaking of his back, Batman questions whether he himself is capable of remaining that savior.

2 Egri (1960: 123).

3 Ibid.

4 Now, you might think Francis Dolarhyde (*Red Dragon*) or Buffalo Bill (*The Silence of the Lambs*) weren't direct obstacles to Will Graham or Clarice Starling, respectively, mainly because the villains didn't know anyone was on their trail until the end. How could they stop a protagonist they didn't know even existed? They do qualify as antagonists, however, because they pre-emptively created obstacles for any investigator by effectively obscuring the physical details of their murders. What wasn't seen was just as obstructive as what was in plain sight. This is typical of the murder mystery and thriller genres.

5 Jung (1969: 15).

 6 Jung (1969: 184).
 7 Ibid., p. 82.
 8 Ibid., p. 154.
 9 Ibid., p. 154.
10 Unless, of course, the game is an already established franchise with confirmed actors or you have actors in mind as north star "comparables" to guide casting.
11 Contrivances, in essence, are unearned story details. A writer can subconsciously employ contrivances to add unnecessary tension or dramatic glitter, but they are nothing more than transparent, empty, and forced character traits, backstory, and/or plot points.

REFERENCES

Egri, Lajos. (1960). *The Art of Dramatic Writing*. New York: Touchstone, p. 123.
Jung, Carl. (1969). *The Archetypes and the Collective Unconscious* (2nd edition). New York: Princeton University Press, pp. 15, 82, 154, 184.

CHAPTER 7

Structure

WHAT IS STRUCTURE AND WHY IS IT IMPORTANT?

Dramatic structure is the sequence of story-driven events that provides a natural escalation to a protagonist's journey. Structure gives a story its shape, or more specifically, a coherent organization of moments that provides the maximum entertainment, character development, and necessary setbacks that make subsequent resolutions enjoyable and meaningful.

A protagonist's journey is not fulfilling if there are no obstacles to overcome. In fact, a protagonist becomes more admirable and more heroic with every escalating challenge that they overcome. The greater the challenge, the greater the effort. The more successful the effort, the greater the heroism. The greater the heroism, the greater the hero.

Structure is just as important as character. In fact, structure is the one element of storytelling that is the least controversial, simply because there is a natural logic to a sequence of events that, if violated, would render a story incomprehensible. Moreover, ignoring obstacles, their escalation, and their resolution would render a story dull, stale, and stagnant.

WHERE GAMES FAIL

Structure is oftentimes given the backseat treatment because of the numerous concessions that writers have to make for gameplay, development rescoping, and budget pressures. But it is also the case that poor precedent was set in the early days of games. Why? Many of the early days of narrative were not written by writers, but more so by game designers who had little-to-no knowledge of story structure or character development.

DOI: 10.1201/9781003438113-7

(Thankfully, the effort to uproot this precedent – and basically destroy it – is ongoing.)

MAIN STRUCTURAL BEATS

When I am brought on to a new project, I make sure to have the creative director, lead designer, producer, and others in a single room, where we hash out the big moments of the game's story. Usually, the team will already have a set of "non-negotiables," that is, required moments that provide the biggest impact on gameplay and on the hero's journey. I then work with them to figure out the main story beats in between these key gameplay moments. From there, we work toward establishing a structure and a natural escalation of events.

Over the years, I have evaluated the following story concepts from some of the best dramatists and story theorists in the field. Not one theorist offers a clean set of story milestones that works perfectly for games. Therefore, I have cherry-picked story milestones from these various thinkers and have added my own to the following list. Bear in mind, these story milestones conform to elements of Western storytelling, which – rightly or wrongly – continue to pervade the global marketplace. Terminology of these milestones might vary from studio to studio.

Act 1

Setup or Establishment of the World – This is not a major story beat, *per se*. However, by establishing the status and tempo of the world, the story immediately orients the player on genre, tone, atmosphere, the hero (unchallenged), and other details that bring heft and specificity to the world in which the hero currently resides (or will reside if brought from another locale).

Inciting Incident – the first significant moment in the story that redefines that *status quo* of the world of the protagonist. This moment has a downstream effect that impacts everything in that world and eventually forces the protagonist to take an action that officially sets the story in motion.

Introduction to Protagonist's Purpose – a protagonist might be morally unscrupulous, pure-of-heart, unimposing, enterprising, or quiet. What is important is determining clearly and upfront what drives them. This is the most important building block of a protagonist's personality DNA. A great example of this is in the first episode of *Breaking Bad*. After his diagnosis of terminal cancer, Walter White makes a clear-cut decision to collaborate with a former student to make and distribute crystal meth. His goal (at least at first) is to generate over $900,000 so that, after his death, his wife, disabled son, and unborn child will have enough money to survive on their own.

Fans of the show will realize later on that Walter White's ambition does not end there. His eyes eventually set on becoming the biggest drug kingpin in the Southwest. But it takes a long while for us to get there. In the meantime, our sympathies are with a dying Walter White in his selfless crusade to make and sell drugs. The goal is very clear as are his priorities. We, as viewers, make the decision to go along with him. Conversely, if the goals are not clear from the outset, it's very difficult to get bought in on the hero's journey when we don't know what they are committed to.

Poorly written heroes do not have defined goals.

Refuse the Call – the moment where the protagonist is offered an opportunity to do something profound and significant, but declines because they feel there is no path to success at that moment, mainly due to a lack of courage or feasibility.

Situation Worsens – the life of the protagonist, after refusing the call, worsens. Either the *status quo* is threatened, a rival emerges, or the hero's sensibilities are offended. No matter the scenario, the protagonist must feel as if life is untenable or unacceptable and reconsiders their act of refusing the call. Perhaps if they re-answer it, they will reverse their current negative trend in life.

Accept the Call – after the situation for our hero or his loved ones worsens, the hero realizes they cannot accept things as they are. They must commit to taking action and putting themselves in harm's way to save those in danger.

If the story is not a violent one, then the comparable scenario to harm's way could be anything that puts the protagonist outside of their comfort zone. They are in a new role, for example, that challenges them in ways they did not expect. Proving that they can handle this role will determine their heroism. But the path forward cannot occur unless the protagonist accepts the new role.

Point of No Return – the protagonist has succeeded in performing their first act of heroism. In doing so, they are too committed (and inextricably linked) to the mission that they cannot turn back. They, therefore, march forward into new territory (either literally or figuratively) to solve the main conflict, where greater challenges await.

Act 2

Adjustment to New World – on their journey to accomplishing the mission, they will need to adjust to their new surroundings. This should not be easy for the hero, as every hardship – big or small – makes the hero more adaptable, more honorable, and stronger.

Escalating Burdens – this new world involves new hardships and conflicts that increase in complexity and intensity the further the protagonist travels. Once again, every new challenge – big or small – is an opportunity for the protagonist to become better at (1) what they do as a practitioner of their craft and (2) who they are as a thinking, feeling person.

Escalating burdens is shorthand for new conflicts that arise and threaten our hero's existence. They can be physical challenges (climbing a mountain, crossing a sea, etc.) or emotional ones (a femme fatale leaves the hero's house with the stolen money, an angry partner feels betrayed by a hero and leaves the mission). They often involve their own micro-stories, especially if the medium is episodic. If the medium is structured like a three-act structure (which most films and games are), then escalating burdens will take up most of Act 2. They are a series of challenges that threatens the hero continually while increasing in danger. Escalating burdens drive the plot forward. They are the logistics of a story and are often a different class from larger narrative milestones.

In other words, escalating burdens are often the "what happens next" instances of story. This is also known as "Rising Action" in traditional cinema story structure.

Exposure of Weakness – every good story has a moment where the hero's momentum stops, and the audiences (or players) are forced to reevaluate the journey and the protagonist. This is the critical lead up to the low point of the story. But, the buildup to the low point is essential; the hero cannot suddenly lose everything and expect the audience to feel something. There has to be a sense of doubt instilled in the viewer long before the low point happens. Here, you can plant the seeds. These momentary weaknesses might seem like nothing, especially if the hero continues to excel. But once a major event occurs wherein the hero's weakness leads to the destruction of a village, for example, the perception of the hero *as a hero* is in grave doubt. Sure, a weakness for wine means nothing if the hero wakes up with a hangover and enters the dark forest the next day only to experience no altered status quo or changed reactions from others. There was nothing at stake, no meaningful consequences of their actions.

If, however, they chose to drink wine that night and got too sloshed to run to the village and stave off a massacre from marauders, such a weakness is unforgivable, but possibly redemptive.

Loss of Trust – once the weakness is exposed for what it is, the protagonist will lose the trust of those around them and of the audience (or players). Exposure of Weakness and Loss of Trust are complementary and symbiotically connected; you cannot have one without the other. Loss of trust should be the emotional antecedent of the low point, whereas exposure of weakness should be its logistical antecedent. Together, they tee up the events that lead to the low point.

Midpoint/Low Point – this is the story beat where – coupled with Exposure of Weakness and Loss of Trust – the protagonist's fortunes are reversed. A single act has led to a full stop to the hero's progress and to the deprivation of or great harm to something important, for example, the decimation of a village they were meant to protect; an abduction of a loved one; the destruction of a weapon; the death of a close friend, loved one, or relative. Whatever the event, the hero should feel their own sense of doubt. Is finishing the mission even possible? Will the hero survive? Will the people who mean the most to the hero survive as well? Or, could those people permanently lose faith in the hero? This is a moment of great despair and the most necessary story beat in terms of escalation. While everything was once rising and the hero was rising with it, a drop as severe as this one truly tests the hero. How they adapt to this low moment, especially if they feel responsible for it, will determine if they are a hero and, if so, what kind of hero they are.

The most effective of low points happens as a result of a hero making a choice they shouldn't have. One's opting to drink wine at the local tavern over guarding their village is a perfect example. The choice reveals a psychology about the hero that will need to be planted earlier. The hero's drinking could either be a sign of an addiction or a casual arrogance where they believe everything's good if there are no signs of danger in sight. Neither scenario makes a hero. In a later story beat, the hero should learn from that weakness and work twice as hard to remedy their mistake or flaw while delivering on their most heroic effort yet.

In the Belly of Jonah's Whale – after the low point, the hero moves forward but in a fog (either mentally or physically). Their pace is slower and there is great confusion as to where they need to go next. Usually, it is a moment of stagnation. It is akin to being *in utero*, where the hero is floating powerlessly without direction.

There is uncertainty in this stage, which may involve physical threats to one's life or mental anguish where one doubts themselves. To survive this moment is to reemerge from it a new hero, better than before.

This concept was identified by the philosopher Joseph Campbell with regard to the Biblical parable of Jonah and the whale. Jonah, in defying God's orders to preach to the people of Nineveh, headed on a boat to Tarshish where he was soon caught up in a great storm. The men on the boat blamed Jonah for the storm, for it was clearly a result of God's wrath, and threw him overboard. Jonah was then swallowed by a whale. Inside its belly, Jonah then repented and pleaded to God to be spared. At last, he got "spit up" by the whale on the shores of Nineveh, where Jonah visited its wicked citizens and preached the word of God.

As Joseph Campbell points out:

> *The conscious personality here has come in touch with a charge of unconscious energy which it is unable to handle and must now suffer all the trails and revelations of a terrifying night sea journey, while learning how to come to terms with this power of the dark and emerge, at last, to a new way of life.*[1]

This story beat is about the hero's facing their innermost demons and slaying them only to be reborn braver and stronger.

Act 3

Redemption Path Begins – once the protagonist has survived the grueling stasis inside the belly of Jonah's whale, they emerge as a new hero, repurposed or rededicated to achieving their initial goal. They have adopted a new zealotry with a tacit code: "I will achieve my goal by any means necessary." Their motivation brings them to the next level of hero status. Where once they were a timid protagonist who rose to the occasion when needed, they are now proactive, single-minded, intense, and strong-willed. They are willing to die for their cause. This story beat can straddle between the end of the second act or the beginning of the third.

Ticking Time Bomb Introduced – our new hero will face an overwhelming obstacle like no other. While they have emerged as a better warrior as a result of prevailing over Jonah's whale, the difficulty in achieving their initial goal amplifies. This is a must; otherwise, the story would run stale quickly if an omnipotent hero has an easy path ahead. The figurative ticking time bomb is either a rapid escalation of the main villain's goals or an introduction of a new threat to vanquish the protagonist or those the protagonist holds dear (e.g., a loved one, a family member, a best friend, or even an entire city).

Escalating Burdens Intensify – the ticking time bomb isn't the only obstacle the hero must face in Act 3. They will encounter numerous warriors, environmental threats, and interpersonal struggles that exacerbate the tension created by the ticking time bomb. These burdens keep getting in the hero's way, reducing the odds of stopping the ticking time bomb from "blowing up." Escalating burdens increase suspense by compelling the player or audience to ask themselves, "Will the hero make it in time to stop the bomb?"

Obligatory Scene/Climax – once the hero has resolved all the escalating burdens and is on the verge of stopping the ticking time bomb, they must face the antagonist. This is the final showdown between good vs. evil, also known as the obligatory scene. In video games, these scenes are known as "Boss Battles"; however, every game has numerous boss battles that ultimately lead to a final one. Other media do not have that kind of creative mandate. It's important, still, to designate the final boss battle as the obligatory scene, so that the dramatic tension can be properly built early and gradually.

This story beat isn't just important from a logistical sense (defeating the villain in order to stop the bomb); it's also important from a moral sense. Evil should not prevail. Every protagonist knows this implicitly; therefore, defeating the villain is a moral imperative. This confrontation is also the climax of the story, aka, its most important moment. It's what your entire story is intended to lead to. One can determine the depth of its importance by identifying what would happen if the hero lost (case in point: instant destruction of the community they were dedicated to saving). The stakes cannot get any higher than this moment.

Reversal – when analyzing Athenian drama, Aristotle identified a key moment in every play where the status of the protagonist shifted, either from good to bad, bad to good, or from any position or perspective to its opposite. This is known as a reversal.[2] This story beat has endured for thousands of years and finds its way in games, books, and movies today. In the last 50 years, no film has had a better reversal than in *Godfather II* (1974). When Kay, the wife of the powerful crime boss Michael Corleone, reveals to him that the baby she lost in pregnancy was not due to a miscarriage, as originally thought, but to an abortion, Michael (the hero) is instantly shattered. No matter what power he could wield as a Mafia boss, what was important to him, above everything else, was family. His reversal went from powerful to powerless within seconds.

Recognition – in response to the reversal, Aristotle observed that the pro- tagonist must have a moment where they must switch from "ignorance to knowledge"[3] in their relationship to the world around them. In Michael Corleone's case, his true understanding behind the loss of Kay's baby forced him to see he was not as powerful as he thought. He was the most feared leader in organized crime. But as a man, his rapacious desire for power pushed his wife away to such a point where she aborted their child so that future generations of Corleones could never wreak havoc on this earth. As a result of this revelation, he lashed out at Kay – both physically and verbally. This uncharacteristic move derived from Michael's recogni- tion of his failure as a husband and man. But that recognition did not stop him from continuing his heartless journey; instead, he doubles down on it and commits the most heinous of crimes: the killing of his brother Fredo, as a result of an unrelated double cross. It is not necessary for the hero to change once they've achieved recognition. What is necessary, however, is that they are *given the opportunity to change*. Whatever action they take then – be it to change or to stay the course – will define the type of pro- tagonist they are.

Resolution of the Bomb – just because your hero has defeated the antag- onist doesn't mean the ticking time bomb has stopped at the same time. There's still work to be done. And fast. The bomb continues to tick as a lingering, imminent threat. If the hero stops to take a breath after defeating the villain, it's too late. The bomb will go off, leading to utter devastation. The hero at this point has nothing to prove. They aren't looking for a pat on the back or payment for services rendered. Their next move is a reflexive, visceral response to save the day … in mere seconds. Taking action should be instant and reflexive and reveal the hero's innate sense of selflessness. It's the community the hero's been fighting for, not the desire to become a hero. But by saving the community, the hero truly becomes a hero.

Denouement – when the ticking time bomb has been resolved, the hero and their community can relax. Everyone will take the next steps to achieve a new *status quo*. We're all familiar with the common tropes. The hero and a love interest kiss. The community celebrates the hero. People take precautions to prevent the rise of the villain. All of these events make up the denouement: the collective sigh of relief paired with the early signs of life returning to normal. Not all stories have a denouement. Some will end with a sense of unease, *a la* the villain rises from the ashes to signal a sequel or the hero is compromised irrevocably. The 1970s conspiracy thrillers – for example, *The Parallax View* (1974) or *Three Days of the Condor* (1975) – exemplify this type of ending.

Please Note: Don't kill yourself trying to get the precise order of these milestones in place. The point is to be aware of their general proximity. The sequence will be dictated by the organic development of your story.

DRAMATIC ESCALATION WARNINGS

The goal of these milestones is to build a strong, meaningful, and believable escalation of the protagonist's journey. They are like coordinates for the story, such as when the character is introduced to the challenge or when the character must face off against the villain. These coordinates provide navigational guidance on how to craft the forward momentum of a story.

While I am stickler for taut structure, I cannot expect other writers and narrative designers to be the same way. What is important – in fact, what is necessary – is dramatic escalation. Is the story steadily moving upward in terms of the stakes of the hero and their pursuit of the resolution of the conflict? Escalation is the baseline; without that (and without conflict once again), there is no story.

In games, however, narrative escalation can be undermined through gameplay. This can happen in a few ways.

Premature Character Introduction

People love bad guys. In games, people love killing bad guys. Bad guys often appear early on as a way to foreshadow more bad things to come. But when the main bad guy appears semi-frequently, it often ruins the moment when the player has to face off against them in a final obligatory scene (aka final boss battle). The powers of the main bad guy are not surprising as you've already been exposed to them prior to the final confrontation. Moreover, if you meet a rogue's gallery of cooler characters in between every appearance of the main bad guy, it's hard to avoid disappointment when the final boss battle occurs.

The same goes for sports games. If the cover athlete of the game happens to be one of the best in the league but not *the* best, the final matchup in a linear tutorial (i.e., an in-depth pregame experience to teach you basic mechanics) will be problematic. There will be a clear logical disconnect if, for instance, you face off against better-in-reality players before the cover athlete.[4] True, the game might be tuned or programmed where the difficulty increases from one player to the next. So, by the time you face off against the (lesser-in-reality) cover athlete, you might not notice the disparity between reality and fantasy because you're struggling to keep up. Nevertheless, it's clumsy storytelling.

Long Missions with No Narrative Interspersed

This is the most common obstacle in game narrative. How can you expect players to remember the details of the story when there is so much gameplay disruption in between beats? Some solutions involve in-game dialogue, where characters talk to you as you traverse an environment. Much of that dialogue is clumsy exposition, as it serves to inform players of mission progress, potential foreshadowing moments, information about the world, and loose (very loose) character development.

Nevertheless, *The Last of Us* (which I will delve into Chapter 10) is extremely successful in this effort. Its ambient dialogue is varied and rich with mystery that slowly reveals the status of the world. It also enhances the tone of every dramatic situation in the game (i.e., intense when danger approaches and uncertain during suspicious quietude). Enhancing tone is the key solution to this narrative problem of long missions. *The Last of Us* makes the most out of every opportunity to tell story. Take, for instance, the situation where the game's protagonists Joel and Ellie stealthily travel from one abandoned building to the next to escape a quarantine zone. They will elude a tyrannical paramilitary force who are killing rebels on the streets. While that player might not absorb every line of dialogue that is spoken by these non-playable characters (NPCs) several yards away, they will absorb what's going on gradually as varied dialogue expresses and reinforces lore and tonal continuity over time. As a player, not only do I know what I'm doing long and short term, but I'm also engrossed in my current mission because the dialogue reflects (or even shapes) how I feel. Most games do not vary their NPC ambient dialogue. It is often uniform and is more about imminent tasks ("Kill them!" or "Take cover!") than it is about revealing details of the world in an organic way or about supporting the tone of the scene.

Once again, writers cannot force people to stop playing and absorb every narrative detail. Instead, like music and great graphics, the narrative must be an enhancement to the immersion of the gaming experience.

Arbitrary Bells and Whistles

Designers love creating cool features, but oftentimes these new features do not have narrative justification. These moments are there to enhance the player's fun, but can be completely irrelevant to the narrative. Yet, because these moments are addictive and fun to play, narrative designers have to justify their existence through story. While the length and frequency of typical gameplay moments can drown out a game's narrative, irrelevant bells and whistles can compound narrative's never-ending fight for prominence.

To solve these issues is to be in a constant state of awareness of the game's development. If there are additions that undermine the story, you must let the team know as soon as possible. If this new course can't be reversed, you must revise what is already written, not necessarily to make the story better but to assure its coherence.

DIFFERENT LENGTHS OF THE ACTS

The three-act structure is a tried-and-true narrative model for most console games.[5] Due to the emphasis of gameplay, quick intros and outros are strongly preferred. Act 1 – which is often 30 minutes in a 2-hour film – provides setup for a game. A player will ask themselves – *What's the world I'll be playing in, what's at stake, what kind of character am I, who are my enemies?* The act ends with a huge complication that thrusts our hero onto an uncertain path where they will face one dangerous mission after another. Sounds similar to film, yes. But the difference in games is – for an 8-hour-plus experience – Act 1 can be as short as 15 minutes. All of the elements I just described are revealed at a rapid pace in order to get the players' fingers moving on the sticks (aka controller) as quickly as possible.

Act 2 is the vast majority of the gaming experience. Ranging from 6 to 40 hours, Act 2 is where the player faces difficult, yet visually stimulating challenges successively. Bits of narrative are revealed along the way, but can get lost in a morass of grinding activities. The key here is to provide consistent content that is revealed in short bites that often repeats or restates itself. This is to reinforce crucial narrative information that can get overshadowed and lost by tremendous volume of gameplay moments.

A steady stream of short narrative encounters is the best way to create a frictionless narrative that players will remember. The narrative vehicles to deliver and repeat this information do not have to be the same. A collected item that a player reads can introduce a plot point; an in-game dialogue moment with an NPC who walks with you to a location can reinforce the info you read in the collected item; and a dialogue tree conversation with an NPC can drive home the information you originally read in the collected item and can take it one step further by revealing crucial character information.

This can continue throughout all of Act 2 up until Act 3, which must end on a high note, both in gameplay and in story. Will the protagonist defeat the villain in the most dangerous of circumstances? This obligatory scene must be the culmination of art, gameplay, sound, programming, and every other discipline in game development. It must give players their biggest thrill after days of playing nothing but your game.

There isn't a lot of narrative in Act 3, but what's left packs a wallop. The following examples are a bit overly simplistic and paint game narrative resolution into an unfairly limited box. Nonetheless, they indicate clearly how each of these plot points corresponds to timeless story milestones in a typical Act 3 (Table 7.1).

From a narrative standpoint, these story beats happen quickly and are closely tied to gameplay. And if gameplay is escalating properly, its integration with narrative should reach its most symbiotic state in Act 3. One could argue that there is a natural order of events when it comes to resolving the end of a story. There is always an extreme escalation, a threat of total destruction, a confrontation, and a resolution of that confrontation (hero wins or hero loses). Games do this very well. If you've diligently seeded the proper narrative beats before Act 3, then allow the final story events to take their natural course. Those events, in themselves, have a natural escalation and structure.

TABLE 7.1   Basic Minimum Story Milestones for Act 3

Story Beat	Structural Milestone
The player is thrust into a new threat that is time sensitive with devastating effects	Ticking time bomb introduced
They then have to save someone or something as obstacles from the new threat get in the way	Escalating burdens
They face off against the main villain	Obligatory scene/climax
They might risk the safety of the person they are saving if they do not defeat the villain	Reversal
Upon defeat of the villain and the saving of the person, place, or thing ...	Resolution of ticking time bomb
... . the hero has achieved a greater understanding of who they are	Recognition
The hero is loved by those they saved	Denouement
The hero walks off into the sunset	Denouement (cont'd)
But a rising threat emerges, foreshadowing danger ahead in a potential sequel	Sequel hook (not required)

NOTES

1 Campbell (1991: 180–181).
2 Aristotle (1996: 18).
3 Ibid (18–19).
4 For example, you are a Major League baseball pitcher who has to face off against several historical Yankee legends. Your first batter is Mickey Mantle and then Babe Ruth. To strike out the side, you have to face this year's cover athlete: Don Mattingly. Now, Don Mattingly was very good from 1984 to 1989 and even won an MVP in 1985. But he was never on the level of Mantle or Ruth. Sports games do this often, mainly because nabbing a cover athlete is hard; studios are lucky to get a star every year. Also, because cover athletes change to match the annual publishing cadence of a sports title, game companies will seldom have the upcoming season's top star on the cover consistently, year after year.
5 Episodic games have their own structure. The structure of role-playing games (RPGs), for example, resembles that of a soap opera or melodrama. The Telltale Games portfolio mirrored the structure of a mini-series or a six-episode season, popularized by the British TV model. More about episodic storytelling is provided in Chapter 8.

REFERENCES

Aristotle. (1996). *Aristotle's Poetics* (M. Heath, Trans.). London: Penguin Books Ltd., pp. 18–19.
Campbell, Joseph. (1991). *The Power of Myth*. New York: Anchor., pp. 180–181.

Other Storytelling Methods for Games

OTHER STORYTELLING METHODS

The traditional three-act structure is far from the only way to structure a game story; nonetheless, it is the most common in the Western marketplace. The following methods either achieve the same goal but through different means or focus on an entirely different type of story experience. For the latter, the basic components of story (like conflict or climax) might be absent, but that does not invalidate the enjoyment of the experience. Narrative, in that case, serves as an additive layer, not a central one.

Episodic Storytelling

Some studios tell their stories episodically, if not as a strategy to galvanize anticipation for the next downloadable content (DLC) drop, then as a way to introduce multiple story arcs that don't necessarily (or always have to) tie into a single objective or conflict. Writers of episodically told media – like television, comics, and even old-school (as in pre-1950) radio dramas and movie serials – craft the highs and lows of their stories around the *cliffhanger*, the adrenaline-fueled action or revelation that ends an episode.[1]

Writers will even draft seasonal goals and pinpoint major plot points at a macro-view. Diving deeper, those writers will affix major plot points to individual episodes, which will have their own microstructures. Episodically told games (or chapter-based storytelling), like a Telltale's *The Walking*

DOI: 10.1201/9781003438113-8

Dead or ArenaNet's *Guild Wars*, do not possess the same frequency of episodic output as TV or comics have. Each DLC is closely intertwined with a new campaign that involves months, if not years, of game development. Or, games-as-episodes are developed at once and each episode is released upon a specific but contained schedule (*a la* weekly or monthly within a limited time frame). The saga of that game continues as a next "season." (Telltale Games embraced this model with additional licensed properties such as *Batman* and *Minecraft* before its initial closure in 2018.) One should consider DLC as a micro-game, not as a feature update. But it is impossible to expect a player to uphold the same level of excitement for the story from one DLC drop to the next. Unreliable release dates disrupt continuity and maybe even player memory. A studio also runs the risk of losing players if the gaps between DLC are too long.

Open World Incentivizing

Player agency allows gamers to explore environments at their leisure, and there is no better example of this than in Open World games. Many of these games have story – traditional ones too. But the narrative information isn't delivered linearly; certain areas of the environment and/or task completion will trigger it.

But a player can ignore these narrative opportunities and just explore as they wish. A narrative designer, therefore, needs to focus less on the structure of the story and more on the incentives that lure players into experiencing it. Narrative designers must devise sonic cues and visual spectacle that, by their nature of being mysterious or just out of the ordinary, entice a player to follow those sounds or visuals to trigger the next story fragment. This requires out-of-the-box environmental storytelling. Collectables and non-playable character (NPC) dialogue might not suffice. One must think, instead, of seductive cues that fit within the world and demand a player's attention. A far-off plea for help that gets louder the more one walks toward it, an abandoned saloon with blood all over it, or a rainbow in a rainy world – basically, anything that speaks to danger or that sticks out from the norm is a good place to start.

Lore Discovery

As I will discuss in "The Future Player" section in Chapter 13, the rise of cozy games like *Animal Crossing: New Horizons* and *Stardew Valley* brings new meaning to story. Neither conflict nor the imminent path to solve it resides in these games. A player will, instead, encounter NPCs, get to know their backstories gradually, and develop mutual kinship. A player is incentivized to play more so that they can increase their encounters with NPCs and "unlock" new backstory fragments. A player will also encounter landmarks and towns that gradually offer fragments of their histories over time. I call this type of storytelling **lore discovery**, as the emphasis is not on conflict but on a consequence-free, self-paced discovery of narrative information.

Kishōtenketsu

As an ancient storytelling method, Kishōtenketsu has had a big influence on how stories are told in China, no matter the medium. Japanese and Korean stories have also adopted Kishōtenketsu, which breaks down as follows:

- Ki – the beginning of the story where characters and world are introduced.[2] This is the Western version of the setup or establishment of the world. But at the end of Ki, our hero will confront the major objective of the story and commit to pursuing it (in Western terms: inciting incident and Point of No Return).

- Shō – this is an opportunity to deepen our understanding of the characters and world through the pursuit of the objective.[3] In Western screenwriting terms, these events qualify as escalating burdens or "Rising Action."

- Ten – this is the last-minute twist of the story that throws it into flux.[4] The closest Western equivalent here is the climax; however, Ten doesn't necessarily require the resolution of the story's conflict, but it does require a major surprise that no one (neither character nor audience) was expecting.

- Ketsu – eventually, the tumult settles and either broken relationships are mended and/or status quo returns to the world.[5] This would be the equivalent of the denouement.

Visually, the structure would look like as depicted in Figure 8.1 (forgive my artwork):

There are similarities between Kishōtenketsu and the Western three-act structure. Story, no matter the culture, always captures a natural progression of events. Where I advise caution with Kishōtenketsu is in the "Ten" section. Last-minute twists can run out of control for Western audiences

Figure 8.1   Kishōtenketsu story graph.

if the criteria for its triggering are too random. While twists are seductive, without seeds or clues planted before, they can disrupt the internal logic of a story, especially if they lead to characters behaving outside of their established emotional rulesets – in other words, acting "out of character."

Pixar Storytelling Method

Some writers find it hard to identify major story milestones before the writing begins. They'd rather let their stream of consciousness run freely until the writing is complete. I'm somewhat loath to recommend that path to new writers, but I welcome the unfettered imagination approach with some guardrails.

As long as writers can understand the power of escalating cause and effect – that is, how one action leads to a meaningful reaction that complicates the story's conflict – then structure will come quite easily. There is a natural progression of events in any story – typically, an introduction of a problem, incidents that complicate that problem (and the hero who tries to solve it), a final confrontation between the hero and the person who caused the problem, and then a resolution of the problem that leads to restoration or reset of the hero's original world (assuming this is a happy ending).[6]

Some writers might argue for a different set of milestones, but each one would agree that there is a problem, its escalation, and its resolution (or failure therein). Pixar, the well-reputed animation company that Disney acquired in 2006, serves as an exemplar of simplicity in this regard. Their "Pixar Storytelling Method" has led to such cinema masterpieces as *Toy Story* (1995), *WALL-E* (2008), and *Up* (2009). How their writers craft a story follows a very simple rubric:[7]

Once upon a time _____
Every day _____
Until one day _____
And because of that _____
And because of that _____
Until finally _____
And ever since that day _____

Let's fill this in with a simple plot:

1. Once upon a time, there was a mouse named Leland.
2. Every day Leland would nibble on pieces of discarded cheese in an alley behind a cheese shop.
3. Until one day, a cat named Leopold chased the mouse out of the alley, deep into the city streets.
4. And because of that, a frightened Leland would hide in various homes and restaurants to evade Leopold.
5. And because of that, Leland ran out of places to hide.
6. Until finally, Leland confronted the cat, saw how skinny and desperate Leopold was, and convinced him to search for discarded cheese together.
7. And ever since that day, the two best friends found plenty of cheese and neither one had to starve or hide ever again.

In this scenario, Act 1 comprises Lines 1 to 3 (and part of 4), where Lines 1 and 2 are the setup and Line 3 is the inciting incident (the introduction of the story's major conflict). This is a compressed story, so one ought to expect that the lion's share of Line 4 would fracture into numerous lines that elaborate on what hiding in "various homes and restaurants to evade Leopold" entails. "Because of that" lines will likely comprise 90–95% of one's story beats – the majority of those being in Act 2. Lines 5, 6, and 7 are part of Act 3, with Line 6 being the climax of the story and Line 7 as the denouement.

If anything, the Pixar Storytelling Method shows us the power of words. "Because of that" serves as a trigger that taps into one's imagination and logic. This method clearly indicates that plot points are consequences of previous plot points and triggers to future ones. In some ways, writing is managing the plot points in a story supply chain, where an inherent logic and escalation dictate the conflict's evolution and resolution.

FRICTIONLESS NARRATIVE

Structuring stories remains a constant creative challenge (and joy!) for game writers and narrative designers. But sometimes, game developers might reject story outright as either an unnecessary expense or as a reaction to the vast majority of gamers, who skip story content regularly. There is a happy medium and that presents itself with the question of how to present the story without interrupting the gameplay. The appetite for narrative varies from consumer to consumer. But it is often the case that gamers do not want their gaming sessions to be halted or distracted in any way. Distractions include bugs or software glitches, unnecessary grinding missions, and even annoying music. Narrative is often seen as a distraction as well. A lot of gamers feel that if they wanted to have a story, they'd watch a movie.

Yet, narrative is beloved by many. And the industry often embraces narrative as a baseline requirement for a solid score on the game review aggregation website known as *Metacritic*. It is so influential, in fact, that a studio will hire former reviewers to play-test an upcoming game solely to predict its *Metacritic* score. As a result, the dev team will make last-minute, targeted improvements on certain features and/or change its marketing strategy.

How narrative integrates with gameplay is something that narrative designers solve for every day. Stopping the gameplay for a cut scene is too disruptive, as it prevents the player from interacting with their screen. In-game dialogue is better, but not perfect. This involves a player to enter a new environment and interact with NPCs. They will gradually reveal, through voice-over or on-screen text, the mysteries of the environment or share with a player crucial information that could influence decisions they make in the future. Being overloaded with information is not ideal for most gamers, who just want to zone out and play. Nonetheless, in-game dialogue is often a successful alternative to the cut scene.

Then there are discoverable items – for example, The Riddler's letters in *Batman: Arkham Asylum* (2009) or the audio diaries or the Voxophones in *BioShock* (2007) and *BioShock: Infinite* (2013), respectively – that can be read or listened to at a player's own pace after they are collected. They can be saved in your inventory of items or can be instantly activated once collected. Discoverable items, or collectables, are a way to steadily deliver bits of the narrative without much friction. There is a flip side, however. If these story bits offer too much content per collection and/or require frequent collection, a player will reach narrative fatigue and stop absorbing the story. A player will likely avoid collecting further, especially if it has no bearing on the gameplay.

Then there is the conversation tree mechanic, which we will discuss in Chapter 9. In brief, when an NPC asks a player a question, the player will have one of two (if not more) choices to select from. The outcome of the conversation could lead to a different story path or provide slightly altered content based on the attitude you just gave in your responses. The results of these decisions form dialogue trees. They're called that because paths can "branch," or form a new direction, based on one's decisions.

If there is neither an influence on the gameplay nor a slight modification on the narrative, then the dialogue is meaningless. The narrative should be designed in a way where it has consequences on the gameplay or can be modified through decision points. At the very least, the conversation should reward a player with a gift (like a weapon or experience points). But a different outcome of the player's journey should be the prime ambition.

One could argue that an ideal frictionless narrative is one that is not on the same screen as the game. The concept of the second-screen experience has been experimented with over the last decade. It is not designated to games only.

In 2012, Disney released the Blu-ray of the sci-fi adventure film *John Carter*, an adaptation of the Edgar Rice Burroughs' novels. The film production was massive in budget (over $250 million, not including $100 million for marketing) and failed to make a profit. While subsequent plans for a sequel were quashed, the home entertainment experience, however, flourished.[8] [9]

One could attribute such success – $19.3 million in home entertainment sales in its opening weekend, $38 million overall – to the innovative features it offered, including the (then) recently anointed *Disney Second Screen* experience. Through the use of a smartphone or tablet app, a consumer could watch the film and receive supplemental content through one's device. For example, audio cues in the film would get triggered by the app when the customer read a journal entry written by the protagonist. The journal also offered interactive character art that consumers could manipulate and gain further context into the *John Carter* universe.

Games are the perfect medium for this and have already explored second-screen possibilities. The widely popular first-person shooter *Destiny* (2014) offers Grimoire cards for players to read on the internet. Unlocked with every milestone achievement, each card would reveal the lore of the world and the characters who live in it.

Migrating to another technology (in this case, from console to computer) provided seamless enjoyment in the *Destiny* experience. A player had the freedom to absorb the narrative whenever they saw fit without interrupting their gameplay.

Second-screen experiences were more popular from 2012 to 2014 than they are at the time of this writing. Today, many games have a companion app that is not critical to experiencing the game; however, it enhances one's gaming experience either by providing reward opportunities, navigational assistance, or reminders to upcoming events in the game. Basically, companion apps are rebranded second-screen experiences.

How do we explain the staid enthusiasm for second-screen experiences? This is the natural evolution of product and feature development. Companies hope that people will break old habits or loyalties to adopt new ones. When the product comes out, there is an initial wave of excitement. People experiment with it and often have a positive reaction. Alas, there is no follow-through, especially if the product has no utility outside of entertainment. Today's slow adoption of virtual reality might shed light on why second-screen experiences did not take off like they should have. People fear change. They like what they have and can only absorb something new in small bits before the appetite increases at a snail's pace or vanishes entirely. By then, the product is no longer in the conversation.

It is also possible that the second-screen experience, in general, was not designed as well as it could have been. What's the incentive for a player to leave one platform for the next, even if the departure is momentary? Is there something they can gain that is meaningful and neither contrived, manipulative, nor distracting? Also, if the second-screen experience must happen simultaneously while playing the game, is that too much pressure to put on a player? Is it overstimulating? Perhaps this is why Grimoire cards, which can be experienced upon one's convenience, are a more successful example.

Yet, what if Grimoire cards were not only a result of a gameplay unlock but also could affect gameplay? Perhaps it would drive more players to the computer to check them out. Or perhaps it is as simple as offering a narrative experience vs. a non-narrative experience on a game's Start Menu.

Players can opt in to a "story mode" experience, play the normal golden path of the game, and consume the narrative on another device. If it is branded honestly and clearly from the beginning, it is possible that players will feel respected. They can then play the game a second time but through the mode they opted out of initially.

In the games industry, preserving the consumer goodwill is paramount. If a developer looks like they are not respecting a player's time, there will be severe consequences, from incessant trolling of a company on social media to widespread boycotting of a game's release. More importantly, preserving consumer goodwill by developers comes from a genuine, heartfelt place: *developers are gamers too.*

How did second-screen experiences emerge in the first place? Quite simply, the mobile revolution. When the iPhone premiered in 2007, the technology quickly became less of a telecommunications device and more of a minicomputer. Multitasking became commonplace. Fast forward to today, when watching television, consumers have evolved from looking up information about an actor on their phone's browser to communicating with strangers over X or Snapchat about the latest battle in *House of the Dragon*. Concurrent multimedia consumption is the true second-screen experience and has become the new path forward. Therefore, those who design and produce entertainment experiences for this new path will flourish if they can harness the media consumption patterns of today's multitasker. It is then only a matter of time when traditional Hollywood entertainment becomes a thing of the past.

Activision Blizzard, creators of the *World of Warcraft* franchise, now an entity of Microsoft's, has explored a different and very successful approach to frictionless narrative. For their extremely popular multiplayer first-person shooter (FPS) *Overwatch* (2016), the narrative was explored in comics and animated shorts that are outside of the gameplay. This approach was not a second-screen experience; it was instead a separate media experience with high production values that could be consumed even if you don't play the game. In other words, these story bits were not triggered based on gameplay milestones or achievements. They were instead introduced to the player on a separate release schedule and broadened the fictional universe of *Overwatch* by telling the stories of its various characters. The narrative was not necessary to experience for the gaming experience, but it was rich enough for players to increase their enjoyment of the IP and gain a deeper understanding of its universe and characters.

As gameplay in general becomes more compelling and addictive, narrative will need to become more frictionless. How to tell the narrative will need to be just as innovative as the software behind it. *Overwatch's* external narrative extensions might hold the formula for the future of game narrative.

NOTES

1 To understand this fully, think back to 1980s television. Even a sitcom like *Happy Days* welcomed the cliffhanger ending on occasion. Fonzie runs his motorcycle off the cliff – will he reach the other side of the mountain? Film freezes, title card reads: "To Be Continued."
2 Kindree, "Is Conflict Necessary?" 2019.
3 Ibid.
4 Ibid.
5 Ibid.
6 Or, a sad ending would lead to the person who caused the conflict to triumph over the hero and remake the original world to how they see fit
7 Coats, "Story Basics #4" 2011.
8 The Numbers, "John Carter of Mars" 2012.
9 Strowbridge, "Blu-Ray Sales: John Carter Acts Up" 2012.

REFERENCES

Coats, Emma. (2011, March 26, 4:33pm). *Story basics #4: Once upon a time there was ___. Every day, ___. One day ___. Because of that, ___. Because of that, ___. Until finally___*. X. Retrieved on February 15, 2024 from https://twitter.com/lawnrocket/status/51788817111330816

Kindree, Jimmy. (2019, January 27). "Is Conflict Necessary?: Kishōtenketsu and the Conflict-less Plot" Retrieved on February 9, 2024 from https://wordsliketrees.wordpress.com/2019/01/27/is-conflict-necessary-kishotenketsu-and-the-conflict-less-plot/

Strowbridge, C.S. (2012, June 20). "Blu-Ray Sales: John Carter Acts Up." Retrieved on February 9, 2024 from www.the-numbers.com/news/128220830-Blu-ray-Sales-John-Carter-Acts-Up

The Numbers. (2012, June). "John Carter of Mars." Retrieved on February 9, 2024 from www.the-numbers.com/movie/John-Carter-of-Mars#tab=video-sales

CHAPTER 9

Meaningful Choice, Branching Narrative, and Downstream Effects

BREAKING IT ALL DOWN

The concept of meaningful choice is critical in game narrative. It is one of the few times that narrative is a proactive force (as opposed to a reactive one) on gameplay.

Meaningful choice is the result of an interactive dialogue exchange between the player and the non-playable character. The interactive exchange allows the development team to provide necessary context and story while giving the player immediate incentives once they complete a dialogue exchange. Such incentives include experience points, gear to brag about to your friends, and/or tools or weapons that enhance the player's abilities (e.g., a sword if it's a medieval role-playing game or a type of sneaker if it's a sports game).

Good narrative design will make sure that a player is given more than just a sword at the end of an exchange. Good narrative design will make sure that, no matter the choices you are given in a dialogue exchange, either option will provide you with **sufficient differentiated content to encourage replayability**. These dialogue exchanges can create branching narrative, which is, in part, a methodology of storytelling that centers on a player's ability to make choices in the game that directly impact the

DOI: 10.1201/9781003438113-9

outcome of the story. In a non-branching narrative (aka linear story), the outcome is proscribed and immutable (open world games excepting). In a branching narrative, however, the outcome could have numerous endings and numerous paths to reach these endings. Branching narrative is often compared to a "Choose Your Own Adventure" book: strategic moments in the narrative (also known as decision points) encourage a player to choose one of many paths to continue the story. In games, branching narrative is most common in RPGs. Whatever the player chooses will eventually lead to further decision points that will offer, yet again, more choices. As a result of the multiplicity of choices, the player has reached a unique ending that is markedly different than numerous other endings that resulted from various routes that could have been chosen in substitution. Each ending, no matter how different, starts from the same, singular point. The first choice a player makes will set the course for a series of downstream effects that will lead to a completely different adventure from one path to the next.

This is called branching narrative because during the story architecture of these decision points, the visual representation of "what ifs" (as in, what if you chose Choice #2 vs. Choice #3) adds up to what looks like countless branches in a large tree. In the pages that follow, I map out what a branching dialogue looks like.

But first, let's say an NPC approaches you at a gate. You cannot pass unless you engage him in a conversation. After every line of dialogue, you will have three choices of responses. Depending on your response, the NPC can continue the dialogue directly addressing the tone that you set and/or deprive you of or provide you with a new clue or opportunity to help you continue your path. For this exercise, I have added notations next to every choice (e.g., 1a, 2a, 3a, 1b, 2b, 3b, etc.). Each lowercase letter will represent a part of the conversation with the NPC (five parts in total, labeled a, b, c, d, e). Once one part of the conversation is done, the player's responses proceed to the subsequent set of the same letter (from all a's to now all b's, for example). The numbers of the notations, on the other hand, range from 1–3 within a discrete part of the conversation and are otherwise immutable as the subsequent parts of the conversation move forward. To reduce complexity (as if this isn't already complex enough!), I refrained from using further notations to show deeper choice variations. Once I reselect a choice from a previous part of the conversation, let's assume there's a reset and none of the alternative options were chosen before. Believe it or not, there is no deep methodology or industry standard here. In fact, these notations are omitted from the visual branching diagram I have provided later on. They are strictly used as guidance for discussion. Let's start:

> NPC: How are you today?

> Choice #1a: Great. How are you?

> Choice #2a: Terrible. My best friend just died of scurvy.

> Choice #3a: Shut up and get out of my way.

Player selects Choice #3a. Then –

> NPC: Hey, that's no way to treat a stranger! Apologize now or I will impale you with my dagger.

> Choice #1b: Methinks I drank too much mead last night. My deepest apologies.

> Choice #2b: You're too stupid to deserve an apology. Now move!

> Choice #3b: Neither option will suffice. I shall leave you to your gatekeeping. Cheers!

Here, Choice #1b leads the player to a new path with no struggle or threat of death, thus moving the narrative along quickly without incident. The subsequent dialogue and story beats will default to the safest path forward. Choice #2b will likely lead to a physical encounter where the player will either win and survive or lose and die. If the player prevails in this possible confrontation, a strong narrative designer must assure that the subsequent conversations will have a defensive tone from the NPCs, and likely, more conflict from other NPCs who will want to avenge the death of their friend, the gatekeeper. This choice is important because it defines the player's attitude and tone that will be adopted in every exchange thereafter. It has a clear **downstream effect**.

On the other hand, if the player chose Choice #3b, the player will return to where they were before but will not be able to progress without taking the amiable, default path (Choice #1b) or the dangerous, hostile path (Choice #2b). Choice #3b, therefore, is the weakest of the choices because it forces the player to retry the unchosen options to move forward without offering any new information about plot or character. Strong narrative branching must allow every choice to (a) lead to different outcomes, (b) move the plot forward, (c) and/or provide more information about the character or world that is not obvious.

A better Choice #3b could have been, *"That dagger of yours? It looks familiar. Was that given to you by Johan Lankersheim?"* Let's make that substitution. The NPC then replies –

> *NPC:* Why, yes it was. You know my father?

> *Choice #1c:* Johan Lankersheim is still alive? I thought he died in the Battle of Renheiser.

> *Choice #2c:* No, but he is the reason why I left my village to travel the world. I learned many spells from his book The Scrolls of Dark Sorcery. It is my goal to become as skilled a sorcerer as he is.

> *Choice #3c:* Gerhardt, is that you? 'Tis I – your long, lost brother Wilhelm!

Notice that each of these responses offers vastly different story paths, almost unrelated to one another. Choice #1c implies that there is great mystery behind Johan Lankersheim. Rumors of his death have been circulating long before this encounter. Why is that the case? If you have a penchant for mystery solving, Choice #1c is the option for you. Choice #2c speaks to the player's desire for self-discovery – "I am a nascent sorcerer but I need to perfect my craft by going into the world and gaining practical knowledge even if that poses great risk to my safety." Choice #3c is about an unexpected opportunity to repair ties with estranged family members. These choices present different paths that may never intersect down the road. You are choosing a very different experience with each one.

These examples should give a clear picture on the basics of meaningful choice in interactive dialogue. It all boils down to the most basic of conditional statements: "If this, then that." In other words, ... "If the player chooses X, then these are the series of different responses I need to write."

Let's return to the beginning of the conversation (aforementioned reset activated):

> *NPC:* How are you today?

> *Choice #1a:* Great. How are you?

Choice #2a: Terrible. My best friend died of scurvy.

Choice #3a: Shut up and get out of my way.

Player selects Choice #1a. Then –

> NPC: I'm doing well, thank you. If you are here to see Wolfgang the Shaman, please provide us the secret word.

Choice #1b: Quince

Choice #2b: Sassafras

Choice #3b: Aha! That is a trick question. Wolfgang the Shaman requires no one to carry secrets!

Player selects Choice #1b. Then the conversation ends like so –

> NPC: I see that you are a farmer of these lands. Please sit in the section for the commoners. You will be asked to leave after 10 minutes. Thank you.

However …

If the player selects Choice #2b, the conversation ends like so –

> NPC: Wow! I see you're part of the aristocracy of this village! Please take a seat in the front row and stay as long as the Shaman wants you to stay. I bow to you in deference.

Or …

If the player selects Choice #3b, the conversation ends like so –

> NPC: Nice try. Guess again.

Choice #1c: Quince

Choice #2c: Sassafras

Choice #3c: That dagger of yours? It looks familiar. Was that given to you by Johan Lankersheim?

This branch starts off by forcing the player to restart the previous branch and choose an overtly correct answer. It's sufficient in this case because the dialogue is deepening the psychology of our character. His arrogance in assuming that he was asked a trick question – and being immediately denied – indicates we're dealing with an inadvertently funny, but relatable protagonist.

The first two choices here will allow the player to enter. So let's explore Choice #3c to its end.

> *NPC:* Why, yes it was. You know my father?

> *Choice #1d:* Johan Lankersheim is still alive? I thought he died in the Battle of Renheiser.

> *Choice #2d:* No, but he is the reason why I left my village to travel the world. I learned many spells from his book The Scrolls of Dark Sorcery. It is my goal to become as skilled a sorcerer as he is.

> *Choice #3d:* Gerhardt, is that you? It's your long, lost brother Wilhelm!

Player selects Choice #1d. Then –

> *NPC:* He survived, but has not been the same since. If you pay him your respects, I will make sure Wolfgang the Shaman will make you a special potion. What say you?

> *Choice #1e:* Next time, but today I'm in a hurry and I need the Shaman's cure for my grandmother's ill humors. The password is Quince.

> *Choice #2e:* Can't you see I'm in a hurry?!? The password is Sassafras.

> *Choice #3e:* I'd love to pay your father my respects.

To the complete conversation tree:

If player selects Choice #1e, the NPC replies –

> *NPC:* I see that you are a farmer of these lands. Please sit in the section for the commoners. You will be asked to leave after 10 minutes. Thank you.

If player selects Choice #2e, the NPC replies –

> *NPC:* Well, well, well. You may be aristocracy, but outside this kingdom, you're as equal as I am. I await that day. Until then, you may take a seat in the front row and stay as long as the Shaman wants you to stay.

If player selects Choice #3e, the NPC replies –

> *NPC:* Good to hear! Follow me and I will take you there.

What makes these choices strong is that you are given three different locations to experience, even if momentarily. If you selected, say, Choice #1e the first time, you have the option of exploring the other two in different gaming sessions and will experience, at the very least, two different visual environments and perspectives of Wolfgang the Shaman. Or, if you chose to see the Shaman right away, you are guaranteed two different dialogue experiences based on the class that you chose: farmer vs. aristocracy. Your gaming experience will thereby be very different in the way people treat you and what you will have access to.

Figure 9.1 presents a very complex breakdown of these choices in a diagram, without the notations I used above. Mapping them out visually will significantly clarify the narrative process. You will notice that when the NPC speaks (indicated in hexagons), the player character (you) will have three responses. That cadence must be continued until the end of the dialogue branch where the NPC's response or action is closely tied to your next move (e.g., exit or battle) and has exhausted further options in that conversation. It is key to keep the number of responses by the player uniform until that final moment of the branch. That's the ruleset the narrative designer establishes with the player. If you violate that ruleset out of convenience, you are cheating. It's okay if answers repeat themselves in different branches of the same conversation. That's unavoidable. Sometimes, a narrative designer might take a circuitous route to get to these lines in service to highlighting different parts of lore that different players gravitate to at different times.

Why all this effort? The crux behind meaningful choice is giving a player enough content so that they are compelled to replay the game through a different lens each time. Not all game narrative is in the RPG genre. But RPG elements often trickle into games that aren't, by nature, RPGs. Character customization and "choose your own adventure" decisions are part and parcel for RPGs. It's the level of depth, however, that separates a

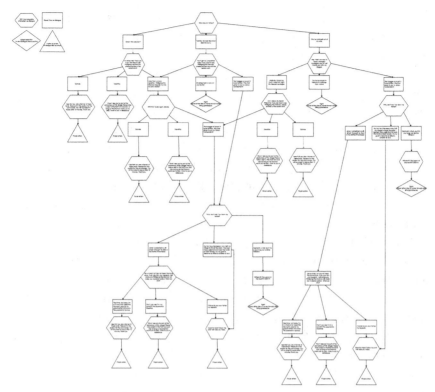

Figure 9.1   Example branching conversation tree. (See full-scale version of this graph at www.routledge.com/9781032571614.)

genuine RPG from a game that has light RPG elements. At minimum, RPG-light games should strive to achieve *meaningful and differentiated* content. If the choices fail to provide sufficiently distinct content or there is basically little-to-no variation among the choices in a dialogue tree, then the choices are inconsequential and cosmetic at best. The result is a weak, unambitious narrative. I'll dive into this deeper in just a moment, but first …

It is perfectly acceptable that the different choices eventually and periodically **dovetail** to the same story milestones. (Again, budget constraints in game development allow for modest branching.) These milestones could be the same inciting incident, crisis point, climax, and resolution. But the paths that lead to those milestones might be differentiated in tone, characters status, and points of view (POVs) of the same event. While not as extreme as different plot points, these three elements are significant changes in the narrative to encourage replayability (Figure 9.2).

Keeping a branching narrative slightly "on rails" is understandable. As mentioned earlier, an ambitious branching narrative has endless, differentiated content that might be too costly to execute.

Now back to the burning issue: what does a meaningful, differentiated choice actually mean? When designing branching paths, ask yourself high-level questions that focus on enhancing the player experience. For instance, if you choose Path B, what are you giving the player that is distinct from, but as entertaining as, Path A? If Path A leads to a destination that gives you a gun, but Path B leads you to the same destination that gives you a knife, you've failed at making a meaningful, differentiated choice. A different tool is cosmetic. It tells us nothing about the character's psychology nor does it reveal a new fragment of the story.[1]

Consider a murder mystery game. Path A takes you to a crime scene through the lens of a detective. There's something odd about this detective. She's brilliant, but you can't quite trust her. Path B takes you to the same crime scene but through the lens of a young boy, who witnessed the crime. The boy notices that the detective has suspiciously taken something from the victim's pocket, yet no one saw this but the young boy. While paths A and B might dovetail to the same locales and moments in the narrative, the different perspectives give more meaning, surprise, and breadth to the story.

If you don't have the budget to write different POVs through the lenses of two different characters, what can you do? Try limiting the experience to one character, but with **different perspectives**. Could the branching dialogue reveal two distinct personalities of the same detective: one that's overly forthcoming, too trusting, and emotional? Could the other be more tacit, seemingly distrustful? This isn't to say that one character is made up of two different characters. Instead, each question in the conversation tree elicits a different response from the same character, and each response reveals a different fragment of her life and psychology. "How's your mother?", for instance, could be an unhappy trigger for a character with an Electra Complex. But if that same person with an Electra Complex is asked, "How's your father?", it triggers a happy attitude. Each path, therefore, is informed by a deep, psychological driver that will influence and differentiate the choices ahead.

Different POVs from the same character (or limited set of characters) can give a cost-effective differentiation of a branching narrative. Less time is spent in crafting wholesale story beats. These different perspectives from

	A	B	C
1	Act 1		
2	Path A (Aristocrat)	Path B (Farmer)	Path C (Respectful Warrior)
3	Sits in the front row to see Wolfgang the Shaman.	Sits far away to see Wolfgang the Shaman.	Meets Wolfgang the Shaman before his public appearance.
4	Offends the person sitting next to him and engages in combat.	The Farmer flirts with a woman sitting in front of him.	The player character offends the Shaman by insulting a reckless battle that his brother led, as it nearly caused his village to be wiped out...
5	The Aristocrat kills the stranger only to discover he was the leader of a group of violent marauders. His followers will attack the aristocrat's village.	The father of the woman, leader of a marauding faction, is offended and vows to scorch his farm and kills everyone in his village.	The Shaman calls upon his protectors, the marauders, to wipe out the player character's village.
6	Dovetail moment: The player character returns to his village to stave off the attack from the marauders.	Dovetail moment: The player character returns to his village to stave off the attack from the marauders.	Dovetail moment: The player character returns to his village to stave off the attack from the marauders.
7			

Figure 9.2 Dovetail moments. (See full-scale version of this graph at www.routledge.com/9781032571614.)

the same character cover the same story beats, but are experienced through a different mindset and, therefore, reveal different context.

Branching narrative development can be a massive undertaking. It involves a huge time commitment and an extensive writing staff to pull it off. Since game companies strongly encourage replayability, branching narrative is the supplement – or even enhancement – to this customer promise. But to achieve its full potential is to lose the average player. As I describe in Chapter 8, players like the least amount of friction in their gaming experience. Story is often friction. Therefore, you should not expect that the average gamer to enjoy or even partake in branching narrative that is intricate and time-consuming. However, light branching, particularly if it triggers new and unique gameplay moments, is the ideal middle ground.

NOTE

1 Yes, there are exceptions. The backstory of a playable character might involve trauma with a knife, and therefore the character could recall events from their past that might add light to the current narrative. But that's stretching it a bit. When narrative designers first start out, there is a tendency to offer Weapon #1 vs. Weapon #2 as strictly superficial differentiation.

CHAPTER 10

Analysis of Narrative in Contemporary Games

WHAT ARE THE CRITERIA OF WELL-TOLD NARRATIVE IN GAMES?

Up to this point, I've provided copious details on crafting solid story structure and creating compelling worlds and characters. These will be useful when we examine the stories of two video games in this chapter. But before we do, it's important to establish additional criteria for what qualifies as a solid game narrative. These can vary from studio to studio, but I always keep in mind the following:

- Are the story milestones exciting and/or compelling?
- Is the character development organic and gradual?
- Does the narrative have a relationship to the gameplay or is it independent of it? To what degree if the latter? Do the actions from the narrative have consequences on the gameplay? Does the gameplay have consequences on the narrative?
- Is the narrative frictionless? Or is the fun being interrupted too many times in order for me to follow a story that is not interesting?
- Does the story fit with the rest of the game? Is it tonally consistent? Is the pacing consistent?
- Most importantly …

DOI: 10.1201/9781003438113-10

AM I EMOTIONALLY INVESTED?

One of the major issues with games is a player's lack of emotional attachment to the story and characters. Oftentimes, a non-playable character can serve a functional purpose, thus justifying their need in one's gaming experience. This type of NPC could be someone who provides a player with information about the locale or mission upon which they are about to embark. Other functions include healing (someone who gives the player medicine to recover from an injury), equipping (someone who gives the player weapons), momentary saving (someone who gives the player shelter from combat), assisting (someone who joins the player in combat and provides cover). The list goes on. But as one can see, these roles render the character as a device of usage. A player will typically ask themselves, *How can I use them in a way to expedite my journey to accomplish my main objective(s)?*

This isn't to say the gaming experience makes a player manipulative or indifferent to human emotion. It is instead an experience that, by design, forces the player to use everything at their disposal to move forward with little-to-no stopping.

Accordingly, within those functions, seldom is there an opportunity to get to know those NPCs. Or, if they are along with the player for their entire journey, it is rare that the player will get a chance to know them in a way that, upon their absence or death, will evoke feelings of loss or sadness.

There are exceptions of course. In *Fable II* (2010), a dog is the player's faithful companion throughout the game. However, after it dies taking a bullet for the protagonist (before being resurrected later on), the world coarsens. The protagonist is no longer a child, but a hero on a mission. Likewise, in *The Last of Us* (which I will delve into later), the death of the protagonist's young daughter in the beginning changes our hero permanently. It sets him on a path that is emotionally indifferent at first, but then reverses once the stakes of survival involve the saving of another girl.

Emotional investment is tricky. What is defined as emotional investment may be different from player to player. The loss of a functional character might spur a player's despair. Now they have no one to rely on for that function, and therefore their series of missions will be harder to accomplish.

But this is the important distinction: loss should not evoke a player's annoyance due to the absence of a function. A true emotional connection is not about making a player's job easier; it is about making their experience more meaningful and fulfilling. A character's presence ought to provide joy, and their absence sorrow.

If genuine emotion doesn't arise, then the character was either not written well enough or, by design, they were strictly a functional device. A writer's or narrative designer's goals are to transcend an NPC from function to meaningful investment.

WHY DO GAMES STRUGGLE AT TELLING EMOTIONAL STORIES?

This is a difficult question not because it's hard to identify but because it puts into light the consumer and developer.

Games are an addictive activity. The products are designed to keep players' buttoning on the controller for hours on end. The dopamine release upon every buttoning activity (e.g., killing an enemy, avoiding gunfire, shooting a basketball, or jumping from building to building) satisfies a primordial impulse in all of us. Accordingly, to tap into these primordial impulses relentlessly is to experience endless joy … at least in terms of addiction.

But these twitch-muscle activities do not allow a player to absorb and reflect upon the environment for anything more than the length of time that the immediate mission allows for the player. There is no epicurean stop-and-smell-the-roses moment. Games create grinding experiences. An art museum or a theater experience (i.e., traditional art) is the complete opposite. In the latter category, a viewer experiences a slower, more methodical process to absorb the stimuli around them.

Games are fast; traditional art is slow. Games are about instant gratification; traditional art is about long-term enrichment. Games are about following directions; traditional art is about making arbitrary interpretations. Games have a definitive set of rules and a victory state; traditional art is unspecific until it's part of the public discourse where its meaning is debated *ad nauseam*.

People play games, generally, not for an emotional experience. They play to have fun. And oftentimes, fun is not about cerebral issues, but about light, fast, and accessible subject matter. That's why the Joseph Campbell-style "Hero's Journey" remains a tried-and-true model for game narrative.

However, this isn't to say we should give games a pass when it comes to emotional investment. There are opportunities to do so (as mentioned in the examples given previously), where emotion can still fit within the gaming experience.

This isn't just about the consumer. They might expect a light, non-cerebral experience because that's what they've been fed for so many years!

Game creators expect or even aim for light experiences too. They grew up on games. In fact, games might have been their primary (and sometimes only) diet of media. Therefore, it's no surprise that the medium's lack of emotional investment corresponds to the developers' lack of exposure to media with emotional investment.

Additionally, many of these folks have a narrow pool of interests when it comes to story. *Star Wars*, *Game of Thrones*, *Harry Potter*, *Marvel Cinematic Universe*, and *The Lord of the Rings* are (obviously) great franchises, but they are the most prevalent go-to examples in most narrative brainstorming sessions. To limit oneself to a narrow pool of stories and genres is to increase the likelihood that one's game narrative will be stale and cliché.

But emotion is not the main reason why these franchises are beloved. Rich characters, worlds, and action scenes continue to evoke loyalty and zeal from fans and developers alike. They can also overshadow the sentiment shared between characters. Thus, if there is no awareness of emotional moments in these intellectual properties (IPs), then there is no chance that emotional moments will cross one's mind when developing the narrative.

That's why it's crucial to involve writers and narrative designers in the brainstorming phase of creating an IP. Their openness to emotional moments and their experience in writing for other fiction-driven media make them invaluable. If they cannot lead the discussions in IP creation, then they need to be the "story whisperer" to every creative director or lead designer who does.

GAME NARRATIVE BREAKDOWN EXAMPLES

I've chosen two games to illustrate how the elements of narrative come together in an actual product in the marketplace. Story milestones, components of great character and world-building, and emotional investment touchstones are the driving criteria. The following two games are vastly different in genre as well as in the quality of storytelling. One is a masterpiece in game narrative, and the other is a Hollywood-bloated misfire.

NBA 2K16

Studio: Visual Concepts
Publisher: 2K Sports (a subsidiary of Take-Two Interactive)

| **Writers:** | Spike Lee, Alrick Brown, Barry Michael Cooper, Rhys Jones, Julius Pryor IV, Kiel Adrian Scott, Sean Michael Sullivan, Tor Unsworth |
| **Year Published:** | 2015 |

Premise

A young basketball phenom nicknamed "The Freq" is on the verge of becoming the next superstar of the National Basketball Association (NBA). But a friend from his past damages his reputation off the court, causing dissension within his family and the team owner.

In a Nutshell

Upon its release, *NBA 2K16* was the latest installment in one of the industry's best-selling franchises in the last decade, *NBA 2K*. This time, Take-Two Interactive upped the ante by offering a story mode (called "Livin' Da Dream") written and directed by Spike Lee.

The legendary filmmaker admitted in the game's "extras" feature that video games were a new experience for him. Did it pay off?

Main Characters

Frequency Vibrations aka The Freq – a basketball phenom since high school, Freq continues to excel in college and makes his way to the NBA as the hottest rookie in his draft class. Achieving all the accolades and fame that come with being a superstar, the Freq navigates the pressures of the league with the help of his fraternal twin sister, his girlfriend, and his agent. He is deeply trusts those around him and expects the same in return. In addition to his near superhuman athleticism, he is a man of honor and loyalty and exercises kindness to those in his close circle, particularly to his parents who gave him everything with the little they had. Due to his extraordinary skill on the court and ability to command instant adoration from those around him, Freq is the narrative's protagonist.

Vic Van Lier – Freq's best friend since childhood. Vic is always finding himself in trouble and relies on Freq to bail him out. However, by the time Freq makes it to the NBA, Vic's hijinks escalate, including spending an exorbitant amount of Freq's money, talking trash about players on social media, and getting caught drunk on video after being stopped by the police. Eventually, his shenanigans force Freq to choose between his friend and his team.

Yvette Ming Ching – Freq's girlfriend. Ever since they dated, she's capitalized on Freq's fame to catapult her own career in the fashion industry. But unlike Vic, Yvette wants nothing but the best for Freq and has proven to be an invaluable advocate for his career. She is often at odds with Freq's sister, Cee-Cee, who doesn't trust Yvette because she believes Yvette is just after his fame and money. However, it's likely the case that she's jealous of Yvette because of her closeness to him.

Cee-Cee – Freq's fraternal twin sister. As soon as the NBA is interested in drafting the Freq, Cee-Cee steps in as his unofficial business manager. The role, at first, is too much for her to handle as she struggles to make the right business decisions for Freq, but she eventually comes into her own. She's at the center of a lot of rifts inside Freq's inner circle, including with his girl-friend and his agent. All she wants to do is protect her brother.

Dom Pagnotti – superagent in the sports world. He is Freq's fast-talking, savvy dealmaker. While he comes across as slick and untrustworthy, he turns out to be Freq's compass through the murky waters of sports business. He always has Freq's best interests in mind even if it defies Cee-Cee's expectations. He will do whatever it takes to build his client's reputation and get him the best deal possible.

Pete and Martha – Freq's kind, selfless parents. Freq is intensely loyal to his parents, even involving them in press conferences. There isn't a specific archetype they represent; they are, rather, a device. They humanize the superhero, make him relatable in ways that Freq could not do himself.

Team Owner – wealthy, intense, no-bullshit owner, who pushes Freq to conform to the standards of his team. On the court is one thing; off the court is another. His players must represent the team gallantly, on and off the court. This poses a problem when Vic constantly hangs out with the team, exploits Freq's popularity, and embarrasses himself in public. The owner forces Freq to take sides eventually: it's either the team or Vic.

Key Story Beats

Act 1

Setup or Establishment of the World – when playing basketball on a local neighborhood court, Freq, a high school student, reveals his goal to make it to the NBA. We see his environment (inner city) and how's he perceived by others (godly).

Introduction to Protagonist's Purpose – When Vic pops up, Freq reveals that his loyalty to his family and friends is a personal priority. In this scene (also part of the setup above), Freq reveals a professional and personal purpose. Vic's mischievousness is clear and serves to foreshadow events to come.

Inciting Incident – Freq's dominant performance at a high school game puts him on the radar of college scouts. However, this one game implies that Freq's excellence was an aggregation over years of playing at a high level.

Refuse the Call – not applicable here. However, one could interpret Freq's listening to numerous college recruiters' pitches and not accepting them as a refusal of a call. He's waiting for all offers to net out before making a decision. This reveals a positive character trait of Freq's: that he's patient and thoughtful. In this game, this narrative beat is more like "Not committing to the call."

Situation Worsens – during Freq's last game in high school, Vic is riding on the coattails of his superstar buddy as an FOF – Friend of Freq – by making deals with shady people. Once again, this is a stronger foreshadowing beat than anything else. Freq's decision to commit to a college is agnostic to whatever shady deals Vic is making; nonetheless, that shadiness will put our hero in a difficult situation in the next act.

Accept the Call – Freq makes an announcement in a home video in front of his family and Vic about the college he will commit to. (The cut scene adjusts to the choice the player makes.) This beat reinforces Freq's "Introduction to Protagonist's Purpose" by making a huge decision that leads him closer to getting to the NBA (professional purpose) and by showing his love and devotion to his family in making that decision (personal purpose).

Point of No Return – a one-on-one conversation with Freq's mom (*a la* docu-style confessional room with the director) reveals how this new step fulfills the dreams and expectations she has had of him since he was young. Now Freq is on his way. This makes Freq's journey not only about him but also about his family. Should he succeed, we will feel the joy that the family feels. Should he miss the boat, we will feel the same grave disappointment that they will feel.

Act 2
Adjustment to New World – Freq's college experience is compressed narratively. It's strictly a device, in that it is just a realistic waystation to the NBA

but offers no character development or interesting story beats to enhance dramatic conflict.

But after winning the championship in college, Freq makes a decision with his agent Pagnotti about Freq's draft strategy, including his leaving school early. The decision is discussed over speaker phone with his parents, sister, and new girlfriend, Yvette. Pagnotti's suggestion to leave college early goes against what the family wanted Freq to do. But this is a unique opportunity based on his unique talent. The traditional path will not get him to where he wants to be. This is the new cutthroat world of the business of sports, no longer the neighborhood playground. The decision to stay or leave college is debated among Freq's close circle. While there's no unanimous answer, Freq decides to leave college early, sign with Pagnotti, and get ready for the draft. Vic's presence in his life is also a cause for debate, as it might affect his draft position.

Freq eventually gets drafted (the draft position depends on player performance in previous games). He signs with his new team in front of an enthusiastic press conference.

Escalating Burdens – now that Freq is an official NBA player, everything starts to change for him, including Vic's recklessness and its effect it will have on his team. The team owner takes this to heart and tells Freq to watch out.

Exposure of Weakness – in the same scene, the owner reveals a filmed arrest of a drunken Vic. He's an embarrassment to Freq and to the team. Freq paid $100,000 to lawyers to make the incident go away. The owner says Vic is banned from the facilities and will arrest him if he's seen anywhere near the team. If Freq helps Vic defy those orders, the owner will cut him from the team. Freq has no choice but to comply because, as he discovers, a morality clause in his contract will hurt him significantly.

Loss of Trust – video game players, at this point, should have a sense of doubt about Freq's judgment. If he can't keep his friend in line and instead spends exorbitant amounts of money to free him from an arrest, what kind of leader or hero is the Freq?

Midpoint/Low Point – Freq's inner circle focuses on how to make him a brand outside of the court. But how to do it forces dissension among the ranks. Cee-Cee's distrust of Yvette and Pagnotti culminates. Pushed too far, Freq lashes out at everyone and doles out orders to Dom, Cee-Cee, and Yvette on how to proceed. He steps up and assumes the role of what's expected of him: a leader. But his rare moment of independence does not solve the chaos; in fact, it invites more of it.

In the Belly of Jonah's Whale – Vic tries to create distrust with Cee-Cee and Dom and says the streets do not approve of how Freq's taking his career. His Jordan sneakers are not being bought, which is a colossal failure. Vic implies that he's a better business confidant than those within Freq's inner circle. When Cee-Cee intercedes, Yvette pushes back and schools her on her terrible promotional strategy for the Jordan brand sneakers. Chaos ensues. Cee-Cee offers a new strategy and proposes to be his official manager. Freq is not cool with that, as he thinks this is a money grab for his sister. Freq's inner circle implodes.

Act 3

Redemption Path Begins – in the same scene, Cee-Cee reveals she does not appreciate when Yvette and Vic are prioritized over her. Freq convinces her that he doesn't need to be protected anymore by her. She needs to accept them. Cee-Cee acquiesces, but only once he reveals that he knows Yvette and Vic are using him. Freq asserts that he's using them just as much.

Ticking Time Bomb Introduced – Vic confronts Freq about why he won't financially support his new endeavor as a hip-hop artist. When Freq denies him, Vic loses his cool by expressing his jealousy over Freq's better upbringing. When Vic doesn't let up, Freq unloads on him, saying he's had enough of his behavior. Vic's leeching is out of control. To top it off, he made a pass at Yvette! The Freq has spent over $250,000 on legal fees and frivolous parties for Vic – and for what? Once Vic feels unappreciated, he blackmails his friend in revealing an old secret: the mysterious death of Dirtbike Donnie. An accidental fall down a stairwell led to his death, and Freq was the cause. Vic covered it up and claims Freq is indebted to him forever. Freq doesn't deny it. Vic then guilts Freq into letting him borrow his expensive car so that he can screw around and have fun. With his emotional stranglehold over the Freq, Vic now has carte blanche to do whatever he wants.

Escalating Burdens Intensify – after a practice is let out early, Freq struggles with his friend's behavior through a time-lapsed montage. Meanwhile, his relationship with Yvette gets stronger.

Obligatory Scene/Climax – the team's owner has a sit-down with the Freq and his inner circle to revisit the off-court shenanigans of Vic. His behavior has gotten worse after a social media insult toward a teammate went viral. Freq, Cee-Cee, and Pagnotti get defensive after the owner makes a veiled threat to cut Freq from the team. Freq stands up for Vic – but Cee-Cee, Dom, and the owner are unified: dump Vic. Freq makes the decision to leave the team.

Reversal – after becoming a free agent, Freq talks with Pagnotti about his next move. Off-screen, Freq promised Pagnotti that he would cut off ties with Vic. He reveals in this scene that he couldn't, due to loyalty. The Freq vows not to make his next move without talking to Vic first.

Recognition – in a press conference, Freq will announce the next team he will play for. But first he shares that the decision was made with the help of Yvette, Cee-Cee, and his parents. He reinforces that their love and trust made this decision possible. This is now the first time where the professional and personal goals intersect. Earlier, it was expressed as two separate goals in the same scene; here, his professional goal could not have been possible without his personal goal. Vic, being suspiciously off the radar for days, was not part of this process.

Resolution of Bomb – post-press conference, Freq gets a call from a police officer. Vic died as a result of speeding in Freq's car, which spun out of control and crashed.

Denouement – after Vic's funeral in their hometown, Freq and Cee-Cee reflect on how "life's a trip" – nothing could prepare them for the curveballs of life. They then meet up with their folks, where Freq shares his appreciation for them, particularly their involvement in his life. After Freq and Cee-Cee leave, they surprise their parents with a gift: keys to a new house and tickets to Montego Bay.

As a post-script, Vic reads from a letter he wrote to Freq, presumably right before he died. He shares how painful his childhood was, particularly regarding his mother who died of AIDS. He thanks Freq for finding love through his family. All he wanted was to be loved and feel a sense of belonging.

Please Note: While the letter is recited and performed by Vic, it's not understood if it's read by Freq or if it's just an inelegantly placed narrative device to give Vic one last say. Why Vic wrote this note remains unclear. This moment is, in Aristotelian dramatic terms, a catharsis. However, it is recited by a supporting character and not by the protagonist. Its presence, therefore, doesn't make much sense except to force players to feel a certain way.

Positives of the Narrative

The dialogue was natural and authentic and allowed for the actors to give seamless performances.

Negatives of the Narrative

This game's only narrative mechanisms were cut scenes. As mentioned before, cut scenes are not beloved by the majority of gamers. Remember: they do not like friction in their gaming experience. What's worse, these cut scenes were 8–10 minutes long! No gamer, even a lover of narrative, will have patience for that. It feels like the publisher was so excited to have a premiere filmmaker as part of their next game that they gave him free rein to do whatever he wanted and turned a blind eye to the needs of gamers.

The type of story that was told is a run-of-the-mill "rags to riches" trope, which is common in the sports genre. It tires very quickly. But that's not the key problem with the narrative here.

First, there is an extremely loose/almost non-existent relationship to gameplay. With the exception of selecting a college team to play with or forcing a trade to another NBA team, the actions a player makes in the narrative have no bearing on what happens on the court. Similarly, what happens on the court is not even recognized in the cut scenes. It would have been nice to lose a crucial game and see what the reaction is in the cut scene. But there was none of that. In fact, it didn't matter what one did on the court; the cut scenes were going to continue with a story that was less about the playable character as a basketball player and more about how business decisions can affect personal relationships. Not a bad foundation for a sports drama, but not compelling enough for a video game. It meshes well with neither the fast-paced nature of the sport nor the gameplay expectations from fans.

There was another major, glaring issue. Players can customize their character in the very beginning of the game. A player can choose their height, weight, and hair style. They can even choose their race. Freq's parents and twin sister are African American. But a player could easily make their character Asian, White, Latino, or African American. If the player customizes their character to be a different race or ethnicity than the Freq's family, this game will not adjust its dialogue or plot points to that choice. So, if a player customized the Freq to be, for instance, Asian American, he will still have two parents and a fraternal twin sister who are African American. Consequences have actions, and player choice is completely ignored in this narrative.

Second, the dramatic structure falls apart halfway through the story after Vic emotionally blackmails Freq with an incident from their past. If Freq listens to the owner and cuts ties with Vic entirely, Vic will (or so he threatens to) expose that Freq killed a local thief called Dirtbike Donnie after a struggle on a stairwell. Freq claimed it was an accident, but Vic never believed him. In fact, he will hold that secret over Freq's head to exploit all the access and riches that come with being a superstar hanger-on.

This is a huge shift in our perception of Vic, who, at first, came across as a lovable yet troubled friend that couldn't get out of his own way. It calls into question Freq's dogged loyalty to keeping Vic around despite the owner's disagreement. Was all of his loyalty and goodwill toward Vic a charade? Was the Freq living in fear of blackmail this entire time?

Not likely. After Vic died in a car accident, Freq honored him at his funeral and was genuinely distraught over his friend's death.

Also, the blackmail card was never used or mentioned after that story beat, which would normally be classified as the low point. Freq continued on with his career without fear or even acknowledgment that Vic had something over him. *In other words, there were no consequences to that story beat.* Why was it even there? Why were we forced to question our hero's integrity and intelligence?

When Vic dies, it's more of a relief than a tragedy. He made our hero look bad on so many occasions, even before he tried to blackmail him. Vic is not a character for whom we should have sympathy. This is a failure in storytelling, mainly because Spike Lee set up the rules for the characters early on and then broke them halfway through. Are we to trust what these characters have to say or do after that? Not likely.

Third, there isn't a real antagonist in this story. Yes, Freq has to make tough, even unfair decisions at the command of his team's owner, but those choices didn't thwart Freq's career or spoil his relationships. Vic might be the closest to an antagonist, simply because he spoils the Freq's reputation and forces him to take sides against his owner. But Vic never really affected his career on the court, nor did he push him away from his family or girl-friend. Vic was basically a nuisance, but not a significant enough opposing force to genuinely obstruct our hero's path.

In Conclusion

NBA 2K16 has a well-intentioned narrative with high production values. But behind its good intentions are deeply flawed structural missteps and characters that are ultimately uneven. Yet, it's important to discuss this game because the video game industry tends to have a secret love affair with Hollywood. So often do publishers and studios go after marquee talent as a misguided strategy to increase sales of the game. But a movie star or popular filmmaker whose name is on the cover is never an enhancement to sales. Gamers don't care about movie stars; they care about great gameplay.

And it is often the case that the exorbitant money a publisher spends on a famous actor or filmmaker takes away from other elements of game development. Such is also the case when well-respected screenwriters of film and television are hired to write the story of a video game. Many of these writers have zero experience in game narrative or in playing games. Much of their work will be thrown away, and game writers and narrative designers will have to come in and change over 90% of the writing. That's why, today, many of these Hollywood writers, by fiat of the game studio, will collaborate early and steadily with narrative designers and game writers to make their work more "game friendly."

Luckily, these types of engagements don't happen that often because the return on investment is very low. Nonetheless, the temptation to hire Hollywood talent exists and should be met with great caution.

THE LAST OF US (2013)

Studio:	Naughty Dog
Publisher:	Sony Interactive Entertainment
Writer:	Neil Druckmann
Year Published:	2013[1]

Premise

An outbreak from a poisonous fungus spreads across the United States. People morph into zombie-like creatures known as "The Infected." The more people they bite and infect, the more their numbers increase. Twenty years later, America has become a post-apocalyptic wasteland, where a paramilitary force known as FEDRA rules with an iron fist. Cult-like factions rebel against their oppressive rules within quarantine zones where survivors are forced to live. Joel, a cynic who lost his daughter in the first moments of the outbreak, makes ends meet by being a smuggler of goods from one zone to the next. When he's presented with a new challenge of taking a young girl to a quarantine zone across the country where she holds the cure to this zombie-like disease, Joel must face his darkest demons and assume the role of father figure once again.

In a Nutshell

The Last of Us was a huge hit of 2013. The game sold over 7 million units in its first 13 months. By 2022, the game sold over 37.5 million units (including 18.63 million units for the 2020 remake).[2]

It was also critically acclaimed, recognized especially for its writing, and, by 2023, was adapted into an award-winning mini-series for HBO. Naughty Dog, a Sony studio based in Santa Monica, CA, was known for their highly successful *Uncharted* franchise. With this new IP led by game director and head writer Neil Druckmann, the studio proved that it wasn't a one-trick pony. They also proved that they are the best studio in the world for game narrative.

Main Characters

Joel – a rugged, grizzled cynic who knows all the angles on how to survive in post-apocalyptic America. Joel lost his daughter during the first hours of the outbreak. Twenty years later, he is a smuggler-for-hire who seldom gets emotionally attached to any person or cause. That is, until Ellie walks into his life.

Ellie – the new daughter figure for Joel. She holds the key to the cure of the outbreak that has infected millions. Tissue from her brain can lead to the creation of a new vaccine. She will need to be delivered safely to a lab to conduct this experiment. It is likely she will not survive the procedure involved.

Marlene – head of the unscrupulous Fireflies, a rebel group who believes they have the cure to the outbreak.

Bill – curmudgeon, booby trap creator, mechanic, prepper and survivalist.

David – leader of a group of random survivors that competes for resources with Joel and Ellie. Many of his men were killed months earlier by Joel. When he discovers Ellie hunting nearby, David subtly plans to exact revenge.

Key Story Beats

Act 1

Setup or Establishment of the World – We meet Joel and his young daughter Sarah in a working-class town in Texas. We understand his status in life when Joel reveals to Sarah that he's about to lose a contracting job.

Introduction to Protagonist's Purpose – They connect after she gives him a watch for his birthday. We know from the very beginning that Joel's emotional purpose is being a good dad.

Inciting Incident – later that evening, a mysterious pandemic hits their region of the United States (the South). Of what nature, we do not know at first; however, Joel attempts to drive out of town with Sarah but is seized by zombie-like townspeople before getting into a car accident. When he comes to, he carries Sarah to the streets as chaos ensues. A military officer confronts them, thinking they are one of the zombie-like townspeople and shoots at both of them. Sarah is killed nearly instantly.

The story flashes forward to 20 years later. The world is a post-apocalyptic wasteland. FEDRA, a paramilitary group, imposes martial law.

Refuse the Call – after infiltrating a seedy underground of a local kingpin named Robert, Joel joins his friend Tess in trying to retrieve guns that Robert gave away to the unscrupulous rebel group known as the Fireflies. After Tess and Joel rough him up, Robert tells them to kill the Fireflies and get their guns back. When talking to a Firefly named Marlene who claims to have access to the guns, Joel doesn't believe that she has them, so she tells Joel and Tess to follow her to an abandoned building where they'll get the guns. In exchange, they must smuggle contraband out of the quarantine zone to a new one across the country. They discover that the contraband is actually a 14-year-old girl named Ellie. Joel agrees to take her to the tunnel to wait for Tess and Marlene but refuses to escort Ellie to this new quarantine zone. Although Ellie might be the key to finding a vaccine to the virus, Joel can't trust Marlene, mainly because she's a Firefly.

Situation Worsens – smuggling Ellie out of the military zone is dangerous as soldiers attempt to stop them. But Tess kills two soldiers after Ellie stabs one of them. They discover, through one of the dead soldier's instruments, that Ellie is infected (but cannot transform into the Infected). Tess and Joel think Marlene set them up. When more soldiers arrive, Joel, Tess, and Ellie have to escape the sector at all costs or they will die.

Ellie reveals that while there are quarantine zones with their own potential cures to the virus, she (due to the mysterious nature of her biology) is the sole link to finding a vaccine.

When trying to escape, they get attacked by uniquely infected townspeople (known as Clickers, a sub-"species" of the Infected) and must undertake various physical challenges. By now, it is clear that a bite from one of the Infected will turn someone into one of them (Ellie being the exception).

Accept the Call – when the person at the drop-off location is found dead, Joel discovers that Tess, his beloved friend and partner, has been bitten by one of the Infected. Joel succumbs to taking the girl to the far-off quarantine zone, so that he can help find the cure for the remaining uninfected people in the country.

Point of No Return – Tess stays behind so that Joel and Ellie can escape. Tess dies in the process. Escaping to the other side of this quarantine zone requires one last perilous journey of killing hostile FEDRA soldiers and more physical challenges (that become harder with Ellie's inability to swim). With the future of humanity resting on his shoulders, Joel knows exactly what his professional goal is: to bring Ellie to the lab in the far-off quarantine zone so that a vaccine can be created. His renewed personal goal emerges as well: Ellie is gradually fulfilling a daughter's role, triggering Joel's instincts as a father.

Act 2

Adjustment to New World – Joel sets the ground rules with Ellie about their relationship: Don't mention Tess and don't tell anyone about her own condition for the fear that she will be killed. They travel through the outside world, where Ellie has never seen the woods before due to the fact that she's been sequestered inside Sector 12 (the quarantine zone they just fled) for her entire life.

Escalating Burdens – Joel and Ellie look for his friend Bill, who can get them a car that they can use to travel across the country. In this search, they come across various physical challenges, booby traps, and armed confrontations but learn to get closer to one another and work with each other.

After meeting with Bill, Joel realizes that they need to gather various parts from cars that can be used to build a working car. Bill joins Ellie and Joel on this quest. This involves more confrontations (including a new creature called Bloaters) and physical challenges.

When Ellie and Joel get the newly refurbished car working, Joel and Ellie continue to develop a stronger father/daughter bond. But when they are ambushed by a gang of non-infected people (also known as Hunters) on an alternate highway, they abandon their car and hit the road by foot, where they must make it to a bridge in the distance. More physical challenges (including an awesome elevator shaft scene) and confrontations take place. Joel eludes the Hunters, but in doing so, the in-game dialogue foreshadows more confrontations to come. Ellie saves Joel by shooting a Hunter who attempted to drown Joel under an overflow of water in an abandoned building. Joel resents being saved by her (or by anyone for that matter). The bitter exchange between the two resembles a heated yet frivolous exchange between a parent and child. However, this time the person with "attitude" is the parent.

Their bond increases when Joel teaches Ellie how to fire a shotgun as they travel through enemy territory of the hunters.

Along the way, Joel and Ellie meet two strangers – Henry and his younger brother Sam – who are doing their best to survive each day. They agree to join Henry and Sam on their way to a hideout, which overlooks the aforementioned bridge. This scene offers more opportunities for Joel and Ellie to increase their bond, fight off enemies, and undertake physical challenges.

The four of them decide to get to the bridge late at night. When a ladder accidentally falls to the ground leaving Joel stranded underneath the bridge, Henry and Sam can't do anything to help Joel. They encourage Ellie to join them and to abandon Joel out of self-preservation. But Ellie refuses and drops down beneath the bridge to be with Joel, as Henry and Sam rush off. Ellie and Joel must survive a harrowing showdown with FEDRA soldiers who are guarding the bridge. Joel and Ellie drop below to the water and are swept to the other side of the bridge, but not before Joel gets knocked out.

When he comes to at the other end, Joel is face-to-face with Henry. Joel aims his gun at Henry as a response to abandoning him at the bridge. They quickly work out their issues in an effort to track down a communications tower.

They encounter more attacks from Clickers and more phys-ical challenges. A drop-down gate forces a separation between the characters: Henry and Ellie as one group and Joel and Sam as the other. Each side must work together and find their way back to each other in a dark abandoned building with Clickers everywhere. This reinforces Joel's instincts of being a parent: he reflexively protects Sam with every threat that pops up. When all four reunite, they set their eyes on getting closer to the communications tower. But first, Joel steps up as a pro-tector of everyone around him to shield them from a series of harrowing encounters with the Clickers.

Joel then offers Henry a chance to find and join up with the Fireflies. If they can make it to Wyoming, Joel's brother (a Firefly) can do the rest.

After a harrowing encounter with more Clickers, Joel serves as a sharp-shooter for the others to help them get to another safe haven. Finally, it's a moment to breathe as Joel lets his guard down and connects with Henry. At the same time, Ellie bonds with Sam and reveals her fears of ending up alone. This is one of the only moments in the game where the pace is slowed down to bolster the emotional connection between these characters. Therefore, if tragedy were to strike anyone of them, the player will feel something significant. Case in point …

Having secretly been bitten, Sam turns into one of the Infected and attacks Ellie. To save her life, Henry kills his younger brother. Henry then turns the gun on himself and commits suicide.

Later … Joel reunites with his brother Tommy at a deactivated power plant and meets his new wife, Maria. Tommy and others have made the power plant a micro-civilization made up of 20 families. In a one-on-one with Tommy, Joel wants his brother to take Ellie off his hands and deliver her to the Fireflies and collect the payment. In exchange, Joel wants some gear. The two argue but put their differences aside when they are attacked by bandits looking to steal resources. Afterward, Tommy agrees to take Ellie to the Fireflies. Joel starts to head back home.

Exposure of Weakness – Joel, realizing that the mission to take Ellie to the lab is too dangerous, turns around and heads back to Tommy's. It's not out of a sense of duty, but rather a subconscious desire to be a parent and relive his life with his daughter. He suppresses practicality and self-preservation to be a dad. And this could kill him.

Loss of Trust – after discovering that Joel almost abandoned her, Ellie steals Tommy's horse and escapes to a ranch. When Joel finds her, she confronts Joel. *What are you afraid of*, she asks him? She then brings up the memory of his daughter and forces him to admit that he wants to give up on her because he's afraid to lose another person in his life. Joel tells her they must go their separate ways.

Midpoint/Low Point – minutes later, the ranch gets raided by bandits. Joel, Tommy, and Ellie trek back by horse to the power plant. Joel has second thoughts and decides to continue on the path he set forth and will deliver Ellie to the Fireflies lab at the University of Eastern Colorado (where the vaccination experiment on Ellie will be conducted). But when they arrive at the lab days (or weeks) later, no one is there. However, someone left a voice recording that reveals that the Fireflies have moved on to Utah.

Joel gets impaled during a fight with random thugs at the university. Ellie must save him by pulling metal debris off of him. Joel steadily loses consciousness while escaping the university. He relies on Ellie to help him through, but then blacks out.

In the Belly of Jonah's Whale – days (maybe weeks) have passed and Ellie finds herself in the dead of winter in a rural town, somewhere far away from (but en route to) Utah. She has become a formidable warrior in the wild. After killing a deer for food, she finds herself confronted by two men. The leader, David, offers antibiotics in exchange for the deer; she agrees. After the other man (James) goes off to retrieve the antibiotics, Ellie and David must defend themselves against an attack by a horde of the Infected. When they do so successfully, David reveals that his group of friends were killed by a man who fits Joel's physical description (the thugs he killed at the University of Eastern Colorado). Ellie recoils when James returns and aims a gun at her head. David tells him to stand down and says to Ellie that she and Joel won't survive much longer in this winter. She escapes and heads back to her safe haven (a house) with Joel.

Joel has gotten progressively worse since he was stabbed at the University of Eastern Colorado. Ellie is doing everything in her power to care for his needs before nightfall (including administering the antibiotics she exchanged with David). When she wakes up the next morning, David's men are near the premises. Armed, they search for Ellie and Joel. She attempts to draw their attention away from the house by escaping through horseback. David's men follow her and shoot at her, eventually killing her horse which thrusts Ellie to the ground. She escapes gunfire and finds shelter in and around a series of abandoned one-level houses. Through stealth and weapons mastery, she kills those who try to attack her. As she defends herself, the player will witness how much she has evolved into a well-honed survivalist and stone-cold killer.

Eventually, her constant eluding of David's men leads her to David himself, who puts her in a sleeper hold and knocks her unconscious. When she comes to, she is in a cage and witnesses someone from his group chopping off an arm from a headless torso. David approaches the cage and offers her some food, which she rejects thinking it's human (later to be discovered as true). David attempts to recruit her to join their group, but she denies him. He leaves her in the cage with her fate to be determined.

When a severely weakened Joel wakes up and discovers that Ellie is gone, he goes out to find her in the brutal winter. In his search, men who are part of David's cannibalistic group attempt to mow him down. He holds his own and shoots at anyone in his way. Joel eventually takes one of the men captive and tortures him to reveal the whereabouts of Ellie before he kills him.

David and another man from his group take Ellie out from her cage and attempt to kill her. She eludes them, steals a switchblade, and escapes to the outside, where she goes in and out of empty sections of their basecamp in the middle of a snowstorm. Ellie uses stealth to kill those who attempt to hunt her down. David eventually corners her in an abandoned steakhouse; she eludes him but cannot escape. She eventually creeps up behind him and stabs him but blacks out due to the fall of taking him down.

Joel trudges through the bitter cold and eventually finds David's basecamp. He kills many of David's men along the way, even as the winter conditions intensify. Joel refuses to give up; finding Ellie is critical.

When Ellie comes to, the steak house is on fire. David, still alive even from the stab wound, tackles Ellie to the ground and chokes her. Ellie gets out from his grasp and bludgeons him to death with a machete. Joel reunites with her while she is in thrall of killing David.

Act 3

Redemption Path Begins – it's springtime now, and Joel and Ellie have finally made it to Utah and are getting closer to the lab. But there's something off about Ellie. She seems distracted, less motivated to soldier on, less in sync with Joel. There's a glimmer of hope when they come across a giraffe eating foliage and grass in an abandoned lot.

Ticking Time Bomb Introduced – Joel stops to let Ellie know that they don't have to go forward with this; they can go back to Tommy's. Ellie moves forward; after all they've been through, it can't be for nothing.

Escalating Burdens Intensify – they press on. Ellie shows him a picture of his daughter. This hits Joel hard. He says he can't escape his past.

They undertake various physical acts and encounter more hostility from the Infected.

An underwater incident involving a submerged bus forces Joel and Ellie to swim through a maze before they get to air. When they do, they are surrounded by the Fireflies. Joel gets knocked out.

Obligatory Scene/Climax – when he regains consciousness, Ellie is nowhere to be seen. He comes face-to-face with Marlene, who questions Joel on how he got this far. Joel attributes that to Ellie's resolve. Marlene reveals that Ellie is being prepped for surgery. The process to create the cure has begun. Marlene also reveals that the reason why Ellie is the critical person for the cure is because of a growth inside her head. This will serve as the basis for the vaccine. However, removing the growth will likely kill her.

Joel rejects this and says he'll just take Ellie back home. But it's too late; this is what's best for society and there's nothing he can do about it. A Firefly militant beats Joel down.

Joel eventually disarms the militant, shoots him, and finds out the whereabouts of the operating room right before the militant dies. Joel heads toward the operating room and kills all those who get in his way.

Reversal – when he gets to the operating room, he shoots the surgeon and rescues Ellie. But her condition is untenable. It's unclear if she's dying or drugged.

After escaping to an empty parking lot, Joel carries an unconscious Ellie in his arms. Marlene stops him by aiming a gun right at him. Just as she's about to shoot …

Resolution of Bomb – we cut to Joel, who is driving Ellie away from the hospital.

In the car ride, as she recovers from the anesthesia, she asks what happened. Joel lies to Ellie and says the Fireflies stopped looking for a cure. Joel says to her they're going "home" (Tommy's place). A flashback reveals what happened during his confrontation with Marlene. Joel shot her, as he cannot risk any of the Fireflies coming after Ellie, even if that means the lives of millions hang in the balance.

Recognition – Back to the present. Their car eventually runs out of gas and they decide to walk the rest of the way to Tommy's. Ellie stops him and talks to her about her best friend Riley, who, when they lived in Boston together, did not survive from a bite from the Infected. Ellie reveals her survivor's guilt.

Ellie then confronts Joel about the aftermath of their escape from the hospital. *Swear to me that everything that you said about the Fireflies is true?* Joel lies and tells her, *I swear.*

Denouement – the game ends on a fabricated moment of uncertainty. Ellie thinks there is no hope, no chance for a cure. Joel cannot tell her the truth and risk losing her, even if that means saving the lives of others. But it reinforces the message that Joel, who had given up on being a parent after the death of his daughter, has been reawakened as a dad. The connection to Sarah (through Ellie) has come full circle. Even though Ellie and Joel are not blood related, their bond is just as strong as any biological father and daughter could ever have. And this connection, as Joel realizes, is sacrosanct. Nothing will come between them, even if it's for the greater good.

Positives of the Narrative

The plot is simple: deliver the girl to safety. It's the difficulty in achieving this goal, however, which makes the game both an exciting adventure and an emotionally wrought father–daughter drama. Survival is the common thread in this game. As such, the slightest threat to either Joel or Ellie is emotionally jarring. If Joel dies, his new daughter figure will not reach safety. If she dies, Joel will relive the trauma of the loss of his biological daughter from 20 years before. The consequences here are not just about the logistics of safety; they are about the sanctity of family at its most rudimentary level. This kind of emotional depth is seldom seen in any medium today – in games especially.

Additionally, the NPC ambient dialogue is masterfully crafted. When a player explores the post-apocalyptic world, they will see its various conditions and the harsh treatment that FEDRA inflicts upon its citizens. While their focus is not necessarily on what minor characters are saying in the background, a player will nonetheless be properly equipped with relevant information about secondary characters and factions. Each line is organically delivered and reinforces each moment's context, mood, and tone.

Negatives of the Narrative

Various missions are repetitive. Their goals are sometimes not meaningful; they are, rather, just another excuse to introduce a new environment with more dangerous confrontations and physical activities. One could easily substitute a Communications Station or Bridge with another locale and not have any bearing on the plot or character development. And the more locations that were added, the more it felt like the game was delaying the achievement of something big and meaningful, story-wise. Obviously, these locales introduce more gameplay opportunities and cool confrontations, but they are hollow by nature because they are just buying time. This is typical of games. The goal is often to be mission-based, not character-based. That's a harsh thing to accept as a storyteller. It is the reality, nonetheless.

Also, the game is very cut-scene heavy. This may not be a bad thing for gamers who love narrative. However, as mentioned several times before, most gamers view cut scenes as interruptions to gameplay. But it just so happens that *these cut scenes are done so well*. If one doesn't like them, then it's a matter of personal taste, not lack of quality.

While the character development of *The Last of Us* is pretty stellar, it's not without its flaws. When Ellie escapes to the ranch after hearing that Joel is leaving her with his brother, one would expect a deeper sense of hurt from Ellie. But instead, her escape is disingenuous; she wants to be found and Joel does so quickly. She wants a platform to show her pain and castigate him for his skittishness toward her. The moment is emotionally false and contrived. But it's just one false move in an otherwise masterwork of video game narrative.

In Conclusion

The Last of Us is a triumph in interactive fiction. It tells a great story, not just for games but for any medium. The excellence doesn't stop there; it's a fun game to play too. This is unique in the games industry. Seldom does a game meet the quality bar for both narrative and gameplay. Telltale Games was known for their world-class storytelling in games before they closed shop, in their original incarnation, in November 2018. But were their games compelling from a gameplay standpoint? I was fascinated with the choices I made and their downstream effects in the episodes of *The Walking Dead* video game (2012). I would then replay an episode and choose different options to see how distinct the consequences were from the first go-around. The game was interesting and artfully executed, but I can't say that I experienced adrenaline-fueled, maniacal buttoning of the controller. Nor can I say that I had fun. That's the essence of games. In fact, that's the intent. When fun-to-play meets a great story, the gaming experience is second to none. And that's why Naughty Dog is in a class by itself.

ADDENDUM: *THE LAST OF US* HBO SERIES (2023)

The Last of Us premiered as a mini-series adaptation on HBO on January 15, 2023. It was an instant critical success and, for a paid cable show, achieved increasingly impressive ratings all the way to its ninth and final episode of the first season.[3] The mini-series was pretty much loyal to the narrative of the game, but did expand the storytelling to focus on minor characters in one-off episodes with slight (but important) changes. Bill, for instance, a business partner of Joel's, who once helped him fix his car in a dangerous part of town, has the entire Episode 3 dedicated to him and his life partner, Frank. In the game, the players do not see them together. All we have is Bill's hostile dialogue about Frank, who – as we discover – abandoned him. Later, the player comes across a suicide note from Frank, which reveals that, after being bitten by one of the Infected, he killed himself to prevent his transformation. The suicide note is a collectable, which means a player can choose to read the note at their leisure or never at all. The true impact of Frank's loss, however, can be felt in the mini-series, where the original narrative changes to conform to an emotionally wrought episode of television. Through time cuts that compress the relationship from years into cinematic minutes, the episode tracks how the two fell in love and survived the societal breakdown together, until the time came when Frank, ill with a mysterious neurological disease, asks Bill to help him commit suicide. Such a tough decision yields a surprising result: the two decide to commit suicide together as a sign of their everlasting devotion to one another. When Bill says to Frank, "You were my purpose,"[4] there is no need to question their suicide pact; living without the other is an impossibility.

In Episode 7, we learn of Ellie's past as a student in the FEDRA military school. There, she developed a deep bond with Riley. But when we meet Riley in a flashback, time has passed since they first met. Viewers discover that Riley went missing from the military school and, when she reappears in Ellie's life, Riley reveals she has joined the Fireflies and will leave the next day to assume her new duties at a post in Atlanta. They have now just one night together, and they spend it in an abandoned mall. Their relationship flourishes and culminates with a kiss – in essence, a confession of mutual love. But when one of the Infected bites both of them, their last moments together are the true expressions of that love. When the flashback ends, Ellie tends to Joel's wounds after a skirmish in Colorado. Riley's fate, we assume, is sealed. But we don't know if Ellie killed her or if Ellie escaped before she saw the full-on transformation of Riley.

Much of Episode 7 was already covered in previous media, but not in the main narrative of the game. Riley's story was dramatized in the Dark Horse comic off-shoot *The Last of Us: American Dreams* (April–July 2013) and in a 2014 downloadable content (DLC) release called *The Last of Us: Left Behind*. Both were solid additions to an already masterfully told main narrative. But there is a difference in emotional impact from DLC and comic to television.

Visual Limitations of the Game Medium

MOCAP performances still invite an "uncanny valley" in visual representation of the human body. That is, common human expressions that should look realistic are not rendered as such. Instead, basic facial and bodily details come across as strikingly alien – sometimes funny, sometimes grotesque. Eyes can look vacant and immobile. Jaws and lips can move out of sync. Arms can gesture robotically. Uncanny valley moments often erode the immersion of the gaming experience.

Player agency can erode the immersion as well. If a player uses their controller to look around the environment, dialogue expressed by the NPC serves to inform the player of what's going on. It is a transactional relationship between NPC and playable character to help orient the player with the task at hand or to deliver backstory of the world without distracting the player's gameplay. But live action film and television cannot get away with such a transaction. The camera moves in a limited capacity under the governance of the director's vision. Audiences see what the director wants them to see, and if the moment requires two people to have an emotional moment, the director will assure that there is no distraction or player agency to remove one's attention from that moment. The camera and POV stay put or are limited in movement. As such, the acting is the primary focus of that live action scene. Replicating that scene in Machinima-style motion capture will likely not achieve the same heights of live action artistry. The player will likely move around the environment, searching for collectables or equipping a weapon. Player freneticism would kill the drama. Even if such a scene in the game limits player agency through a non-playable cut scene, the awkwardness of the uncanny valley erodes its emotional impact.

Ingredients for a Successful Adaptation

Like the game, the mini-series is a triumph. Had one never played the game before, the storytelling and the acting are so compelling that the work thrives on its own merits. The mini-series was nominated for 24 Emmys, including "Outstanding Drama Series – 2023" and "Outstanding Writing for a Drama Series – 2023."[5]

The Last of Us has legitimized video games as worthy source material for Hollywood adaptations. Prior to the mini-series, video game adaptations into films were huge disappointments. *Uncharted* (2022), *Max Payne* (2008), *Warcraft* (2016), *Street Fighter* (1994), *Double Dragon* (1994), *Prince of Persia: The Sands of Time* (2010), *Far Cry* (2008), and *Silent Hill: Revelation* (2012) were either box office bombs or critical failures (or both!).

In some instances, when profits meet fan enthusiasm, the film adaptation can have a long shelf life. The billion-dollar-plus blockbuster *The Super Mario Bros. Movie* (2023) did not reap praise from critics, but millions of fans across the world thought differently. On the online review aggregator Rotten Tomatos, the movie scored a 59% among critics, but a whopping 95% among fans.[6]

In 2019, Netflix premiered a live action streaming adaptation of *The Witcher*. Three seasons later, the series has received numerous nominations from such entities as the Saturn Awards and Primetime Creative Arts Emmys Awards. It is not a strict game-to-series adaptation, however. *The Witcher* is based on the Andrzej Sapkowski novel series (1986–2013) of the same name. Yet, as a game series, dating back to 2007, it has received numerous awards for writing and remains one of the biggest selling game franchises of all time.

Arcane (2021–), an animated series in the world of Riot Games' *League of Legends* (2009–), was also a successful outing, having won the Emmy for Outstanding Animated Program in 2022.[7] However, there is a bigger gap to leap over when adapting from a game into a live action series. Visual representations and performances can undermine expectations if the live action translation isn't accurate or loyal to the original source material. But for those not familiar with the game, there is a limitation in believable subject matter and performances in animation. Visual spectacle and fantastical events are the focus for the medium, and they can easily distract viewers from bad storytelling. This isn't to say *Arcane* is bad (quite the opposite, in fact!), but relatable events and emotionally genuine performances are conveyed more successfully in the live action *The Last of Us* mini-series over the animated *Arcane* series.

So, while games are gaining ground in terms of Hollywood respect – and granted, that is an inane barometer of success, yet it is the reality for widespread pop culture adoption – *The Last of Us* remains the north star to which all other games ought to aspire. (That is, if widespread pop cultural acceptance is a goal for a game studio.) It is a video game original with a great story that maximizes the unique affordances of the interactive experience. It is easily adaptable to another medium, thanks, in part, to its compelling and vital characters, an overriding urgent conflict, a dangerous and immersive world, and a main character with a unique personal goal.

As to why other adapted properties failed, one can attribute that to a filmmaker's disrespect of the video game medium. Players want to have fun, yes. But consider an adaptation that injects wackiness into characters and pushes non-stop (often cartoonish) activity where the characters are but a cog in the visual chaos. This spells failure. The filmmakers are looking to compact a 24-hour-plus gaming experience into 2 hours and, consequently, gorge audiences with spectacle and adrenaline-laced moments *ad nauseum* to compete with the original source material.

The Last of Us, like *The Witcher*, may have an unfair advantage by having been adapted into a live action mini-series. An extended storytelling experience provides Joel and Ellie's journey with moments to breathe, where audiences can get to know them at a gradual pace (in 9 hour-long episodes vs. a single 2-hour movie) and where danger and dread inform their every move, absent of uncanny valley moments. With all those considerations, there isn't a panic from the showrunners to overwhelm Joel and Ellie's journey with constant noise and busyness. If it had been a film, it is likely their story would have been short-changed in favor of action scenes with the Infected. Such movies wind up being nothing more than a money grab. The relationship between these two characters, however, deserves better. Naughty Dog and Sony made the right choice.

NOTES

1 A remake of the game came out in 2022 with no difference to the narrative despite its significant visual enhancements. I reference the 2014 DLC *The Last of Us: Left Behind* later on in this chapter in relationship to the HBO mini-series. But I did not analyze its story, as it falls outside the scope of the main narrative.
2 VGChartz, "The Last of Us Series" 2023.
3 Porter, "'The Last of Us' Passes 'House of Dragon'" 2023.
4 Mazin, "Long, Long Time" 2023.
5 Television Academy, "The Last of Us – Emmy Awards" n.d.b
6 Rotten Tomatoes, "The Super Mario Bros. Movie" n.d.
7 Television Academy, "Arcane: League of Legends" n.d.a

REFERENCES

Mazin, Craig. "Long, Long Time." (2023, January 29). Season #1, Episode #3. The *Last of Us*, created by Craig Mazin and Neil Druckmann. Production Companies: The Mighty Mint; Word Games; PlayStation Productions; Naughty Dog; and Sony Pictures Television Studios. Distributor: HBO.

Porter, Rick. (2023, March 13). "'The Last of Us' Passes 'House of Dragon' in Full-Season Viewers." Retrieved on February 10, 2024 from www.hollywoodreporter.com/tv/tv-news/the-last-of-us-season-1-finale-ratings-1235351440/

Rotten Tomatoes. (n.d.). "The Super Mario Bros. Movie." Retrieved on February 10, 2024 from www.rottentomatoes.com/m/the_super_mario_bros_movie

Television Academy. (n.d.a). "Arcane: League of Legends." Retrieved on February 10, 2024 from www.emmys.com/shows/arcane

Television Academy. (n.d.b). "The Last of Us – Emmy Awards & Nominations." Retrieved on February 10, 2024 from www.emmys.com/shows/last-us

VGChartz. (2023, April). "The Last of Us (Series)." Retrieved on February 9, 2024 from www.vgchartz.com/game/226267/the-last-of-us/?region=All

CHAPTER 11

Breaking In

BECAUSE NARRATIVE DESIGN AND game writing are creative endeavors, they face the same ups and downs for employment that musicians, actors, screenwriters, and artists do. Granted, getting a staff job with a publisher mollifies some of that anxiety. However, unless the publisher or studio you're working for is story-centric or has multiple titles that you are tending to, brace yourself for rough waters ahead. Storytellers play second fiddle to pure designers, programmers, and audio engineers. As stated many times before, gameplay is king. If the game can live without story, then polish your resume when your company needs to tighten its budget.

Now, this isn't to say you shouldn't pursue game writing or narrative design. It just means to move forward and prepare yourself mentally for a volatile industry. Your first concern should be getting your foot in the door.

ENTRY POINTS

The industry's massive financial growth for nearly two decades[1] is due to its increasing global popularity and steady replacement of film as the pop culture go-to. According to a 2023 report by the Entertainment Software Association and the NDP Group, global consumer spending on games in 2022 far surpassed global movie spending – $335.51 billion to $77 billion.[2] So while the industry is massive, one would think the barrier to entry is low when, in fact, that's not the case.

Finding game writing opportunities is no different from finding other kinds of jobs. LinkedIn,[3] Indeed.com, and Zip Recruiter stand the test of time for job searches. Discord servers devoted to various specialties and communities in game development are good sources too. Submit your

DOI: 10.1201/9781003438113-11

resume and cover letter online. If either sparks interest, the hiring manager will view your portfolio.[4] If they like what they read, they will assign you a writing test to complete at home. You will then need to exhibit familiarity with the company's games. Play them and watch walkthroughs online before you write a single line of dialogue. The goal is to absorb voice, tone, and personality of the characters of their established franchises or of the spirit of their company's brand if the franchise is new. Your script must show a command of all three and, if the IP is established, must properly (and elegantly) reference canonical events, characters, landmarks, weapons, vehicles, etc. of the world. Sometimes, tests will require a player to integrate narrative content with prescribed mechanics. To prepare for this, play games with similar mechanics and then observe how their writers communicated the narrative. Apply the same methods to your sample. Don't be afraid to ask questions to the hiring manager along the way. Tests shouldn't take more than 4–8 hours of your time (in total, spread out over 2–3 days), but exceptions happen not infrequently. If you pass the test, then you'll be subject to a series of interviews. Show respect for the company's IP, share which games you're playing and which you're passionate about, and illustrate why your particular talent is uniquely suited for the job. Be a good listener. Take the interviews seriously but don't take yourself too seriously. It's okay to smile. The company is looking for a good teammate. Are you someone who's fun and reliable during tough moments on weekends and late nights? Are you the person they want in the foxhole with them? When it's all done, prepare thank you notes to send off through LinkedIn or email (if business cards were exchanged). Then, hope and pray.

That's the conventional route. And there are no guarantees for its success, but you have to do it anyway.

So, assuming you don't have a family member or good friend who owns a game studio who can hire you, there are typically four other paths to breaking in:

- *The university path.* Enroll in a college or graduate school that offers degrees in game development and internship opportunities at game studios. There are a growing number of schools that offer these programs including the University of Southern California, Rensselaer Polytechnic Institute; University of Utah; Michigan State University; Full Sail University; University of Central Florida; and Carnegie Mellon University. (I provide a larger list in this book's final chapter.)

- *The tester path.* Apply for jobs as a game tester, where your primary responsibility will be playing games, testing them for bugs, and reporting these glitches to the relevant feature owners. (This position is also known as a quality assurance analyst, or QA analyst.) By starting as a tester, you will work yourself up to a junior position in another department (usually design or engineering) upon which your path to creating content for games begins.

- *The experienced-professional-from-another-field path.* These folks include programmers, artists, writers, project managers, and others. They often make a seamless fit due to their breadth of experience from another field. These professionals offer a different set of skills and perspectives that are helpful in making a product better and innovative.

- *The make-your-own-game path.* If you have money saved up, it might be worth creating and distributing your own game on a mobile device or on Steam, a video game distribution platform run by the Valve Corporation. While this might seem like an expensive endeavor (and it is!), it is an investment for the future. You will be developing a series of transferable skills that is used often in game development. These include project management, producing, designing, writing, marketing, trademark oversight, directing voice-over talent, etc. If you are an outsider and your game is playable, game developers will appreciate your effort. You now have something in common: surviving the backbreaking, overwhelming, and sleepless process known as game development. *Developing empathy is just as important as adopting skill sets.*

But no matter your background or experience level, getting hired depends a lot on the emotional quotient (EQ) you bring to the interview. You will meet people of various backgrounds and expertise who are attempting to get a "feel" for you as a potential coworker, and the attitude you project could make the difference of getting hired or getting rejected.

Attitude

People in the game industry work extremely long hours. The demands are constant and often are a hybrid of technical and creative challenges. Using both the left and right brain hemispheres can cause one's focus to be diffuse. So, the last thing a developer wants to deal with is an unnecessary distraction … in the form of a coworker.

Game professionals are looking to work with those who check the ego at the door, aren't precious over their work, and are flexible and nimble when curveballs are thrown their way (which is basically all the time).

An interview doesn't often reveal these attitudes, at least not in a genuine sense. That's why past work experience and, more importantly, reference checks will confirm (or deny) that the candidate is in possession of the right qualities.

What is often revealed in interviews, however, is the general attitude someone has toward games. This is often a trap for people who come from another industry, many of whom have never picked up a controller before. A holier-than-thou attitude can often emerge; same with the attitude of "Well, my kids play (fill in game here), therefore I am qualified to tell you how I feel about your product." No.

You will never be hired based on what other people think of games; you will be hired based on what *you* think of games. If you cannot deign to pick up the sticks or if you look at games as a lesser medium (which many prospective candidates do), it is best to look elsewhere for employment. The long hours, the countless internal product reviews, and the conversations with employees are extremely humbling. Games are constantly in flux, even after content lock (thanks to periodic software updates). This means one has to have an appetite and the intestinal fortitude to muscle through constant criticism, last-minute innovations, and endless technical bugs.

Games are fun to play. Making them, however, can be drudgery.

Familiarity

It's required that a prospective candidate study up (i.e., play) the product/franchise they are interviewing for. What's more, they ought to have a broad sense of the competition. Candidates will often be asked about what improvements they would bring to the next version of the game they're interviewing for and what innovations they would offer to differentiate it from the competition.

It's also important to be "in the know," so that you can speak to how the game compares to others in its genre and in the industry at large. Innovations from a game in one genre can inspire innovations in another. *Destiny*, for instance, influenced multiple games in numerous genres to adopt hero customization. PlayerUnknown's Battlegrounds, aka PUBG, made their mark on the industry in 2017 by popularizing the multiplayer "battle royale" fighting genre. Soon after, Epic Games saw the potential in it and repurposed a survival game of theirs called *Fortnite* into a cooperative battle royale game. Billions upon billions of dollars later, *Fortnite*, after taking the video game industry by storm, forced a few big-time game publishers to create their own battle royale games to stanch hemorrhaging stock prices.

It's also important to come prepared to discuss your craft and how you would leverage it to add value to the game. *As a narrative designer, what will you do to make the story of this franchise better? How will you improve the narrative mechanics so that story is more seamlessly intertwined with gameplay?* So, be ready to discuss games that you've played recently and what you thought were missed opportunities in the storytelling. This will show an interest in the medium as well as a command of your craft.

Lastly, as I will discuss in Chapter 12, it's important to have experience in certain technologies that will mostly likely be outside of your area of interest. Excel, Jira, Microsoft Project, Visio – all of these are tools that are used frequently in game development shops. Excel, for instance, enables the sharing of story content with other disciplines, who work in nothing but spreadsheets. Jira allows project managers to see how well you are progressing toward major deadlines. These tools might seem counterproductive for a writer, but they are a necessary evil for the betterment of the team. Never forget: *games are a highly collaborative industry.*

Larger Perspective than Games

As a narrative designer, you will be driving countless brainstorming sessions with creative directors, game designers, artists, and even engineers. It is common for these people to know the medium of games really well, but when pushing these folks to think outside of the industry, you will get the same set of IPs thrown at you: *Star Wars, Harry Potter, The Lord of the Rings*, and a superhero movie or two (or 30!).

The pool of resource material is very limited, and as such can be stifling creatively. But these professionals aren't hired to be well rounded in the narrative of other media. Rather, you are! It is important to have a broad exposure to and knowledge of well-told stories in various media. How an author decided to unravel a story beat, no matter the genre, will be instructive for whatever narrative you are trying to map out.

And I cannot say this enough: read books. And read books that are not only sci-fi, fantasy, or horror. Today's game narrative suffers too much from copying of the same tropes of the same genre of other games. And if it's not from other games, it's from the same episode of *The Walking Dead* or a short story by HP Lovecraft. Not a bad place to start, but the reading and watching must continue to other destinations – foreign destinations especially (i.e., not sci-fi, fantasy, or horror). Be comfortable with reading literature. Homer and Shakespeare offer the clearest and oldest examples of character and story structure, upon which modern-day drama (be it television, film, theater, or fiction) is built. Reading non-fiction is perhaps even more important. Real-life legends in history can be inspirations for characters in your narrative. Understanding their psychology and their backstory will fuel your imagination and make your characters' motivations more believable.

IF YOU COME FROM ANOTHER MEDIUM, WHAT SHOULD YOU EXPECT?

Television and film writers often have a hard time making the transition into games mainly because the script in traditional media is sacrosanct. It is the cardinal blueprint of production. True, dialogue gets changed all the time when you're on a film set. But the trajectory of the story (typically) remains intact once the camera rolls. People know what to expect in the next scene.

In the game world, the script (when there is one) does not command that degree of respect. Instead, the central document to which all the stakeholders refer is the game design document (GDD). This is a comprehensive document that provides the creative vision of the game as well as breakdowns for each mode and feature. It is the "source of truth" for every discipline on the game team. The GDD is in constant flux, mainly because features in the game either expand or contract based on ongoing industry trends or focus group testing. Once again, the games business is the business of software development. When technologies evolve, this forces everything else to change with it. A game can expand in scope anywhere in its development, in which case new content will need to be created and current content will need to be updated. Conversely, if the technologies contract (due to schedule, personnel, or budget), teams will cut or diminish features and modes. Narrative is often the first to get hit.

A writer from another medium will not be able to survive in this world without being nimble. Changes happen all the time and narrative is not immune. This can be frustrating for traditional screenwriters, who may be accustomed to altering scenes or bits of dialogue, but never wholesale changes of the mechanisms that deliver narrative, such as changing a cut scene into a non-voiced, non-animated branching conversation with an NPC. This involves a massive amount of work and can seem ludicrous (and often is!), but it is not out of the ordinary. Again, games are software. Tech always comes first.

What's more – and I can't stress this enough – traditional screenwriters will also have to be comfortable with writing in different software that isn't writer-friendly. Most of the time, narrative designers and game writers will be writing in a spreadsheet. Microsoft Excel (and, at a growing rate, Google Sheets) provides a wide breadth of data in individual cells that are relevant to different disciplines in game development. As discussed in Chapter 4, a spreadsheet makes it possible to monitor a single line of dialogue throughout the content creation pipeline. With every written line, you will have a corresponding asset ID, which will be the identification signifier that designers and audio engineers use to implement in the game. The localization team, as well, will use that same asset ID when translating a single line into numerous languages.

Although crucial to the collaborative process, spreadsheets are the most counterintuitive software for a writer. Filling in a narrow cell with dialogue is a lifeless process. Writing is often about human emotion, and there's nothing farther from emotion than a spreadsheet. Not to mention, it stymies the momentum of the writing process when one must endlessly manipulate the cells to accommodate new collaborators from different disciplines. Game developers often don't relate to this, and it's incredibly frustrating to deal with these constraints day in, day out.

I recommend those not familiar with spreadsheets to write their content in other software (like Word, Final Draft, or articy:draft) and then copy and paste their work into the appropriate cells. This is not ideal, but it is par for the course. And it is something writers need to be comfortable with if they wish to pursue this field.

Once again, games are software, and the development of software is not always an organic fit for creatives who thrive on the open canvas. Software development, on the other hand, has very structured and pronounced confines. To thrive as a writer in this world is to embrace those confines.

NOTES

1 "Nearly" is the operative word here. As of this writing, the industry is going through a post-COVID "cooling" that has resulted in mass layoffs at Microsoft, Riot, Twitch (Amazon), Gearbox, Niantic Labs, Unity, and countless others,

from mid-2023 to early 2024. That said, the industry's massive profits continue to far exceed those in film

2 Entertainment Software Association, "U.S. Consumer Video Game Spending" 2023.

3 And a good hashtag strategy on LinkedIn to find relevant posts can go a long way, e.g., #narrativedesignjobs #gamewritingjobs #narrativedesigner #gamewriter.

4 A portfolio often comprises an online collection of writing samples that showcases dialogue mastery and an understanding of interactivity. Twine games, 5-to-10-page sample scripts in proper screenwriting format, and walk-through videos of games you've worked on all suffice. Make sure to include what you can within the boundaries of signed NDAs. Otherwise, use spec material that conforms to the above. Include a link to your portfolio on your resume, cover letter, and as part of your email signature and LinkedIn profile.

REFERENCE

Entertainment Software Association. (2023, January 17). "U.S. Consumer Video Game Spending Totaled $56.6 Billion in 2022)." Retrieved on February 9, 2024 from www.theesa.com/news/u-s-consumer-video-game-spending-totaled-56-6-billion-in-2022/

CHAPTER 12

Rules and Tools for Success

B ECAUSE OF THE INTENSE collaborative nature of games, a narrative designer cannot write without confines. This can be constrictive for those who come from another medium such as film, fiction, or theater where the immediate process of writing is owned and governed by the author. Game narrative is typically a reactive discipline. Ideas often originate from a creative director who sets the vision of the game. This vision will include the type of game (first-person shooter [FPS], real-time strategy [RTS], platformer, etc.), its premise, the type of experience for players, and the golden path.

Creative directors are also on task to incorporate data and marketplace trends to shape their vision. These business interests can't be ignored. Game companies can invest tens, if not hundreds, of millions of dollars in a single title. The directive that emerges – *a la* a *Fortnite* copy, or the next futuristic FPS, or a mobile Match 3 game – will be the north star for the creative director.

Writers and narrative designers are often not consulted in this early phase ... and much to the game's detriment. Premise and golden path are, by their nature, so rooted in worlds, characters, and stories that it is only logical that they'd be workshopped with writers. Once again, the game world is a world of software. There are certain processes in place in which

DOI: 10.1201/9781003438113-12

content is created. Bringing writers in *after* the vision is created should be a relic of the old school way of game development, but it is not. What can be built, technology-wise, is often the starting point. The creative follows. This is not a universal (nor ideal) process for all game studios, but it is still the most common.

FLEXIBILITY

With that in mind, narrative designers and writers must be okay with contributing after the vision has been cemented and working within confines that may not be narrative-friendly. Not all cool games make for great stories. (That said, not all great stories make for cool games.)

Thus, the first rule of success is flexibility. Realize that when you come to a team, while you are desired for a special skill, you are not a priority … at first. Game developers will never realize how crucial narrative is until it's in the game, weeks before content lock. Then they will hound you to make improvements until the very last hours before everyone is "pencils down."

During this time, you'll be thrown a ton of change requests that might undermine the narrative. With time ticking away, you'll have to use the limited options in your quickly dwindling arsenal. The revision process will involve (a) figuring out ways to accommodate those last-minute changes in various narrative mechanisms, (b) identifying their downstream effects on the writing, and (c) writing those changes in a way that is neither awkward nor excessive so as not to bore or confuse the player.

That's the goal, but then reality sets in. Consider, if you will, an environment that has been cut at the last minute along with a crucial cut scene. A narrative designer will need to redistribute all of its relevant story information to other narrative mechanisms found in other environments in order to maintain story coherence. The information from that cut scene will eventually transform into – wait for it – an inelegant moment of exposition, either through voice-over from in-game dialogue or through user interface (UI) text.

This is only hypothetical, but it is similar to the types of compromises one should expect. Few people understand how fragile a story's architecture is. One arbitrary addition to or subtraction from a game feature could potentially cause the narrative structure to collapse. This is a constant challenge for storytellers. Finding ways to sustain the integrity of the story will be a tireless effort amidst the chaos of the game development cycle.

BRAINSTORMING SESSIONS

Once you join a game studio, you will quickly discover that the whiteboard will be your best friend. Ideas will be generated at rapid speed when the team is in the blue-sky phase of product development. Anything goes at this point. The transcribing of ideas, the mapping out of flows, and the prioritizing of creative pillars will decorate the whiteboard. Each brainstorming session will feature a new set of ideas ... and handwriting. The most important contributions from the team are not the quantity of ideas, but rather the parameters of the creative vision, which is often in an amorphous, unclear state. Creative directors ought to lead these initial discussions. This could take weeks to cement. Afterward, the narrative will start to emerge.

The narrative designer's greatest impact will be in organizing the ideas behind each creative pillar as it relates to story. She will draw connections between these ideas and subtly advocate for quality. The latter issue requires the narrative designer to reject ideas that are nonsensical, unachievable, off-brand, and/or downright offensive. She will be the gatekeeper of practicality, common sense, and good taste. She will also need to find the optimal actualization of narrative. If the product, for instance, is a family-oriented Match 3 mobile game, a narrative designer will need to add story within the limited confines of UI text. *Where and how*, she will ask herself? Does each Match 3 victory trigger a fragment of backstory or lore of the fictional universe of the game? After five achievements, does the player receive a letter from their fictional mom saying how proud they are? "If only you could break my record of twenty-five straight wins ..." Corny as that might sound, the player is given a specific goal rooted in a story, mainly about honoring their fictional mother's wishes. A narrative designer must always look for these opportunities and then ask tough questions to the team, such as, "What more can narrative do here?" At this stage, the job is to minimize the amount of missed opportunities for story.

The tough questions and their answers set a strong foundation for the brainstorming sessions. Once those basics are answered, it's then a matter of getting more specific with the narrative and how it works within the different elements of gameplay. The team will look to you to be the subject matter expert on story, and you will need to push back when the gameplay overwhelms or diminishes it. Without these brainstorming sessions, games will be created in silos. Seldom does that make for a fun player experience.

ROBUST DOCUMENTATION

Game developers love documentation. And why not? It provides the blue-print from which game features or systems are created. In addition to the GDD, ancillary design documents will describe features in great detail and will be shared among all disciplines within the studio. Centralized docu-mentation – also known as "sources of truth" when agreed upon by relevant stakeholders – provides visibility and updates for everyone involved, and will welcome feedback and contributions from members of the develop-ment team.

Many writers who join a team for the first time think they have but one goal: to write scripts or on-screen text. But that process is usually *the result of* copious narrative documentation. The following is a list of the types of documentation a narrative designer or game writer will take on before the actual scriptwriting begins.

Story Bible

A writer will often be tasked to write the lore of the world of the game. Their only fodder in the beginning will most likely be a premise, similar to an elevator pitch, which is a clear, concise, and vibrant description of your story's premise. Hook your audience into something exciting. The goal then is to take the premise and create a mythology that is designed for that game only.

This mythology will include the visual descriptions of the locales of the games, their backstories, the biographies of the primary and secondary characters, an in-depth story summary, beat by beat, and the descriptions of the sequels (implying that the game is a franchise and not a one-off).

The latter is important, as it provides a direction beyond the project at hand and will therefore force the writers to plant seeds in the first game that can blossom for each sequel. Remember: blockbuster games are franchises, and you'll always want to be thinking in those terms. (Indie games are the exception, but seldom do indie studios have enough budget (read: money) to support a full-time writer.)

Story bibles are living documents. They evolve as the franchise evolves. Characters and worlds will be added to it. And as the story summaries per each game are added, the bible not only serves as a guide for writers, artists, and programmers but also serves as a brand source for marketing teams, merchandising partners, book publishers, or film companies who plan to bring your game to life in their respective field(s). Therefore, story bibles should be well-organized, up-to-date, and comprehensive.

Crucial Component to Story Bible: Visual Structure

Writers share a common language. Inciting incident, climax, obligatory scene, etc., are structural terms that we toss back and forth to one another as a way to understand or improve the structure of a story. But for those who are outside of the field, it can be a challenge to explain what these terms mean.

What I have found most useful is mapping out the structure of a story through a diagram. **Structural milestones will be inserted on the graph, as if they were coordinates on a map**. Those higher on the graph serve as big, exciting moments or reveals for the story. I then draw a single line that connects these various coordinates together.

There are various reasons behind this exercise that go beyond communicating structure to outsiders. The visual map is an opportunity for writers to see the pacing of structural milestones and to "flip" coordinates or fill in story beats in between coordinates to prevent inactivity of the story.

Figure 12.1 is an example of a visual graph. There is no one right answer on how to map out your story. Different types of stories dictate their own pacing and milestones. However, there are some basic requirements that need to be on your map. First discussed in Chapter 7, the following story milestones are the *bare minimum requirements* for any visual graph. To recap:

Inciting Incident – what is the event that puts the journey of your protagonist in motion?

The Point of No Return – the moment in your story where the character has made a commitment to their mission and cannot back out. Doing so would be cowardly or dishonorable. But from a sheer practical standpoint, if the hero regrets their decision and decides to turn back, then the story ends right there.

Midpoint/Low Point – this is the moment in the hero's journey where they have been momentarily defeated. It seems as if the future is grim. If they can get over this hump, they will renew their sense of purpose and come out a stronger hero.

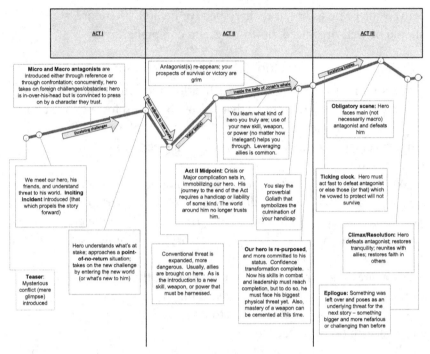

Figure 12.1   Story structure map. (See full-scale version of this graph at www. routledge.com/9781032571614.)

Ticking Time Bomb – the hero must act fast, now that the villain has introduced a new threat. The intensity and tempo of the hero's journey increase exponentially. The stakes are too high for the hero to fail.

Obligatory Scene/Climax – the moment where the hero has solved the most difficult challenge of the entire story and instantly changes the power dynamic of the world around them. For example, a nuclear bomb has been launched toward New York; the hero (most likely a superhero, in this case) changes its direction in the nick of time and then disarms the missile before it can explode. The citizens of New York, once terrified for their lives, can now breathe a sigh of relief.

These five story beats provide the necessary escalation of the protagonist's journey and set a course for clear moments that test the hero and make them more compelling. Everything else in between is up to the writer. But to have a solid foundation in the story's structure, the writer must assure that these five story milestones are stakes in the ground, wherein there should be little-to-no adjustment once the story is set.

Granted, changes will always happen. But these milestones should serve as guides toward the completion of the story. If there is something new that develops and causes, for example, the climax to change, this should not cause tremendous disruption where you lose sight of what the story is about. The goal of having immutable (or nearly immutable) stakes in the ground is to force yourself to be creatively disciplined and make strategic decisions that enhance what's already there. If a milestone changes and forces the significant revision of other milestones, it is likely that (a) that story was not well-thought out to begin with or (b) you need to change the entire story due to higher business demands or budgetary restrictions.

Always do your best to stay loyal to the strict story pillars you establish early on. Otherwise, there will be no end to the writing. There's too much at stake for you and your fellow game devs. You don't want to be the bottleneck of the content creation pipeline.

Other Components to a Story Bible

Collaboration can be a wonderful thing, but it does have its limits, especially when there are countless opinions from people with no experience in the task at hand. Narrative is a prime target. Everyone has an opinion about it, everyone is quick to judge, and everyone is quick to criticize. And seldom is everyone on the same page.

It's hard to juggle numerous opinions at once. Strike that – *it's impossible*. But what is possible is developing documentation that provides the team with great visibility into the progress of the development of the narrative.

Tone Document

Tone should be one of the first pillars of the creative direction of a game. The senior creative team – which includes, among others, the creative director, executive producer, senior producer, lead designer(s), animation director, and art director – should come up with this pillar in the early days of conception. Tone is a creative driver; it is the common denominator that bonds other parts of game development together. It is also a north star that helps keep in line all of the other creative disciplines such as art, narrative, and sound.

In the *God of War* series, the tone could be described as intense, dark, contemplative, and fierce. In *Legend of Zelda* franchise, the tone is adventurous, dangerous yet optimistic. In *Dead Space*, as with most horror-survival games, the tone is menacing, scary, and stressful. In each of those descriptions, the expectation for every creative discipline is to fulfill that tone and infuse it in nearly every part of the creative. At times, other disciplines might look to the narrative designer to help define the tone or at least crystallize it.

One-Pager

Now, while *Call of Duty: Trade War* or *Fortnite Battle Royale for the Elderly* might sound catchy, a pithy idea means nothing if there's no heft behind it. A one-pager will help you communicate a viable premise and the makings of a good story. Told in under a page comprising 500 words or fewer, this summary will focus less on narrative design and more on marketing. So, use active verbs, avoid long sentences, and keep the language simple.

There will be a ton of iteration on this, not surprisingly. Some might quibble with the premise, while others might argue about the characters. The whole point of this document is to start a conversation. Most folks may be too close to the subject matter to see what they're creating. An outsider, like a game writer or narrative designer, will bring weaknesses to light. By taking a team's callow pieces and putting them together (after adding a dose of coherence and writerly flare, of course), the narrative designer will provide an unvarnished premise of the game. It's then up to the creative leadership to optimize for success.

Elevator Pitch

This was discussed in the section "ID the IP" in Chapter 3. As a reminder, you'll need to provide a basic description of the story in 40–50 words in no more than two to three sentences. It can be part of the one-pager or live separately. I recommend opening your one-pager or intro to the story bible with an elevator pitch. It gives a strong and clear message as to what the story is. Your goal is to write something easily understood and compelling while setting the tone.

Take once again, *The Last of Us*. After a pandemic causes infected humans to destroy the rest of civilization, a survivor is hired to smuggle a young teenage girl out of an oppressive military quarantine. Their brutal journey across the country forces them to redefine their relationship to the world and to each other.[1]

Clear, exciting, dangerous – that's a great takeaway. This elevator pitch may not tell the entire story of the game, but it tells enough. It describes something that people will want to play.

The movie industry has been doing this successfully for years. They've even developed a shorthand for popular movies that piggyback on previous blockbusters.

Die Hard on a ship = *Under Siege*
Lethal Weapon meets martial arts = *Rush Hour*
Toy Story under water = *Finding Nemo*
Breakfast Club meets vampires = *Twilight*

This shorthand technique is not something I would necessarily include in your elevator pitch. However, successful comparables help your listener understand the parameters of your new IP and its general proximity to success. What's important is for the author to ask themselves, *How can I get people excited about this project and let them know it's a blockbuster in the making?* That starts with communicating what's unique and viable[2] about the game while still tying it to a successful IP of the recent past.

Character Bios and Sample Dialogue

Another crucial document that you should prioritize is character biographies. What are their backstories and affiliations? What's their psychological makeup? How do they communicate through sample dialogue? The goal here is to establish an agreed-upon voice of the characters. Creative directors, designers, artists, and others will need to reach consensus on these in order to assure that the tone of the characters' voices is consistent with the tone of their work.

It is also extremely helpful to write sample dialogue so that the creative leads can determine whom they will want to cast for those characters (assuming the game has a budget for cut scenes or other voice-over opportunities). Characters aren't just created when you play them for the first time. They have a past, and that past often informs their personality, their linguistic style, their decisions, their friendships, and their rivalries. A good writer doesn't just make up those moments on the fly. One must put serious thought into how these characters came to be.

Genre and Platform

Is the game an FPS for PS5 and Xbox? Or a point-and-click mystery for the PC? Tell the reader what kind of game it is and on what platform(s) a consumer will play it.

Backstory of the World

The environment that a player finds himself/herself in must be designed intricately. After all, without a visually interesting world, why play it? Every environment reflects the tone of the story and can hint at its past. When playing *Fallout 4*, for example, you see a barren wasteland with abandoned buildings and vehicles. How did this world become post-apocalyptic?

As mentioned in Chapter 6, the environment or world is a character unto itself. It has a past, a personality, and a purpose. What happened there before the game began should inform the current plot. If the land was decimated by an evil force, it's likely that that force will reappear and your protagonist will have to confront them.

If the environment is futuristic and hi-tech, how does your protagonist relate to this world? What is their role here? And what drove this world to its current state?

If the environment is a moment in history – like the American West of the early 1900s (*Red Dead Redemption*) or Ancient Egypt (*Assassin's Creed Origins*) – is your character a significant part of it? Or, are there well-known historical events that happened before the start of the game that your character was directly affected by?

The backstory of the world is crucial to establish. It not only affects the characters in the game but also gameplay events and visual and audio cues that add specificity (and, at times, authenticity) to the world. Your description will not only inform the narrative but also will assist artists, audio engineers, level designers, and gameplay designers to do their best work.

THE SOFTWARE TOOLS

For the Basics

Writing games usually involves the usage of Microsoft Word or Google Docs for story summaries and character bios. Scriptwriting software like Final Draft always comes in handy as does software like articy:draft, which helps to map dialogue choices and branching narrative.

And as discussed previously, proficiency in Excel or Google Sheets goes a long way when writing dialogue. Not only is the spreadsheet the most effective data input tool, but it is also the perfect centralized hub for different disciplines to work from and track the implementation history of each line of dialogue or on-screen text.

For Productivity and Visibility

Strict milestones dictate the development of the game. These milestones include (but are not limited to) pre-production, production, alpha (the final stage in which new content can be inserted), and post-launch updates and downloadable content (DLC).

Within each of these milestones, there are sprints where teams commit to the creation or development of specific deliverables within a brief time frame. This is a very tech-centric process devoted to tracking progress (through an agile planning tool like Jira or Asana) and supervised by a project manager or producer. Writers and narrative designers live within a nebulous world of sprints. Tracking the writer's work doesn't smoothly correspond to tracking the work of a programmer or game designer. In general, tracking work is an imprecise process, but it is often used to provide budget support and potentially spotlight the value of a discipline. But this can be easily corrupted. A designer assigned to numerous Jira tickets might look like they add more value and impact than someone with fewer Jira tickets, which isn't always the case. I call this the **Blades of Grass Dilemma**. Which sounds more impressive – "I mowed the lawn today"? or, for that same-sized plot of land, "I mowed 27,482 blades of a grass today"? It's the latter, of course. Few people understand proportionality or have the time to assess what the work of others entails. Breakdowns of tasks to ridiculous granularity are par for the course in this industry. Not to mention that not all tasks or crafts require the same complexity.

Not all jobs are equal, but one shouldn't undersell what they do either, as this can influence a future layoff or feature rescoping. Therefore, narrative designers should be prepared to think in terms of reasonable granularity and plan for minute itemization of their storytelling to show value. "Write first part of Act 1 by March 4" will likely trigger a quizzical stare from a producer. Instead, unpack the work, even if it's an estimate that changes down the road. "Complete first batch of 1,000 lines of Act 1 by March 3," "Edit first batch of 1,000 lines of Act 1 by March 4," "Send 1000 of Act 1 to localization by March 4," and continue the same breakdown until you meet a realistic deadline by which all lines are to be written, edited, and localized. This might seem mundane and inane, but unpacking goes a long way toward job protection.

Another reason why narrative can struggle within the tech productivity framework is that story is often not a driver of a feature that involves serious technical requirements. Narrative can inspire the creation of features. But once the basics of the feature are articulated, a pure designer takes it from there and works with engineers to build it. Once the shell of the feature is coded, narrative designers and writers will then fill in that shell with content.

Productivity tracking/task management tools are vital to game development, despite the potential for corruption. Writers tend to work in isolation; however, as long as they are organized and in constant communication with other collaborators, deliverables will be accomplished on time. But team members aren't accountable only to one another. Director-level staff needs to have visibility into each person's progress, so that they can determine where help is needed and where budgets can expand. Task management tools provide that visibility to help guide critical management decisions.

Moreover, there are people outside of your team that may not work with you on a daily basis but could have a secondary connection to you. They will need to check in on your progress of tasks to see if there is anything that might block them in the near future. Motion Capture studio managers have very strict deadlines. If they know you are writing a cut scene, they will need to know when it is due (via Jira or the equivalent) so that they can adjust their schedule to film it. It is likely they are accommodating multiple games within the same company.

If either the sprint process or task management system is too difficult to adopt, you can ease into it by setting up an editorial calendar and filling it with specific due dates for deliverables. Using Outlook Calendar is a great tool for this. However, you'll eventually need to transpose those weekly or daily tasks into Jira or another task-management tracking software, so that project managers know what you're up to. In this day and age, tech professionals cannot avoid agile planning software.

For Brainstorming and Presenting

For brainstorming and mapping out high-level structure, diagramming software is the perfect tool. It provides a clear, visual representation of a story flow. Once story milestones are set, you'll map out of the sequence of events in Visio, OmniGraffle, or Gliffy only to discover what works, what is missing, and what needs to get fixed.

For presentations – of which there will be a countless number – Power Point, Google Slides, Adobe, and Keynote remain the industry standard. Everyone in a development team will have to make internal presentations at least a few times in a dev cycle. Building a deck with compelling images is practically required these days. So, if you're someone who's just comfortable with writing words, make sure to team up with a visual professional to make your presentations compelling. This is crucial. Most of a narrative designer's work *will not be read until the end of the dev cycle* where the quality assurance team is hard at work, making sure there are no flaws in the writing or in its execution. A clear-cut, visual pitch will mobilize the support you need from leadership early on in the dev cycle.

NOTES

1 Metacritic, "The Last of Us" 2013.
2 That is, achievable to make within a typical product cycle.

REFERENCE

Metacritic. "The Last of Us." (2013, June 14). Retrieved on February 9, 2024 from www.metacritic.com/game/playstation-3/the-last-of-us

CHAPTER 13

The Future of Interactive Storytelling

THE FUTURE PLAYER

The future of narrative design, of course, hinges upon the future of the player. The difficulty lies in the fact that players are a constantly moving target. Studios as well as publishers are, therefore, always on the hunt for the next big blockbuster and must think several steps ahead of the competition. A lot rides on their predictions to match player desires once the game is released. All in the timing. This is at least a three-year commitment to a self-perceived "game changing" idea or set of features, as it takes an average of three years to develop an AAA game. Things change, of course. In fact, the only guarantee in games (and in life) is change. But games are a special breed since their development comes from a culture of constant flux due to tech innovations and a proactive, hyper-finicky customer base. Typically, changes to features will beset a game deep into alpha, sometimes delaying its release. Games are a competitive business, so these frenetic, last-minute changes are par for the course.

But there is no guarantee that these changes will please a player. And there are no guarantees that a hyped-up new technology will please a player either. Microsoft placed a massive bet on the Kinect in 2010 only to discontinue it in 2017. Yet, it sold 35 million units,[1] a speciously successful

DOI: 10.1201/9781003438113-13

stat. The Kinect did not (*ahem*) connect with players for myriad reasons, including its instability and lack of software that appealed to core gamers.[2] Neither physical gesture nor voice command to move the gaming experience forward enticed enough players to buy the product. They still preferred the traditional hands-on-controller style of gaming.

Kinect was a great technology, but it was arguably not a gaming one. Or, it was possibly a technology too ahead of its time in the games space. One could say the same for virtual reality (VR), a transformative immersive visual experience, but not practical or enticing enough to dethrone mobile technology and traditional console gaming technology, neither of which possesses as sophisticated a hardware as VR. VR headsets have had a low adoption rate since its release in 2016 when 5 million units were sold worldwide.[3] By 2023, Deloitte Insights predicted that cumulative units sold would be 22 million worldwide, rendering the technology a "niche"-based interest for customers.[4] While sales have increased, they have not done so significantly to validate VR as a popular product category. So, when predicting the next trends – be it VR or a supposed gaming enhancement like the Kinect – one must dispel the old conventional wisdom. Be it bigger, newer, or laden with bells and whistles, the latest shiny object doesn't always mean it's better than what's already out there.

The same rule applies to traditional screen media. When looking at the current state of film and scripted TV, one thing remains abundantly clear: audiences are diffuse. There are no more "water cooler moments," that is, people will not watch the same shows during the same time slot as others do, like they did from the 1950s to the early 2000s. (Live events of magnitude, like the Super Bowl, are the exception.) Audiences today also possess myriad tastes and, therefore, do not yield to content that attempts to cast the widest net. One can attribute the new media consumer's selectivity to the explosion of streaming services and, before that, to the advent of YouTube. Eyeballs are everywhere, and for a media company to survive, they cannot create content for either the majority or plurality of audiences, but rather for loyal fragments. And the more intense a loyal fragment is, as the video games industry has witnessed, the more profits are to be had. The consumers that are part of these intense loyal fragments are better known as "whales," and they are responsible for an inordinate number of in-app purchases or microtransactions within a single game. Whales who play mobile games, for instance, can comprise 50%–70% of a single game's in-app revenues.[5] That figure is even more astounding when those whales represent just 1%–2% of an average mobile game's playerbase![6]

Disruptive forces are afoot. As one will see, the powers of the consumers attribute to these forces just as much as new technology does. Exciting and, yes, scary times ahead.

Player as a Disruptive Force

Gamers are savvy and loyal and command tremendous influence in the video game industry. When their expectations aren't met, they leverage their purchasing power and social media to staggering effect.

Seeing through the Smoke and Mirrors of Silicon Valley

As the examples of the Kinect and VR headsets indicate, players easily reject trendy technology if it has no meaningful impact upon their gaming experience. Smoke and mirrors, bells and whistles, whatever the nomenclature, over-hyped trends immediately engender distrust and scrutiny from gamers, who are often the first to witness or interact with industry buzzwords and acronyms before the rest of the world does. Artificial intelligence (AI), non-fungible tokens (NFTs), augmented reality (AR), and (yes) VR made their way into games long before they showed up in apps or online tools for non-gamers. If a company plans to push a new buzzword-worthy technology upon the gaming community, the C-suite executives ought to expect major pushback if the technology does not enhance the gaming experience.

Technology that *substitutes* the traditional controller or UI/UX will not be as well received as technology that *amplifies* it. Just compare the Nintendo Wii to the Switch. The Wii adopted a wireless controller (or "Remote") that resembled something in between a baton and a stubby TV remote control. Its default nature or form factor was vertical and required the use of just one hand for many of the Wii's games. The Remote, however, was flexible in motion capabilities – a major departure from the two-handed horizontal controller that gamers had been used to with the PlayStation, Xbox, and previous Nintendo gaming systems. Precision-type controlling was not part of the Wii experience, unless a player bought a separate controller or horizontal attachment that resembled the traditional design of those associated with a PS3 or Xbox360.

The Wii was a kid's and family console primarily, thanks to the kinetic nature of the hardware and software. In other words, those games were meant to be played standing up and moving around, oftentimes with others.

No game spoke to this more than the *Wii Sports* title that was bundled with the first versions of the console. Its tennis and boxing offerings, especially, provided hours of mindless fun. While the Wii was a success from 2006 to 2013, Nintendo reaped greater sales with the Switch. After launching in March 2016, the mobile console (or tablet) distinguished itself from the competition immediately with its capability to "moonlight" as a traditional screen (read: television) gaming experience. As of December 31, 2023, it has sold over 139.36 million units worldwide, whereas the Wii, in its life cycle of 11 years, sold 101.63 million units.[7] The Switch captures both the mobile and larger screen gaming experiences, and its controllers possess a more traditional design than the Remote did. The Switch has sold nearly 30% more units than the Wii did in less time.

All of this is to say that evolution often wins out over revolution.

Players Have More Power than Ever Before
A 2021 study found that worldwide players spend on average 8.45 hours per week gaming.[8] In the US, those numbers are significantly higher. While COVID is likely to have inflated that average, the NPD Group found that US gamers spent as much 14.8 hours a week in 2020, up to 16.5 hours in 2021.[9] However, in 2019, before the pandemic, that American average was 12.7 hours per week, once again surpassing the worldwide average.[10] The average time spent on gaming from 2019 to 2021 ranged anywhere from 660 hours to 858 hours per year in the US alone! [11] That's devotion. As such, games serve as emotional connective tissue between entities, that is, player to player, player to players, and even player to company. Games are, for some, a life source, and the moment a game company disrespects their playerbase, players will unite and effect profound change.

Remember, for example, when one-time XBox president Don Mattrick touted the soon-to-be launched XboxOne as an "all-in-one" entertainment system during the E3 unveiling in 2013? In his talk, Mattrick emphasized its potential for innovative television and film programming while underplaying its gaming capabilities.[12] Outcry over social media followed. Players vowed to boycott the console. Then other controversies started to emerge, including the console's price tag, which was loftier than that of the Sony PlayStation 4 ($499 over $399). When Mattrick left Microsoft for the CEO position of Zynga in November of that year, XBox gamers let out a sigh of relief. Did they influence his departure? It is hard to determine, but Microsoft had already been in the mode of parting ways with department heads a year earlier (also in November) with the departure of Steven Sinofsky, former president of Microsoft's Windows division, after early signs pointed to a disastrous launch of Win8. Sea change in leadership is nothing new, but long-term product anemia is hard to predict. Sales of the XboxOne always lagged behind the PlayStation 4's – greatly lagged behind, in fact, selling fewer than half of total PS4 units sold,[13] even after the prices of both consoles reached parity. If the product launch hadn't been so controversial, it's possible the XboxOne would have stood a better chance at catching up to the sales of the PS4. Executives today exercise greater caution.

Hardware may endure the slings and arrows of player uproar, but it's not alone. Software (read: games) does as well. In 2012, after fans decidedly rejected four different endings to the role-playing game (RPG) *Mass Effect 3*, the developers at BioWare sent off an extended downloadable content (DLC) that changed those endings and added new content, varying from "tweaks" to "major additions."[14] Fans continued their swagger in 2014, after the launch of *Destiny*. Peter Dinklage, famed actor from HBO's *Game of Thrones*, voiced the Ghost character to the displeasure of countless fans. Dinklage arguably gave a lifeless performance and was replaced by famed voice-over actor Nolan North when the DLC of "The Taken King" launched in 2015. A download of the DLC not only added new content to one's console, it also updated previous data. This included a wholesale replacement of Dinklage's voice-over in the original game. Bungie, the studio behind *Destiny*, denied any criticism of Dinklage's performance. They claimed that his Hollywood projects prevented a long-term commitment to the franchise, so it was better to replace him with North, whose availability promised long-term continuity through additional DLC drop and sequels.[15]

Whatever one is to believe, studios and publishers are in the service business – the service of making players happy. Players don't just play games. They view the product emotionally and will either follow it to the end of time or unify with others to upend its sales. Game companies, therefore, are in no position to isolate their playerbase.

The Future of Story

We should all take great joy in seeing the player as vehicle for change in the industry. But what role will story play in their gaming experience? Is it too cynical to ask if it will even have a role?

Yes, players appreciate story just like any other media consumer. Often, however, they will not appreciate story interrupting their gaming session. That's why cut scenes, no matter how artfully crafted, face a harsh reality: the skip button … which a good portion (if not, the lion's share) of gamers are not afraid to hit. Collectables and environmental storytelling, as mentioned in Chapters 3 and 8, are more successful methods to deliver narrative without causing any friction to the player. These narrative delivery methods will likely persist in decades to come.

But are those methods enough?

Story Redefined by TikTok?

The bigger issue isn't how to deliver story in the future, but *how to define story*. With the advent of TikTok, YouTube, and Twitch, players derive tremendous enjoyment from amateur-style acting, cinematography, and story. With screens fracturing people's attention spans, the well-told story, which have thrived in books and film, is diminishing in both appreciation and exposure. Americans are reading fewer books a year these days – 15.3 books per reader in 1990 down to 12.6 in 2021.[16] It's safe to say that many Americans are not reading any books at all. With that diminishing interest, it should be no surprise that American culture leaves itself susceptible to the rise of new forms of entertainment. Since 2005, YouTube has heeded that call, only to be followed in the last few years by TikTok. A 2022 study showed that GenZ annually spent 1,574 minutes on YouTube, 755 minutes on TikTok, and 437 minutes on Twitch.[17]

TikTok, a Chinese video hosting company owned by ByteDance, is rising in popularity since its release in 2016. Meanwhile, many politicians in the US consider it a national security risk, alleging that user data and user locations are being shared with the Chinese Communist Party. Some states have enacted TikTok bans on devices of government employees (including those at state universities).[18] The U.S. Department of Defense has issued the same mandate.[19] No doubt, TikTok is a disruptive force – maybe even a genuine threat. But, for the purposes of this book (admittedly, something less urgent), one should not underplay its impact upon storytelling either. TikTok videos are often bites or brief moments, infused with splash or a punchline with little setup. Like Tweets, they are stimuli primarily and sensationalistic one-offs and gags to spur attention. Story cannot thrive in single bursts.

Indeed, TikTok is entertainment, but can be (mis)perceived as possessing the storytelling basics of film or TV, simply because it communicates through a screen. But even with those few common denominators with cinema (e.g., character, setting, action), consumers should not confuse its videos as legitimate evidence of story. Without a conflict, escalation of events to solve the conflict, or meaningful character growth, a single TikTok (or even a series of related TikToks) struggles to adopt meaningful components of storytelling. This brings up a major concern: the more people imbibe stimulus masquerading as storytelling entertainment, the more future generations will classify and believe it as such. They will grow up malnourished in this regard, and when presented with a serious story told through a longer experience like a film or novel, they will not be equipped to assess its quality. In fact, future generations might dismiss it off the bat, thereby keeping greater distance between them and stories with heft, stories that nourish (i.e., literature and art).

Lore Discovery

Yet, the meteoric rise of cozy games like *Animal Crossing: New Horizons* (2020)[20] and *Stardew Valley* (2016)[21] indicates that players still crave good characters and stories ... well, backstories. A cozy game experience is like no other: a player will "unlock" lore fragments of each non-playable character (NPC) just through a simple encounter. Over time, as more encounters accrue, these fragments reveal the NPC's past and the mysteries of the world. Concurrently, players will develop a long-term, emotional connection with an NPC. The lore fragment is its own version of a collectable, and the story in these games is all about the process of **lore discovery**. The urgency of conflict and the immediacy of its resolution no longer have any bearing, as self-paced player agency reigns supreme.

Many players appreciate the lack of an imminent conflict and the urgency it evokes. Self-paced player agency provides a stress- and punitive-free experience and encourages exploration and improvisation. In a sense, cozy games exemplify player agency in its purest form. A player can choose to accomplish tasks or not, to roam free or not. An optimal experience might involve experiencing an imminent story or pursuing tasks of high importance. In this case, "optimal" means as intended by the game designers to provide the most content and ideal pathway(s) in experiencing it. For some players, an optimal experience means one with the most agency to explore the world as the player sees fit. This type of player controls the pace of their experience without penalty. This is profound.

So as screens continue to disrupt attention spans, as TikToks (woefully) redefine story, and as cozy games create a consequence-free experience, the way stories are delivered in games will need to change. Fragmented lore delivered over time, quick bites of narrative, and compelling characters are here to stay. One day soon, game developers will design games centering on a stress-free conflict as the norm. "Stress-free conflict" might seem oxymoronic; yet, if the player can resolve the conflict at their own pace, then "stress-free" and "conflict" align. Urgency will be missing, but if that's what players want, the industry will make it the standard.

That said, traditional storytelling in a consequence-free environment must be communicated as the game's optimal experience. In other words, if the player is given the choice to roam freely in the world and defeat the corrupt sheriff at the player's own pace or roam freely at their own pace and *not* defeat the corrupt sheriff, then the studio will need to create a series of fun gameplay mechanics and rewards that can only be achieved if the player makes efforts to defeating the sheriff. However, the studio cannot deprive the core experience from the player if they don't want to defeat the sheriff. The player just won't experience the added fun and rewards of hunting him down. The sheriff-as-conflict is part of the ideal experience, not the core experience – if not designed that way, then marketed as such.

If such a design is impossible, then one must consider migrating the narrative outside of the gaming experience entirely. This would enable external narrative fragments to serve as rewards to the player either after gaming sessions or upon progression milestones. The delivery mechanisms could be story-driven emails or unique codes sent (i.e., texted, emailed, etc.) to players to unlock a piece of media (e.g., animated short, short story, small comic) on the game's website. Consumer-based technologies from the likes of Amazon or Apple could integrate themselves in games and deliver story content too. But until an Alexa skill or iWatch app is designed as a meaningful, friction-less experience (i.e., an evolved companion app experience), migrated story content will have to embody traditional but fan-centric forms (again, animated shorts, digital comics, online short stories, etc.), delivered through a central hub of the intellectual property (again, website).

OTHER DISRUPTIVE FORCES TO GAME NARRATIVE

Interactive Television as Games?

Because game narrative is mostly a reaction to gameplay, the future of game storytelling depends on gameplay innovation. It is likely that story will remain a secondary focus for most games. But as games become more integrated with mass culture, will there be an expectation that some games will have to be less interactive and more story-driven in order to appeal to a wider audience?

Or, will interactive TV shows like *Black Mirror: Bandersnatch* be that bridge between interactive entertainment and non-gamers? If so, then is it possible that choosing your own adventure in an episode of television can be classified as a gaming experience?[22]

If the intention of the medium is to tell a story and there are no other typical gameplay mechanics like cooperative play, collection, or puzzle solving, then interactive television is not a game. If there is no reward for choosing a right answer (or a penalty for choosing the wrong one) in an interactive conversation, then it is not a game. If the participant doesn't achieve a clear victory state or sense of achievement at the end of an episode, then it is not a game.

But will these criteria hold true when more people participate? Especially if these new people want something different than what traditional board games and video games have to offer? No. Absolutely not. Games are games. Interactive television is television.

That said, we are living in a highly gamified culture. Game mechanics – like leveling up, earning badges, customizing content based on decisions – have infiltrated business, education, and even health (Fitbit, anyone?). Hotels gamify loyalty programs. Financial service companies leverage chatbots through a very primitive form of branching conversation trees. By leveraging the arcade redemption game mechanic, airlines entice customers to pay for hotel rooms with frequent flyer miles that they achieved over time. So, while there are distinct lines between what is a game and what is interactive entertainment, one cannot deny that the influence of games is everywhere in today's society.

The Rise of eSports

eSports (or competitive gaming) is trending significantly and changing spectator sports as we know it. Games like *Overwatch, League of Legends,* and *Dota 2* are captivating millions of fans across the world, who just watch people play video games over Twitch, YouTube, or in person at competitive tournaments. If you didn't catch that, *millions of people are watching people play video games.* This is a new world, and it is expected to grow to $4.81 billion by 2030.[23]

While these games often possess a rich lore, none of these titles features any meaningful narrative during the competition. Why? Because audiences do not have the patience for it at that moment. They want to see players compete. Therefore, with the growing popularity of eSports, is there a place for storytelling in the future? Yes, but not in the traditional sense. Narrative designers and game writers will need to adopt craftier ways to drip feed story throughout a game as frictionless as possible. Does one cut out the narrative entirely from the game and reserve it for another medium, like animation or comics, similar to what *Overwatch* does or a Netflix series like *League's Arcane*? Or will it come through as constant in-game dialogue enhanced by on-screen UI text? Sure, but will the story be absorbed when it's competing with so much activity?

One needs to look to social media to understand the player's threshold for words and ideas. Will it all boil down to bite-sized information that is sent out frequently? Will a standard game narrative one day be fractured into micro-episodes or story flashes – no more than 30 seconds of a cut scene, no more than a 5-second splash of UI text, or no more than a 30-second interactive conversation? Will TikTok win after all?

Rapidly shrinking attention spans are redefining fun. Game creators must keep players happy by keeping them constantly active. The cut scene, a former narrative driver, has lost its luster. Narrative designers cannot rely on that to tell their stories entirely – or, in most cases, at all. Nor can they view themselves as screenwriters anymore. We are content designers and interactive designers who specialize in a game feature known as story. Due to this sea change, we must abide by this warning: Never do you want a gamer to "lean back" (passive) in a "lean forward" (active) experience.

But to what extent does a writer shrink the content to where it still contains meaning? This remains unclear.

Artificial Intelligence

While eSports, TikTok, and interactive television present a potential content disruption to narrative design, there is even a more challenging disruption beyond what to write. *How* stories will be written invites greater uncertainty than what those stories will be. As of this writing, AI has taken the world by storm. Some view it as an exciting technology; others are a bit more reserved. Then, there is a loud minority of the population that cringes upon the sound of those two letters together. "End of times!" is their typical reaction, either felt or said outright.

Yes, AI is not without warranted controversy. The surprising ousting of Sam Altman from the company he founded, OpenAI, and then his subsequent rehiring (both in November of 2023!) proved that the buzz around this technology is nothing short of dizzying.

ChatGPT and Google's Gemini (formerly Bard) impress the world with small tasks, like writing essays or answering simple history questions. These large language models (LLMs) exhibit quicksilver processing of thought-provoking requests. "What were the three main causes of the Persian Gulf War in 1990?" will generate a cogent 500-word response with three medium-sized JPEGs.[24] In general, the output possesses an authoritative tone, which, before recent updates, would occasionally spew out well-written but factually inconsistent statements. The danger was in the users' inability to fact-check the content. They'd believe what they read was gospel and would share those falsehoods with others.

Then there's the danger of plagiarism. Many students shamelessly lift direct quotes from ChatGPT or Gemini, or steal the entire content without attribution. (Though, it's doubtful that attribution was something they thought about in the first place.) Sometimes, the AI can forget to cite its sources as well.[25] In fact, a list of companies and celebrities – including the New York Times, George R.R. Martin, and Sarah Silverman – continues to grow, each of whom is suing OpenAI and Microsoft for copyright infringement.[26] [27]

Narrative Game Development

Regardless of these risks, some video game studios have embraced the technology. Ubisoft and NetEase are exploring how to leverage AI-generated dialogue for NPCs. Ubisoft claims the AI will assist in the writing of barks through their proprietary tool called Ghostwriter, but only as a first stab at content creation.[28] The thinking is with the AI writing barks, human writers will have time to write more involved narrative tasks.[29] But once those are complete, human writers would polish the bark writing.[30]

It's not clear whether NetEase will apply the same human touch to their barks as Ubisoft will. They have, however, admitted that, in their game *Cygnus Enterprises*, players will experience dialogue variety from NPCs, thanks to AI-generated content.[31]

While some might view this as a job killer for game writers, one must bear in mind that AI-generated content will run the risk of dry, lifeless, and homogenous dialogue. Most Gemini and ChatGPT outputs possess the same sentence structure, paragraph lengths, tone, and attitude. The message is simple and the buildup leads to a predictable conclusion (for non-fiction, a rehash of what was written; for fiction, unambiguous saccharine endings or absolute tragic endings). AI prose exemplifies tidiness.

AI-generated dialogue faces a similar problem. NPCs are characters, and each character has their own backstory and personality. Personality evolves over time; as such, so do linguistics traits (like inflections, word choices, pauses in between sentences, etc.). Context also informs dialogue. Whispering to a loved one while they're in the recovery room, for instance, will bring about a different tone, speed, and word choice than whispering to the same loved one during an opera. The former is a tense situation focusing on health (maybe even survival); the latter is about social etiquette. The desire to comfort carries more weight than the desire not to be rude. Good dialogue ought to reflect that distinction.

All of these traits – backstory, personality, inflection, evolved experiences, context, etc. – inform a single line of dialogue and they ought not to be rendered so easily as data points shoved into an algorithm. Just based on the current state of LLM text and my own experience working for game companies, I guarantee that no AI-generated dialogue for NPCs today will survive without the human touch. The experiment will work at first, but the more players engage with these NPCs and the more they are exposed to stale and homogenous reactions, the more players will complain.

Players will be engaging with a world and characters with whom they will form a bond. Once those characters come across as artificial and unintelligent, a studio will lose their playerbase.

Taking a Stand

Hollywood takes a different stance than the video game industry does. During the Writers' Strike of 2023, members of the Writers Guild of America (WGA) made sure to add safeguards against AI as part of their top priorities in negotiating for a new collective bargaining agreement with the Alliance of Motion Picture and Television Producers (AMPTP). A nearly half-a-year work stoppage resulted in meaningful concessions from the AMPTP. From Section 5 of the "Summary of the 2023 WGA MBA," the WGA demands the following:

- *AI can't write or rewrite literary material, and AI-generated material will not be considered source material under the MBA, meaning that*

AI-generated material can't be used to undermine a writer's credit or separated rights.

- *A writer can choose to use AI when performing writing services, if the company consents and provided that the writer follows applicable company policies, but the company can't require the writer to use AI software (e.g., ChatGPT) when performing writing services.*
- *The Company must disclose to the writer if any materials given to the writer have been generated by AI or incorporate AI-generated material.*
- *The WGA reserves the right to assert that exploitation of writers' material to train AI is prohibited by MBA or other law.*[32]

The 2023 strike focused a lot on disruptive technology in general, mainly streaming services and proper compensation therein. In the past, the WGA took on a reactive posture to technology. The 2007–2008 WGA Strike required the need for proper compensation in "new media," mainly content that had been (and was going to remain) distributed online. This time, the WGA has met the disruptive force (AI) before it has spread meaningfully into scripted entertainment.

Will games also take a stand? So much hinges upon the player, of course. Will they notice AI-generated content? Will they care if they do? AI could meet the same fate as other trendy tech acronyms like NFT, AR, or VR did. In other words, once the hype fades, the tech is here to stay but its adoption is minimal. Hard to say what will occur. However, the explosion of AI technology in the next few years will likely inform the long-term future of its usage in narrative and, more importantly, in the world.

FUTURE JOB REQUIREMENTS OF A NARRATIVE DESIGNER

Adopting Technical Skills

With new disruptive technologies emerging every day, companies are going to require more technical responsibilities from narrative designers than before. While I defined the narrative designer in the beginning of this book as a creative professional first and foremost, I cannot discount the fact that the need for technical chops increases every day. Competency in scripting languages (see below) has become a popular requirement with many companies. Some might expect the narrative designer to implement the narrative content in their game's engine (e.g., Unity, Unreal, Lumberyard).

Others might expect a robust spreadsheet that enables pure designers to do it themselves. Whatever the case, narrative designers can't expect to work off of Microsoft Word only. One might work within a company's suite of proprietary tools or those from different companies.

It bears repeating: games are software. And as software becomes more expansive for the consumer, so too will the challenges for the developer. Will a pure creative role like a narrative designer become a hybrid one: half creative, half technical? The proportions are definitely shifting in the favor of technical know-how. Thus, it doesn't hurt to master one's storytelling chops as well as adopt supplemental technical knowledge. Some technical skills include familiarity with JavaScript, Lua, C#, and Python. As mentioned in Chapter 12, creating tasks on Jira or Asana is becoming the norm too, and, of course, spreadsheet mastery can never be appreciated enough.

Creating a Narrative Tool-Set

The gaming experience has quickly evolved from a solitary experience to a social one. Consoles connected to Wi-Fi enable millions of players across the world to play with or against one another in real-time missions. This multiplayer gaming has brought gaming culture to a whole other level. The rise of Twitch – Amazon's streaming platform where people broadcast their live play on an online personalized channel – rewards the multiplayer experience with exposure to (potentially) millions of channel subscribers across the world. When players are not on Twitch, they are sharing their recorded gameplay moments on YouTube in the hopes of getting enough subscribers to increase ad revenue and to become a social media influencer – an entity that has enough social media clout and exposure to attract brand deals. If a player opts out of the social media influencer path, they are nonetheless sharing their gaming experiences through screenshots or video clips on all social media platforms. The result is a continuous conversation with like-minded players across the world.

Players are creating their own "stories" these days. Story in this case isn't anywhere near what this book has discussed. In the context of social media, a player views story as, essentially, news about themselves. *What feats have I accomplished today that would generate attention from friends and strangers?* These events are personal and attention-getting (and borderline exploitative), and can be so powerful a force that traditional story wanes in comparison.

Yet, people crave story, be it their own or one that is created by another. That demand will never end. But the three-act structure? Or well-crafted episodic storytelling *a la Breaking Bad, Better Call Saul,* or *Succession*? Rigor is missing from current social media content creators; it's been replaced by catharsis and authenticity of self. Can the trend reverse? Unlikely if game publishers and studios need to market their games. "Content creators can do anything as long as they plug our game." Game companies jump at the chance to integrate a tighter connection between gaming and social media year after year. And they'll redirect funds from parts of the game's budget to funnel into this marriage. Narrative will be the first to be affected by this because, as mentioned in the "Frictionless Narrative" section in Chapter 8, anything that is perceived as an obstacle to a player's experience is the first to get cut.

Additionally, narrative designers will have to contend with the industry's continual redefinition of story. In addition to the impact of TikTok, the term "story" has been coopted and warped by marketers and brands in the tech industry for nearly a decade. Appealing to a consumer as a storyteller or emphasizing the importance of a consumer's "personal story" is just a cheap ploy to lure people into buying or using the products and services of a brand. Social media companies are particularly guilty of this: *Instagram Stories* is a perfect example. But stories aren't being generated here. "Stimuli," once again, is the better word for it. ("Self-indulgence" is another.)

Nonetheless, social media platforms continue to be effective in empowering consumers to become creative artists. Many now offer video production tools that were once inaccessible to the average person. People couldn't film themselves before the advent of the smartphone unless they bought a camcorder. Posting it without horribly compressing the file was tremendously difficult until YouTube came around (and then, later, TikTok). You soon could get an instant audience by sharing a link of your YouTube video on Facebook. Facebook Live then became a free live streaming service, where you can engage with fans while you're filming.

This is Do It Yourself (DIY) filmmaking at its finest with little-to-no cost for the average person. As long as you have your own mobile phone, Meta extensions (Facebook, Instagram, Threads), X, Snapchat, YouTube, TikTok, and others provide users with a tool-set to be their own filmmaker, celebrity, and storyteller. Games will eventually do the same. The act of creating a game will take longer to develop, but that hasn't stopped the industry from empowering their players to be game designers – from heavy touch (*Minecraft, Roblox*) to light touch (initial character customization in games like *Madden* and *Anthem*). So much of the gaming experience now centers on players who record their gameplay and share it on social media, while showcasing their self-crafted environments or characters with a self-designed, signature artistic style.

This is a huge opportunity for narrative designers. While it flies in the face of what pure storytelling is meant to be, we nonetheless will survive if we own this space. What tools can we design for our players that empower their experience and make them a creator? What are all the elements of a gaming experience and how do we tie them together? What curation tools can we create that allow players to enhance their power of engagement with others on social media? It's possible that future narrative design may become less about the writing and more about the designing of "story templates" for others to use and craft experiences around.

IN SUM

Narrative designers and game writers must prepare for disruption, from technological advancement to customer whim to new definitions of story. If TikTok and cozy gaming continue to rise as does the need for players to create their own story experiences, narrative designers and game writers will have no choice but to meet those needs. The question is do we, as writers, impose what we think is best to uphold the tried-and-true story experience or do we go with the flow and potentially relinquish (or partially relinquish) what we know as good storytelling, especially if TikTok or AI leads the charge? A happy medium exists. It takes just a few product misfires to pave the way.

NOTES

1 Reisinger, "Microsoft Has Finally Killed the Kinect Xbox Sensor" 2017.
2 Weinberger, "The Rise and Fall of Kinect" 2018.
3 Futuresource, "Sales of Virtual Reality" 2017.
4 Arkenberg et al., "Will VR Go from Niche to Mainstream?" 2022.
5 Mihovil, "What Are Mobile Game Whales" 2024.
6 Ibid.
7 Nintendo, "Dedicated Video Game Sales Units" 2023a.
8 Limelight Networks, "Average Weekly Time Spent Playing Video Games" 2021.
9 Insider Intelligence, "US Video Gaming Industry in 2023" 2023.
10 Ibid.

11 These numbers are likely to drop by the time of this publication, since the world has said goodbye to COVID lockdowns and work-from-home engagements. Numbers are not likely to drop below 2019 numbers, however.

12 Chaey, "Microsoft Unveils Xbox One" 2013.

13 Warren, "Microsoft finally admits Xbox One sales" 2022.

14 GR Staff, "What 'Mass Effect 3's New Endings Actually Changed" 2012.

15 Good, "Why Is Destiny Replacing Dinklage?" 2015.

16 Jones, "Americans Reading Fewer Books than in Past" 2022.

17 comScore, "Average Time Spent on Social Media Platforms among Gen Z" 2022.

18 Richmond, "University of Wisconsin Latest to Ban TikTok" 2023.

19 Vincent, "Pentagon Issues Rule to Ban TikTok" 2023.

20 44.79 Million Copies sold. Source: (Nintendo, "Top Selling Title Sales Units" 2023b).

21 20 million copies sold by November 2022. Source: (Chalk, "Eric Barone Says" 2022).

22 In January 2024, Stephen Totilo of *Game File* reported that Netflix was no longer developing interactive shows. Source: (Totilo, "Netflix's Interactive Choice" 2024). Nonetheless, my questions in the subsequent paragraphs (written in the first edition of this book back in 2019) remain relevant.

23 GlobalData, "Esports Market Size" 2023.

24 As tested on January 10, 2023.

25 Hagey et al., "Publishers Prepare for Showdown" 2023.

26 David, "George R.R. Martin and Other Authors Sue" 2023.

27 Shapero, "New York Times-ChatGPT Lawsuit" 2024.

28 Barth, "The Convergence of AI and Creativity" 2023.

29 Ibid.

30 Ibid.

31 Yu, "NetEase Games' Cygnus Enterprises Adds an AI Companion" 2023.

32 Writers Guild of America West, "Summary of the 2023 WGA MBA" 2023.

REFERENCES

Arkenberg, Chris, Allan V. Cook, Paul Lee, and Ben Stanton. (2022, November 30). "Will VR Go from Niche to Mainstream? It All Depends on Compelling VR Content." Retrieved on February 11, 2024 from www2.deloitte.com/us/en/insights/industry/technology/technology-media-and-telecom-predictions/2023/vr-content-development-lagging-vr-hardware-market.html

Barth, Roxane. (2023, March 21). "The Convergence of AI and Creativity: Introducing Ghostwriter." Retrieved on February 11, 2024 from https://news.ubisoft.com/en-us/article/7Cm07zbBGy4Xml6WgYi25d/the-convergence-of-ai-and-creativity-introducing-ghostwriter

Chaey, Christina. (2013, May 21). "Microsoft Unveils Xbox One, An All-in-One Entertainment Console." Retrieved on February 11, 2024 from www.fast company.com/3009983/Microsoft-unveils-xbox-one-an-all-in-one-entert ainment-console

Chalk, Andy. (2022, November 9). "Eric Barone Says He 'Can't Believe' Stardew Valley Has Sold 20 Million Copies." Retrieved on February 11, 2024 from www.pcgamer.com/eric-barone-says-he-cant-believe-stardew-valley-has-sold-20-million-copies/

comScore. (2022, December 21). "Average Time Spent on Social Media Platforms among Gen Z Users in the United States in August 2022 (in minutes) [Graph]." In *Statista*. Retrieved on January 08, 2024 from www-statista-com. libproxy1.usc.edu/statistics/1359924/time-spent-gen-z-social-media/

David, Emilia. (2023, September 20). "George R.R. Martin and Other Authors Sue OpenAI for Copyright Infringement." Retrieved on February 11, 2024 from www.theverge.com/2023/9/20/23882140/george-r-r-martin-lawsuit-openai-copyright-infringement

Futuresource. (January 20, 2017). "Sales of Virtual Reality Head-Mounted Displays Worldwide in 2016 and 2020 (in million units) [Graph]." In *Statista*. Retrieved on January 08, 2024 from www-statista-com.libproxy1.usc.edu/sta tistics/697159/head-mounted-display-unit-sales-worldwide/

GlobalData. (2023, January 31). "Esports Market Size, Share, Trends and Analysis by Region, Revenue Stream, Gaming Genre and Segment Forecast to 2030." Retrieved on February 11, 2023 from www.globaldata.com/store/report/ esports-market-analysis/#:~:text=The%20Esports%20market%20size%20 by,16.7%25%20over%20the%20forecast%20period.

Good, Owen S. (2015, August 11). "Why Is Destiny replacing Dinklage? 'Hollywood Nonsense,' Says Producer." Retrieved on February 11, 2024 from www.poly gon.com/2015/8/11/9129947/why-is-destiny-replacing-peter-dinklage-nolan-north-bungie

Grguric, Mihovil. (2024, January 23). "What Are Mobile Game Whales and How to Catch Them?" Retrieved on February 11, 2024 from www.blog.udonis.co/ mobile-marketing/mobile-games/mobile-games-whales

GR Staff. (2012, June 26). "What 'Mass Effect 3's New Endings Actually Changed." Retrieved on February 11, 2024 from https://gamerant.com/mass-effect-3-new-ending-changes/

Hagey, Keach, Alexandra Bruell, Tom Dotan, and Miles Kruppa. (2023, March 27). "Publishers Prepare for Showdown With Microsoft, Google Over AI Tools." Retrieved on February 11, 2024 from www.wsj.com/articles/publishers-prep are-for-showdown-with-microsoft-google-over-ai-tools-6514a49e?reflink= desktopwebshare_permalink

Insider Intelligence. (2023, January 24). "US Video Gaming Industry in 2023: Gaming Devices & Video Game Content Viewership Trends." Retrieved on February 11, 2024 from www.insiderintelligence.com/insights/us-gaming-industry-ecosystem/

Jones, Jeffrey M. (2022, January 10). "Americans Reading Fewer Books than in Past." Retrieved on February 11, 2024 from https://news.gallup.com/poll/388541/americans-reading-fewer-books-past.aspx#:~:text=In%202021%2C%2017%25%20of%20U.S.,2016%20to%2027%25%20in%202021

Limelight Networks. (2021, March 16). "Average Weekly Time Spent Playing Video Games Worldwide As of January 2021 by Gender [Graph]." In *Statista*. Retrieved on January 08, 2024 from www-statista-com.libproxy1.usc.edu/statistics/246706/weekly-gaming-time-worldwide-gender/

Nintendo. (2023a, December 31). "Dedicated Video Game Sales Units." Retrieved on February 11, 2024 from www.nintendo.co.jp/ir/en/finance/hard_soft/index.html

Nintendo. (2023b, December 31). "Top Selling Title Sales Units." Retrieved on February 11, 2024 from www.nintendo.co.jp/ir/en/finance/software/index.html

Reisinger, Don. (2017, October 25). "Microsoft Has Finally Killed the Kinect Xbox Sensor." Retrieved on September 4, 2023 from https://fortune.com/2017/10/25/microsoft-kinect-xbox-sensor/

Richmond, Todd. (2023, January 24). "EXPLAINER: University of Wisconsin Latest to Ban TikTok." Retrieved on February 11, 2024 from https://apnews.com/article/technology-politics-united-states-government-china-privacy-26b0ee0d4c8421fa7f58b06f76651dc1

Shapero, Julia. (2024, January 9). "New York Times-ChatGPT Lawsuit Poses New Legal Threats to Artificial Intelligence." Retrieved on February 11, 2024 from https://thehill.com/policy/technology/4392624-new-york-times-chatgpt-lawsuit-poses-new-legal-threats-to-artificial-intelligence/

Totilo, Stephen. (2024, January 8). "Netflix's Interactive Choice." Retrieved on February 11, 2024 from www.gamefile.news/p/sea-of-thieves-playstation?curator=toomuchtv&utm_source=substack&utm_medium=email

Vincent, Brandi. (2023, June 2). "Pentagon Issues Rule to Ban TikTok on all DOD-Connected Devices, including contractors." Retrieved on February 11, 2024 from https://defensescoop.com/2023/06/02/pentagon-proposes-rule-to-ban-tiktok-on-all-dod-connected-devices-including-for-contractors/

Warren, Tom. (2022, August 15). "Microsoft Finally Admits Xbox One Sales Were Less Than Half of the PS4." Retrieved on February 11, 2024 from www.theverge.com/2022/8/15/23306068/microsoft-xbox-one-sales-lifetime-versus-ps4-sales

Weinberger, Matt. (2018, January 3). "The Rise and Fall of Kinect: Why Microsoft Gave up on Its Most Promising Product." Retrieved on February 11, 2024 from https://finance.yahoo.com/news/downfall-kinect-why-microsoft-gave-183900710.html#:~:text=The%20Kinect%20was%20a%20huge,and%20the%20novelty%20wore%20off

Writers Guild of America West. (2023). "Summary of the 2023 WGA MBA." Retrieved on February 11, 2024 from www.wga.org/contracts/contracts/mba/summary-of-the-2023-wga-mba

Yu, Nathan. (2023, August 17). "NetEase Games' Cygnus Enterprises Adds an AI Companion to Its RPG Shooter." Retrieved on February 11, 2024 from https://inworld.ai/blog/netease-games-cygnus-enterprises-adds-an-ai-companion

CHAPTER 14

Transmedia

THE CHANGING MEDIA LANDSCAPE

I'll define transmedia in just a bit. Let me first explain why the effort induces an immediate headache. It's not that its definition can't be easily explained; rather, it's just that those who matter most, historically, have not been receptive to it. And when I refer to "those who matter most," I mean entertainment professionals with access to capital and production infrastructure. These are Hollywood executives stuck in the '90s, who think they're the only game in town when it comes to entertainment. They are people too wrapped up in traditional media and don't see the signs of its demise or, at least, its imminent and radical transformation. This small thinking is definitely a sign of profound arrogance. "Nothing can take away our grip on the world's culture! We own it!" is a common sentiment. Yet, they have no explanation on how game sales have continually eclipsed movie box office revenue for over 15 years now.[1] [2] [3] It's true that Hollywood still holds the monopoly of glamour and access to bigger stars than those in the digital world or games do. The traditionalists' grip on pop culture is weakening, however.

In 2014, a survey[4] conducted by *Variety* Magazine discovered that young millennials and older Gen Z'ers are more familiar with stars on YouTube than stars on television or film. This revelation shook the industry. It was a telltale sign that Hollywood, as it then operated, would soon fall behind.

The biggest reason for this change is easy access to media through mobile phones. Netflix, Amazon Prime, and Hulu offer great apps that can be consumed through phone, tablet, or streaming device, making it easy to

DOI: 10.1201/9781003438113-14

binge-watch one's favorite show anywhere – in bed, at a dentist's office, in traffic, at the airport, etc.

Digital content, however, is not just TV shows reformatted for a different device. Digital content also refers to original content that appears initially on platforms like YouTube and is tailored to the consumption patterns of its viewers. The length of the videos could range from seconds to hours, but they are usually 3–5 minutes long. They could be serialized and produced by major brands like Vice Media, AwesomenessTV, or Machinima (may they rest in peace) – each offering original, exclusive content online.[5] Or, they could come from individuals like Issa Rae (*Awkward Black Girl, Insecure*), Abbi Jacobson and Ilana Glazer (*Broad City*), or Ben Sinclair and Katja Blichfeld (*High Maintenance*), who created successful shows on YouTube that eventually were adapted into TV shows for HBO and Comedy Central. Amateurs also create their own episodes with varying degrees of success. Those who do well are known as social media influencers and are effective conduits for brands trying to reach larger audiences. First, YouTube. Now, TikTok.

The appeal of digital content is a combination of bite-sized length, no interruptions from commercials, casual production values (if any, for most shows), specialized content (e.g., subject matter or genre), and continuous output not restricted or dictated by network hiatuses.

There's one more critical element: access to the creators. Often, a creator of a series, especially if it's non-fiction (e.g., home repairs or dog rescue), will respond directly to viewers and subscribers to their channel in the comments section under their videos. Also, if they have a social media presence (which is pretty much required in that world), it is not uncommon for these content creators to directly engage in dialogue with fans. It is these social media tools that allow the shows to endure. The more subscribers a show attracts to its YouTube channel, the more ad revenue the creators share with Alphabet (YouTube's parent company). Social media channels are the critical connective tissue that allows fan engagement to thrive.

For all these reasons, digital content is a powerful medium. It listens to the viewer and can directly respond to them, thereby making the content-viewing experience relatable.

While fan engagement isn't a necessary factor in a transmedia experience, it is a compelling one. And if the creators of the show can respond to fans in the voice of their characters, then it's even more compelling. It potentially gives an audience member investment in the franchise. Could an exchange with a fan be part of the fictional canon of the IP? Could a fan's suggestion influence the next installment of a show? It's possible (barring legal restrictions, of course). Voting for one's favorite contestant on *American Idol* or *Dancing with the Stars* is fan participation at its simplest form. Fans can shape future developments of a series by voting for who stays on the show and who gets kicked off. But actual plot points? Shows like *Psych* (2006–2014) and the remake of *Hawaii Five-O* (2010–2020) have asked fans to vote for an ending of an episode. But are these gimmicks or are they meaningful interactive storytelling moments?

The traditional Hollywood types would define them as gimmicks. Although they wouldn't be wrong, they'd be short-sighted if they remain complacent. Gimmicks will never innovate how stories can be told. Younger audiences demand more. They consume media on different devices while multitasking. They are constantly plugged into what's going on with their favorite shows and its cast through social media. They'll play games as they wait for their next show to stream. Millennials and Gen Z'ers have radically reset the media landscape in terms of expectations. The traditional entertainment model does not work for them. Transmedia, however, does.

TRANSMEDIA AT ITS MOST BASIC LEVEL

There are different approaches to transmedia, which this chapter will explore later. But at its purest level, transmedia storytelling is the communication of a single-story experience[6] across various media and platforms.[7] To be clear: this isn't across different parts within a single medium (such as 22 episodes of a season of a single television show). Rather, it is across different *deliverers of media* such as television, books, digital content, games, film, and live events where upon each deliverer provides a different section of that single-story experience. (My *Matrix* graph in the pages that follow demonstrates this in detail.)

This requires a storyteller to designate specific fragments of the story to specific media deliverers and then customize those fragments to the grammar of the respective media deliverer. *Why*, one might ask? An episode of television has different rules of storytelling than does a 3-minute video, a feature-length film, or a comic book. To defy those rules is to break each medium's authenticity.

A consumer engages with a specific medium to fulfill certain expectations. A podcast cannot communicate a combat scene as well as a graphic novel can. Yet, an actor's voice from a podcast can be a tonal force that makes characters on a page feel alive and familiar, something that would be lost if a consumer were to read the dialogue in a graphic novel. A big-blockbuster film might be able to check off both boxes of character performance and visual spectacle, but if a consumer wants to control the pacing of the action, they'll read a comic and flip the pages at their own speed.

Relationship with New Technology

Transmedia is a byproduct of tools that allow for communication. These tools – be they smartphones, televisions, radio, movie screens, online forums, live forums – are constantly innovating. This too is a by-product, but of how people communicate.

Does anyone remember Friendster? Or MySpace? These were the social media precursors to Facebook and offered similar functionality, such as emails and public posts among friends. They were a distant (and laughable) memory by the time the mobile revolution hit in 2007. Facebook (now parent company Meta) flourished, nearly a year after it opened its doors to a world outside of the college arena to anyone 13 years and older. As the mobile revolution evolved in the next few years, so did social media. In addition to Facebook, Twitter (now X), Pinterest, Reddit, Snapchat (owned by Snap, Inc.), TikTok (owned by ByteDance), Twitch (owned by Amazon), Instagram (also owned by Meta), and others have become the primary media for hundreds of millions of people around the world and have permanently reshaped the way people communicate with each other. Now emojis are common replacements for written words, as are pics and video as well.

One could argue that the mobile revolution is still sprinting along while newer technologies – including extended realty (XR) tech such as virtual reality (VR), augmented reality (AR), and mixed reality (MR) – struggle for mass adoption. With each of these new platforms, there are different rules of communication … or rather different ways to communicate that are adopted organically and not imposed by the creator(s) of the platform.

Transmedia storytelling reflects – and even mimics – these organic rulesets because it is doing what good storytelling often does: it promotes the authenticity of a platform. In other words, one is not (likely) going to write a two-person script in 280 characters through a single handle on X. That example is more appropriate for a play, TV episode, or film. But X is very much capable of delivering drama. Imagine a fictional couple "talking" on X through two different accounts, where dialogue is started by one of the characters and then replied to by the other. The dialogue escalates into an argument about the man's recent flirtation with a coworker. Insults and revelations of backstory start piling up on a single tweet thread. Each person rotates by offering a new reply to the other. Soon, followers of these accounts start chiming in. The drama becomes shared, as followers (who are real, mind you) take sides. These followers are not playing fictional characters; they are, instead, interacting with the fiction *as if it were a real part of their lives.* It is now an all-out social media war that was once a catty fictional drama between two lovers. Real people are involved now. They are adding to the fiction – if not through plot points, then through enhancement of the tone and mood of this exchange. This "drama" may not be delivered by actors in three acts, but it is just as thrilling and exciting on a new medium that has its own grammar.

But this dramatic moment is not yet transmedia storytelling until the drama spreads to other platforms. So, imagine if one of the fictional characters decides to have a private conversation with followers on Instagram, even posting pictures of his disgruntled yet handsome self. He is unintentionally drawing affection from some of his female followers. They send him overtures of love and even request that he break up with his Twitter girlfriend.

The girlfriend finds out on Instagram what's going on and confronts the boyfriend on Snapchat. The video catches the boyfriend by surprise. Offended by the girlfriend's distrust, he escapes from the camera and takes to X to announce to his followers that he is breaking up with her. Mind you, his breakup tweet is the actual breakup, a live announcement that is news to everyone … including the girlfriend!

This "simple" drama unfolded, escalated, devolved, and exploded in three different, but related media platforms: X, Instagram, Snapchat. The fact that the drama migrated from one platform to the next is just enough to qualify as transmedia storytelling. (And the cheapest form too!) Going from one social media platform to the next is the bare minimum, as the experience of each of these media is virtually the same, comprising: bite-sized info communicated over a short, but intense amount of time; fan participation capabilities; and mobile phone content creation (aka lower production values). The technological experience for each of these outlets varies slightly, so the content will vary slightly as well. But transmedia story-telling should aim for something more ambitious, where the rulesets of each medium differ significantly from one to the other. This maximizes the unique affordances of each medium and prevents stagnation of the story.

When Bigger Budgets Prevail

Big entertainment companies have the financial resources to pull off a compelling transmedia campaign. But they often fail to do anything more than a superficial marketing campaign with zero canonical tie-ins. Ideally, a huge tentpole product (such as a movie or video game)[8] will have a series of transmedia extensions that surrounds its release.

But if the franchise has a series of tentpoles that will be released in a couple of years of one another, a transmedia extension could fill in the gaps to retain the fanbase and pique their interest with new canonical stories. The transmedia extensions could be anything from a comic series that continues where the video game left off or a series of web shorts that builds up to the opening of a blockbuster film by providing backstory to the fictional universe. More about this is provided later.

There are a few ambitious examples of IP creators who have designed the transmedia campaign well in advance and have designated a certain part of that fictional universe to be conveyed through a certain medium. In between each tentpole was significant transmedia "connective tissue" to feed the fanbase. The best example of this is *The Matrix* (1999).

Filmmakers Lana and Lilly Wachowski had a specific story experience in mind when they first conceived of the franchise. Its fictional universe was so vast that one film would not suffice in telling the entire lore. After the success of the first film, the Wachowskis decided to continue the story across different media touchpoints that, ultimately, hit the sweet spots of their hardcore fanbase.[9] Hence, in 2003, a live action sequel, an anime, and a video game were born (for starters). *The Animatrix*, written but not directed by the Wachowskis, composed of nine animated shorts, expanding the fictional universe of *The Matrix*. The anime provided enough story fodder to build up to the release of the original's sequel, *The Matrix Reloaded*, also in 2003. That year continued to be very busy with the release of the video game *Enter the Matrix*, which explained some mysteries of the previous films and cleared up any head scratching over continuity[10] in preparation for the final film of the trilogy, *The Matrix Revolutions*. Two years later, in 2005, another game, *The Matrix: Path to Neo*,[11] came out, along with a massively multiplayer online game (MMO) entitled *The Matrix Online*, which contained enough backstory for the final film, *The Matrix Revolutions*, to retroactively[12] qualify as its prequel. From 1999 to 2004, the franchise also had a series of webcomics that provided ancillary narrative to give fans additional adventures of characters they loved. But the comics did not have a direct connection to the films, anime, or games. (The exception being "Bits and Pieces of Information" written by the Wachowskis, but that was adapted into the short film "The Second Renaissance" as part of *The Animatrix*.)[13] While the quality of the films tended to dwindle one after the other, *The Matrix* franchise validated the power of transmedia by showing that an IP is not defined by one medium. Its DNA dictates what other forms it should take (Figure 14.1).

Why Are Video Games a Natural Fit for Transmedia?

Most games, as with most media, are not designed with a transmedia component. Some might argue that the marketing campaign for a game qualifies as one. However, the occasional tweet or Instagram post that promotes the game in the voice of the company isn't even close to a transmedia campaign. Overt marketing is just an obvious series of branded media overtures to persuade fans to buy a product. But if the campaign was executed through the voices of the game's characters? And in different media? With permanent impact on the lore? That's a different story. That's actual storytelling. And depending on how immersive the campaign is (i.e., how long the characters are conveying the fiction), the storytelling could even be good.

Successful game franchises over the past decade have leveraged transmedia to great success. Titles like *Assassin's Creed, Halo, Mass Effect, Batman: Arkham Asylum*, and their respective sequels have generated impressive sales figures. One can attribute their success not only to the quality of their games but also to the transmedia efforts of their studios. Each made sure to publish books and comics and produce animation or digital content to build up to the release of a game. Yes, these satisfied a marketing purpose; however, these transmedia extensions also expanded the universe of these games and even became memorable products in their own right. In November 2007, *Halo: Contact Harvest* by Joseph Staten debuted on The New York Times' Best Seller list at number 3.[14] This book was not an adaptation of one of the games. It was a separate narrative that took place 27 years before the 2001 hit *Halo: Combat Evolved*.

While the book came out two months after *Halo 3* – that year's anchor property for the franchise – the book's November release helped increase game sales leading into the Christmas season. By early January 2008, the

Figure 14.1   Story chronology of *The Matrix* franchise.[27]

game sold over 8.1 million copies.[15] As of this writing in 2024, *Halo 3* has sold over 14.5 million copies.[16]

The video game industry is a testament to the fact that transmedia is a risk worth taking. But how the industry got to embrace transmedia is a result of the culture of the industry and its fans.

Competitive Edge

Games are a hypercompetitive business. Companies are always looking for the newest advantage over their rivals. The industry is also one that welcomes innovation, from graphics to audio to gameplay. Story is also part of that innovation, but not in the traditional sense.

Story in games is less about the conventional way stories are told (as described previously), but more about its fictional universe and characters. *What is it about this world that draws me in and makes me want to live in it? What is it about the weapons of the characters that I want to use for myself? What is it about the villain's mysterious presence that I want to learn more about?* Not all games engender this type of curiosity. But a select few make sure to answer those questions not just in the games but in the transmedia, all in an effort to increase immersion.

However, transmedia-friendly franchises like *Halo*, *Assassin's Creed*, and *Mass Effect* don't typically tie their transmedia into a single-story experience or a **unified story experience**. The transmedia extensions are usually opportunities to explore deeper into a franchise's universe. One will find origins of world events or revelations of character backgrounds. But we have yet to see a protagonist's journey that is told continuously from one of these media to the next.

Game developers don't want to lose customers by immersing them in a game story that won't make sense unless they read the book or watch the animated series that came out before. The safest bet instead is to create a series of side stories featuring supporting characters of the game, backstories to central characters, or origin stories of referenced landmarks or historical events within the game's fiction. Each opportunity for story should be self-contained to one medium (as it's ancillary to the main game). These different story extensions qualify as a **fractured story experience** and is the most popular transmedia strategy to undertake because it requires less homework from players, who can consume these media off-shoots at their own pace. Fractured story experiences are still important because they provide context to the world and answer small mysteries about the game universe (e.g., *Halo's* John-117 reveal).

Is it too much to ask of consumers to experience all of the franchise's media in a certain sequence in order to appreciate it fully? Maybe. But it's an important challenge to solve in the future, as the new generation of media consumers are so tied to their tech and are consummate multitaskers. One day, it will not be outrageous for them to watch a full season of a Netflix show and visit social media channels to experience the fictional characters' online activities as a meaningful tie-in to the next season of that Netflix show. And when the next season picks up, it's likely that there will be enough drama in there that is independent of what happened on social media so that new followers won't feel left out. But you can bet the farm that a substantial amount of that show's minor storylines will have significant references to the social media drama.

Traditional console games might ultimately stick with the self-contained transmedia off-shoots that they do now. But with the promise of VR, AR, and MR, a seamless and enduring transmedia experience might not be far off. So far, of the three, AR has shown that it can deliver financially on the promise of its technology, thanks to *Pokémon GO* (2016–), a blockbuster mobile experience based on the beloved Japanese franchise *Pokémon* – short for "pocket monster." Since the game's launch in 2016, in-app purchases on various mobile platforms (including Google Play and the Apple App Story) have ranged worldwide from $550.45 million within its first year to its height in 2020 at $908.94 million to post-COVID revenues of $566.38 million in 2023.[17] VR's biggest app of all time, *Beat Saber*, pales in comparison. Since its launch in 2019, this widely popular rhythm game accrued total earnings of $255 million as of October 2022.[18]

How *Pokémon GO* works: players use their smartphones to locate Pokémon in places (aka PokéStops or PokéGyms) in their natural, live environment but are translated in the visual language of the virtual Pokémon world on the screen of a smartphone. This requires players to go outside and interact with parts of their natural environment, near or far. To top it off, they can physically work side-by-side, in real time, with other players to catch these Pokémon together (either through a "king of the hill" mechanic or – if a gamer is working alone – through flicking a ball at a Pokémon). Not much of a narrative experience – even with the presence of the colorful Professor Willow – but revolutionary nonetheless. The developer, Niantic Labs, chartered this AR territory back in 2013 with *Ingress*, a massively multiplayer online real-time strategy (MMORTS) mobile game, which had a rich lore but no identifiable protagonist. To play, gamers must choose a side – either the Resistance or the Enlightened – and collaborate with others on the same side to obtain alien fragments known as Exotic Matter. The Resistance wants to prevent it from getting into the hands of the Enlightened, who want to use it as a way to enhance or transcend human beings. However, the Resistance believes that, due to the alien nature of Exotic Matter, any integration with human biology could spell the end of the human race. Players track and collect these digital fragments of Exotic Matter through their phones, a practice known as geocaching (which *Pokémon GO* thrived on as well). Collection locales correspond to real-world locations but are repurposed through their phone as part of the *Ingress* sci-fi environment.

In addition to its AR capabilities, *Ingress* was also a successful transmedia experience focused on the constant friction between the Resistance and the Enlightened through live action videos and live event gaming. Story installments were delivered through videos, akin to news pieces that depicted the progress of each side at a high level. The lore was independent of the actions the player made. But by working with thousands of others across the world, players could influence the narrative. Subsequent videos would acknowledge (usually on a daily basis) which side was winning in the hunt for Exotic Matter and in the struggle to defend or transcend humankind. However, moving the needle in the ongoing battle between the Resistance and the Enlightened would be a group effort with no callouts to individual players. The daily video responses were, accordingly, generic to player action, but specific to the lore of the world.

The joy of *Ingress* hinges upon online collaboration with strangers across the world. Based on the time of day one plays, a player could always find others in their faction who are also on the hunt for Exotic Matter. They'll be collecting in real-world places and will rely on others to do the same in their part of the world. The rarer the Exotic Matter, the more sense of accomplishment players will have. This type of cooperative play was unprecedented in the mobile space at the time of its launch in 2012. *Ingress* is a revolutionary experience not only because of that but also because it paved the way for AR to become a customer-facing reality.

The more the technology expands, the more the players will demand that their stories adapt to these technologies. *Ingress* and *Pokémon GO* brought players into experiences that were simultaneously real world and augmented. But why stop there? If players are interested in a continuous ongoing search, how far away are we from adding social media into the mix to help players, for example, find other Pokémon? Could there be a "mole" on X that gives cryptic clues to the fans, informing them of the vague proximity and time of when to find a rare Pokémon?

Could there be a virtual marketplace where one could trade Pokémon, even getting backstory for each character through an animated series? For rare Pokémon, is their story told through a comic that increases their value and desirability?

Even if the appetite for this kind of social media integration isn't there yet, AR is fertile ground for innovative transmedia storytelling. One more blockbuster experience is all that it takes to help AR, as a product category, reach critical mass.

Early Adopters

Most people who consume transmedia are often early adopters of new technology. They view anything that is innovative in the realm of story – for example, how the content is delivered and what the technology is that delivers it – as a necessary experience to consume. Transmedia fans are story zealots. They have an insatiable appetite for the *omnipresence of story*, also known as immersion. A fictional character's tweets will gain just as much devotion as a new episode of an animated series from that character's fictional universe.

And games, perhaps due to their addictive nature, have always attracted a more intense, zealous consumer. Not all gamers are story zealots (or even fans of story). But those who are will likely consume everything about the brand of that game – shirts, toys, books, comics, movies, TV shows, podcasts, social media channels, and more.

A video game is also that rare entity that is both a vehicle for story and, in itself, technology (read: software). Games can also be media extensions of beloved brands that came from another medium like film (such as *Star Wars*; Marvel Universe; DC Universe). But games are more often the original medium from which other media extensions emerge (e.g., *Halo, Mass Effect, Assassins Creed*, and *Skylanders*). The *Halo* franchise has spawned numerous books, even one – as mentioned before – that made it to The New York Times' Best Seller list. It has also spawned a successful toy franchise with Mega Bloks. In 2012, the Emmy-nominated *Forward unto Dawn* captured the attention of millions as a digital mini-series on YouTube and Waypoint (*Halo's* proprietary information site). It served as live action lead-in to the much-anticipated *Halo 4*, one of the first games available exclusively for the Xbox One. And most recently, as of this writing, a

Halo series drama developed by Showtime finished its second season on Paramount+. In between game releases, fans of the franchise have had plenty of transmedia material to satisfy their *Halo* appetite. While most of that material is not tied together in any sequential order (in fact, some of the books are centered on past wars that are only referenced in the games), one could argue that *Halo* set the standard for transmedia storytelling for the games industry. More on this later.

Greatest Transmedia Campaign Ever?

During a job interview, a game producer once asked me what I thought was the best transmedia experience in the last five years. This was in 2011, so I quickly rummaged through my memory and recalled all the huge successes in transmedia since 2006 – *Halo 3* and the *I Love Bees* alternative reality game (ARG); *The Dark Knight* and *Why So Serious?* ARG; *lonelyGirl15*; *Prom Queen* … Then it hit me.

In late 2007, Barack Obama eclipsed Hillary Clinton as the Democratic favorite for the 2008 Presidential election. Every story about him – be it in commercials, news pieces, interviews – painted a very compelling portrait of a junior senator from Illinois who had a chance at making history. While the conventional media swooned over him, social media showed that Obama wasn't just a news item or novelty; he was a personal hero to voiceless millions who were excited about a genuine change candidate. Through sharing news pieces about him and engaging in conversation with friends over Facebook, voters cemented their loyalty. They would serve as devoted soldiers in his army of "clicktivists" or social media warriors in today's nomenclature. Without having any connection to his campaign, fans would do their part to get people excited about his candidacy. They did it out of pure enthusiasm for a man who rekindled people's faith in the democratic process.

Fans would soon create their own videos – granted, without much production value – that complemented those that the Obama campaign created themselves. The online discussions and videos were owned by a younger demographic, particularly young Gen-Xers and Millennials.

By the time the results of the Iowa caucuses came in, Barack Obama had quickly emerged as the clear frontrunner. Losses in New Hampshire, South Carolina, and many Super Tuesday states had tightened the race in Hillary Clinton's favor. But by February 12, 2008, after winning District of Columbia, Maryland, and Virginia, Obama signaled to the world that his momentum was just beginning. His path to becoming the first African American candidate for President of a major political party was sealed.

Thereafter, Obama's presence was everywhere – social media, TV ads, live events (rallies, interviews, debates), even in video games.[19] His story was clear: change. No matter what outlet he was on, people knew that voting for Barack Obama was about voting for a completely new look, new way, and new attitude of what it means to be president … and to be an American. Americans were in the midst of a terrible economy, created by the old guard. Nearly seven years of unpopular wars decimated our morale. This was brought on, once again, by the old guard. Barack Obama was a superhero, who would free us from the grips of selfish politicians, warmongers, and corrupt bankers.

His campaign was transmedia storytelling at its finest. His story was clear in every media touchpoint: we knew who the characters were (protagonist: Barack Obama; antagonist: the Establishment *a la* Hillary Clinton, George W. Bush, and John McCain), and we saw the rise of his heroism amidst escalating burdens (the 3 am White House Telephone Call ad; the Muslim extremist accusations; the collapse of Lehman Brothers).

The year 2008 was an exciting time to be a voter, to be an American. It was also an exciting time to witness one of the greatest stories about a politician to unfold before our eyes. My telling this is neither an endorsement nor a rejection of Barack Obama. It is, instead, a depiction of how transmedia storytelling can be a powerful force in our lives.

THE BASICS

What can writers learn from the Barack Obama campaign as it applies to transmedia storytelling? While not all IP or brands are the same, there are several immutable guidelines to adopt when telling one's story across different media platforms.

Identify the main medium of the anchor property. What is the main medium through which the hero's story is told? Is it a film that will have sequels? If so, then the transmedia extensions will serve as their connective tissue. Similar thinking must be applied to a TV show. Will digital videos tie one season to the next during a hiatus (like in *The Office: The Accountants* in 2006)? Or will it be webcomics to galvanize excitement from episode to episode, as we saw from 2006 to 2010 with the TV series *Heroes*? Or is the focus on a figure, like a presidential candidate? In this case, the anchor property is where that type of figure (read: politician) will get the most attention. Typically, that is through television. Each major appearance (like a debate or a nomination acceptance speech) will be the climactic moments to which all the transmedia extensions build up.

Make the hero clear and upfront. One should let their audience know whom the story is about at any given moment and why we should care about them. Without this, the creator has nothing.

A story must migrate from at least two different media platforms in a meaningful way. Telling a story from one television series to another is not an example of transmedia. That is a strict example of a crossover. It's a very popular strategy in television, in particular, as it drives audiences from one show to the other in the hope that both shows retain new viewers after the crossover storyline is complete. *The Practice* and *Ally McBeal* did this in the late '90s, as did *Magnum PI* and *Simon & Simon* in the '80s. It's more common today within the Marvel Universe. Before the Netflix relationship with Disney came to a close in 2019 – which eventually led to the creation of the Disney+ streaming service – beloved Marvel characters like Daredevil, Jessica Jones, Iron Fist, and Luke Cage made appearances in the others' shows as a lead up to *The Defenders* (2017) Netflix TV series. (Cameo crossovers happen not too infrequently on Disney+ on shows like *Loki* (2021–2023) and *She-Hulk: Attorney at Law* (2022)). In the DC universe, Flash and Green Arrow had been crossing over into each other's shows on the CW since the 2014/2015 season.

But transmedia storytelling requires more. In fact, the name itself implies traveling across ("trans") different media. *Quantum Break* (video game/TV mini-series) and *Batman: Arkham Asylum* (game franchise/comic series) are popular examples of a story continuing from one medium to the next as an expansion of or buildup to the gaming experience.

Be consistent with the sentiment across all platforms. If one divides a story into four parts and assigns each part to a new medium, make sure the spirit of the story remains the same. Viewers or players might consume these parts out of order, so one will want them to feel something about the hero's story that's consistently told. One should reinforce the positivity the viewers have about the hero and the world.

Discoverability is everything! If the consumer is only familiar with one medium of a campaign (e.g., digital videos), one needs to make sure there is information somewhere within that medium (either as an end credit or as part of the description underneath the video itself) to drive people to the other media. And one needs to make this process as easy to find as possible, even if it compromises some of the immersion. Navigation is crucial.

Know the endpoint and make sure everything leads to it. Knowing how and when one's campaign ends will dictate the following: (1) when certain media is released; (2) what the media type is, per release; and (3) what part of the story will be released. This requires a very specific plotting of each release and can resemble the story milestones described in Chapter 7 – "Structure" – of this book. If, however, one is not putting out a single story, but multiple stories, then they must keep the endpoint in mind and view every media release before the tentpole premiere *as its own medium.* It's important to map out the 30,000-foot view of the experience from beginning to end. A structure diagram similar to what is provided in Chapter 12 will be a good starting point. Then one should ask themself: Under which act of the experience does the media extension fall? Does it continue where the previous medium left off? If so, assign structural milestones inside each extension. Or is each extension completely new and separate from one another? Then they should adopt the grammar for that medium and craft a self-contained structure for it. Refer to Chapter 7 to adapt one's story beats accordingly.

Encourage fan participation. The IP has "made it" when fans start creating their own media related to it. This shows organic brand activism. IP stakeholders will want to encourage this more because a dedicated fanbase, even if small, will consume the IP in large doses and endlessly advocate for it. These brand activists could be social media influencers, who discuss the product over YouTube, Twitch, X, TikTok, Reddit, Discord, and Instagram and consequently promote its brand to their vast following. Another incarnation of a brand activist is a fan fiction author, who writes alternative plotlines to an established book often without the author's permission. While changing the names of the characters and adding slight alterations to the plot can lead to a massive success without fear of a lawsuit,[20] most fan fiction has no intention of getting published or catapulting a fledgling author to stardom. Its goal is to pay homage to an IP that has brought tremendous joy to a devoted following and to encourage them to let their imagination run wild with the characters they love so much. What this generates is long-term excitement for a brand or IP; therefore, when its next installment is launched, devoted fans will be champing at the bit to buy/see/play/read it and tell their friends about it, thereby increasing the consumer base. Movies, games, and books are no longer self-contained media experiences. At bare minimum, the creators will be reaching out to fans through social media. Fans will, in turn, continue the conversation *ad infinitum* with other fans. If they feel slighted in any way, sales, ratings, viewership, or any other form of consumer goodwill will diminish. With so much competition out there, a brand or IP cannot afford to omit fans at any point of its promotion.

Know the grammar of each medium through which the story is migrating. Writing for television is not the same as writing for games. Writing for games is not the same as writing for comics. Writing for comics is not the same as writing for a live event. Writing for a live event is not the same as writing for a podcast. You get the picture. Each medium requires a different ruleset, including length, where to focus one's attention, what the modality is (visual, audio, etc.), and more. When a story crosses numerous media pathways, fans will not appreciate a "shoe-horned" story experience in a comic if they know it's a better fit for a film. The IP will be judged not just as a holistic experience, but also for its disparate parts.

THE PURPOSE

It's very easy for storytellers to "geek out" on how their story is told. (Often, this zealous focus can take away from the quality of the story itself, so beware.) Without knowing one's audience, however, a person runs the risk of creating a transmedia experience just for the sake of it. That's a waste of time and money; even more so, a vacant transmedia experience diminishes the story and burns consumer goodwill. *Defiance* (2013–2015) is a perfect example of this. This obscure TV show on the Syfy Network thought it could push the boundaries of storytelling by offering a supplemental, but thinly related MMO. Neither the TV show nor the game was any good, and abysmal ratings and miniscule daily active users of the game killed the franchise.

Therefore, it's crucial to identify the business case for the transmedia campaign before one pursues it. Consider:

- *Brand reinforcement and brand omnipresence.* Once one identifies the anchor property of the experience, they need to use the transmedia connective tissue not only to continue the story of the anchor property but also to create awareness of it. They need to have a presence on all social media platforms to reinforce the brand but should refrain from typical marketing. "*Superhero X comes to theaters on March 23rd*" is exactly what to avoid. Instead, one should use the voices of the characters from *Superhero X* to engage the audience and include the requisite hashtags and @s to drive viewers to the typical marketing accounts. They should always remember they are telling a story, so it's crucial to sustain the immersion.

- *Expansion of the fiction.* Before the launch of every *Assassin's Creed* video game sequel, game publisher Ubisoft partnered up with comic publishers, traditional publishers, and animation production teams to expand the fiction in their respective medium as a way to spur excitement for the game. It worked both ways, of course: a popular video game franchise would also spark sales for the other media. Through licensing, the books and comics also offered a secondary income stream for Ubisoft. But the primary goal of these transmedia extensions was to create awareness for new customers of the game. If, for instance, someone stumbles upon the book or comic and likes what they read, perhaps they'll buy the game.

- *Consumer goodwill.* Transmedia experiences are effective because they appeal to a consumer's convenience. Thanks to social media and mobile technologies, one can visit the social media accounts of an IP at their leisure; same too with reading a webcomic or watching a digital short on their phone. These disruptive technologies have upended the traditional "water cooler moment," where people would convene in the office to discuss what happened in last night's episode of a favorite show or an opening of a highly anticipated movie. With the exception of a popular sports event (like the Super Bowl or the final game of the NBA Finals) or an awards show (like the Oscars, though those numbers aren't as strong as they once were), there is little in the media marketplace today that is universally watched at the same time, thus preventing the gathering of people to talk about it. Audiences today are fractured. Today's surfeit of media has made consumers highly selective, hyperspecialized, and incredibly demanding. When they devote their time to a movie, game, show, or book, they're all in. They will binge-watch a series in an entire weekend, read all the social media responses about it, and consume all of the other supporting media. With that level of commitment from consumers, content creators cannot – under any circumstances – under-serve their fanbase. There's a ton of competition out there, so the fans can go elsewhere quickly. Also, the fans' level of enthusiasm of an IP corresponds to the IP's longevity. Fan intensity and positivity have a strong financial impact on an IP. They will buy all the merchandise related to it. Capturing and sustaining their enthusiasm are not only about profit, however. The more valuable currency is conversation. The more the fans discuss an IP on social media (or even traditional media), the more others become aware of it and consume it. If the fanbase senses they are being disrespected, conversation will not only sour but also will eventually halt. By then, the IP is dead in the water.

- *KPIs.* Lastly, one will need to determine what will make the transmedia experience a success. Key performance indicators (KPIs) such as increased followers on social media, sales figures for transmedia extensions (like e-books or ad revenue for a YouTube series), and merchandising sales are good markers of the effectiveness of the transmedia. More importantly, did the anchor property get considerably more ratings/box office receipts/sales as a result of the campaign? Determining specific numbers for each KPI will help drive the budget and make sound creative decisions. Regarding the latter, creative decisions can be altered in the middle of a campaign if certain characters or plot points in the transmedia extensions are not being well received. Granted, the changes cannot be wholesale and will be moderate at best. For instance, if a character from a graphic novel is not trending well two months before the premiere of a film, it's impossible to change that character in that upcoming film. However, the social media accounts for these characters can change instantly or at least address what's not tracking well. Last-minute viral videos can mollify discontent. At the very least, the data from these consumer reactions can effectuate meaningful changes in the next media installment. Fans might have to wait a while, especially if the anchor property is a film or video game. Sequels take time to develop.

TWO KINDS OF TRANSMEDIA EXPERIENCES

When crafting a campaign, a writer needs to determine how immersive one wants the experience to be. Do they want fans to have 100% engagement through the characters of the fiction? Is there a breaking-the-fourth-wall moment where characters will talk to fans to inform them of, say, a launch of a related app? Or will that marketing ploy kill the fiction? Above all, they must identify how patient and enthusiastic their fanbase is. Are fans dedicated enough to follow every coordinate of the story's migration? Are they tech-savvy enough to engage in interactive moments? Are they extroverted enough to participate in a live event? A proper gauge of the fans' appetite will dictate what kind of transmedia experience to create.

A Pure, Singular Story Experience aka Unified Story Experience

As mentioned earlier in this chapter, a pure transmedia experience aims to tell one unified story across different media. Imagine if the first season of Disney's *Daredevil* was repurposed accordingly: Matt Murdock's initial rise as Daredevil and threat to archnemesis Wilson Fisk happen in five episodes of a Netflix series. Then, the media consumer continues the Daredevil's path toward taking down Fisk in a video game. But before Fisk is arrested (like in the first season of the show), the media consumer experiences Daredevil and Fisk's final confrontation in a graphic novel.

Realistically, only some fans will travel with the story from one medium to the next. Pure transmedia experiences are for the true fans, the afore-mentioned story zealots, the "content whales,"[21] and they will go along for a ride with an IP until the car runs out of gas. But for everyone else (i.e., the majority), one cannot design the story experience to have its biggest moments in its smallest media. That's just not good business savvy. Whether it's the death of a sidekick or the destruction of a home planet, certain moments are so profound that they must be delivered through the medium that attracts the most eyeballs and the biggest dollars (once again, the tentpole or anchor property). That medium is usually a film, video game, or TV series. Comics, novels, digital series, amusement park rides, and other extensions have a supplemental purpose in transmedia to explain past story beats, reconnect fans with beloved supporting characters they find fun and charming, reveal mysteries of the lore, or carry forward minor plot points introduced in the anchor property.

I classify these transmedia off-shoots as **"in the wild"** because they can easily live independently of the anchor property, even if they push forward minor plot points to or from it. A creator may never know if a player or consumer found their way to the tentpole product through the transmedia extension. Nor can the creator control how a player or consumer will experience the story. Do they play the game first and then check out the comic series? Do they read the comic series first, put it down, and pick up the game months later and forget the connection between the two? Again, there's no controlling the behaviors of fans. And that should not be a pri-ority for creators. Examples of pure, singular story experiences with "in the wild" transmedia include *The Matrix* franchise (three films, three video games, and an anime are directly connected in telling a unified story); the game *Batman: Arkham Asylum* (2009) and the comic *The Road to Arkham* (2009); *Forward unto Dawn* digital series and *Halo 4* video game (both released in 2012); *Til Morning's Light* (2015) video game and its audiobook *Til Morning's Light: The Private Blog of Erica Page* (2014); *lonelygirl15* (2006–2008) digital series and its alternate reality games (ARGs).[22]

To guarantee that fans will travel from the original medium to another, one may want to **design for a closed ecosystem** – as in, a multimedia or multimodal experience within one product that is interacted upon the moment someone buys it (or streams it or downloads it). *Quantum Break* (2016), for example, is an experience that is part video game, part TV series. A player could not watch the series on television at a specific time of day. It was sealed on the disc on the game, and episodes would unlock after a player successfully accomplished objectives. Everything was "on rails," which meant a player couldn't unlock an episode without playing through a specific proscribed path. The YA novel *Cathy's Book: If Found Call (650) 266-8233* (2006) by Sean Stewart and Jordan Weisman was designed as a closed ecosystem as well. Readers could take part in an ARG just by following clues from the pages of the book.

Fractured Story Experience

The other type of transmedia experience, also mentioned earlier in this chapter, takes into account that most fans will not have the bandwidth or interest to follow the evolution of a single-story experience across various media. However, because they like the characters of the world so much, fans will consume whatever they can just as long as it doesn't require too much time or devotion. A fractured story experience is the most popular form of transmedia storytelling. Creators cannot expect the consumer to buy every comic, watch every digital series, or play every level of a single game to a franchise they've paid good money for. The average consumer does not want the pressure to follow everything. Expecting too much of them is inviting disaster. People consume entertainment to escape, not to do homework.

Under this framework, this transmedia experience doesn't tell a single story that ties all the disparate media together. This framework relies, instead, on lighter connective tissue between the tentpole[23] releases. Supporting characters, commonly traveled worlds, and shared fictional events that are referred to from tentpole to tentpole are sufficient connective tissue. Fans won't feel like they are missing out if they didn't play the last installment of the *Defiance* MMO even though they watched every episode of the show. Or an introduction of a new character (Hana Gitelman) in a *Heroes* episode will be exciting for fans of the TV series, but it might seem redundant to those who read the webcomic religiously. The stories in the MMO and webcomic take on a life of their own, but must be designed thoughtfully in order to feel related to their anchor properties.

The Clone Wars (2008–2020) animated series has done a fairly good job at expanding the *Star Wars* prequel mythology in between *Episode II: Attack of the Clone Wars* (2002) and *Episode III: Revenge of the Sith* (2005). One doesn't have to watch the animated series to understand what's going on in the sequels. However, *The Clone Wars* is an excellent source of expanding the fictional universe of *Star Wars* and providing retroactive "aha" moments when lore references are made in the films.

And, of course, there are experiences that can be too fractured. Take, for instance, *The X-Files* (1993–2018). At the height of its popularity in the late 1990s, *The X-Files* TV series did something that no series did at that point: it had a mainstream release of a blockbuster film – *The X-Files: Fight the Future* (1998). In fact, it generated over $189 million in worldwide box office revenue.[24] Despite its success, the movie was written as a self-contained story so that newcomers to the franchise didn't need to watch the series to understand what's going on. However, loyal fans of the show found the writing to be disjointed and inelegant. The momentum of the conflicts with old enemies, such as the Cigarette Smoking Man, was undercut and derailed in an effort to focus on new villains in the film. By the time the next season started, there was no reference to any of the new characters from the film. It was as if it never existed. The film was basically a 2-hour episode with the occasional swear word.

The X-Files film was an isolated moment in the lore of the show, and ultimately a cheap exploitation of fan loyalty. For something as big as a feature film seen by a fanbase as vast as any TV show up to that moment, the show creators were obliged to move the franchise forward. This means that whatever happened in the film must have, at least, a minor downstream effect on the next season of the series, such as expansion of the lore or new juicy secrets about characters we've been invested in for five years. That was not the case. Sadly, this was a missed opportunity as was the next film *The X-Files: I Want to Believe* (2008).

Sacrificial Lambs

There will be some media that won't get high ratings or purchases. That's not their goal. They exist solely to bridge the gaps between one big-budget medium to the next. The American version of the TV series *The Office* (2005–2013) produced a digital series entitled *The Accountants* (2006), which premiered in the summer before the third season. The ten episodes of the digital series aired on the NBC website on Thursday and were no more than 3 minutes apiece. The series won a Creative Emmy for "Outstanding Broadband Program – Comedy" in 2007.[25] The producers of the show continued to produce a new digital series for subsequent seasons. In 2008, the digital series was split into two installments: once in the summer, once during a mid-season hiatus. In 2009–2011, the two installments varied in release dates. Each installment was a different story arc and continued to focus on the supporting characters of the show.

The purpose, from a narrative perspective, was to provide deeper explorations of characters that didn't have much screen time in the regular series. From a business standpoint, the digital series was a device that galvanized fanbase loyalty and excitement. It didn't matter if the content was short; it just mattered to feed the fans so that they could continue watching the show. That, in many ways, is the bulk of the work of transmedia: to provide continual content in between seasons or tentpole sequels. "Feed the beast," as I call it. Fans want to be nourished and tended to. Without a high-budget film running a perpetual story 24/7, the next best thing is "bread-crumbing" content to fans through transmedia continually.

MEDIA RELEASE STRATEGIES

A compelling transmedia campaign will design everything around the anchor property. The lead-in to its release is the most important part of the entire campaign. Books, a digital series, or a comic series excite the fanbase and "prime the pump" for the anchor property's release.

As part of the *Alien* franchise, the producers of the film *Prometheus* (2012) launched a series of digital shorts on YouTube, months before the film's opening in June. Each served as a backstory fragment of the life of the film's antagonist, Peter Weyland. The number of hits was modest, but the box office for the film surpassed $400 million. It's possible that the digital shorts, which featured actors from the movie, suffered from issues of discoverability, not of quality.

Games have done a much better job at prepping the release of tentpole products than film or TV has. *Halo, Mass Effect,* and *Assassin's Creed* have achieved long-term success in extending the universe of their games through books, comics, board games, animated features, and web series. That's why the transmedia release schedule is very critical. How to carry the interest of fans is part art, part science. When are fans more likely to buy the IP's books and comics? This is a question answered through competitive analysis. When are one's rivals putting out their next game? When is the market least saturated? Which months does the IP's prime demographic spend the most money? These are the science questions.

The main art question is "How does one prevent overexposure of an IP?" Fans are fickle. When they've had enough, they'll let the IP owners know by not consuming their product. By then, it'll be too late because there will be no other chances to regain their interest. That's why it's important to involve user researchers early on to test the "stickiness" of an IP and use their data to pivot strategies. A robust transmedia campaign is ideal, but if one's team is not in sync with their fanbase's level of oversaturation, it doesn't matter how great the content is. The IP is done.

Smart transmedia campaigns cluster content around the release of the anchor property. There's usually a book or comic series release a week to a month before the game comes out. Additional media will come out a day to a month afterward. A good example is a weekly digital series, like *Halo: Nightfall* (2014) (see Figure 14.2). The weekly episodes should provide enough momentum for the IP to endure well after its release date. Reviewers and fans will take it from there. There might be more related media that come out toward the end of the year as a way to generate interest for Christmas.

If the IP is an ongoing franchise with a big tentpole product release every three years (as many big games have), then studios can fill in the gap years with the releases of lesser-budgeted games for console, mobile, or PC. *Lower hanging fruit is the key here.* As such, books and comics will come to market as well, not only to support these smaller game releases but also to pique the interest of the fanbase and retain their loyalty until the next tentpole product release. The following graph is a transmedia timeline for the *Halo* franchise, one of the biggest tentpole franchises in Microsoft's entire games portfolio (as well as one of the biggest game franchises ever).

Figure 14.2 *Halo* transmedia timeline. (See full-scale version of this graph at www.routledge.com/9781032571614.)

Its two-plus decades as a successful video game franchise are not only a testament to its being a great game; its sustained transmedia storytelling through books, comics, and digital series has been a crucial factor as well. The graph starts from the initial release of *Halo* (2001) and ends at the release of *Halo 5* (2015), a limited focus to illustrate the height of *Halo's* popularity as a video game series. Due to the vast output of the franchise, not all of the transmedia extensions are represented here (Figure 14.2).

FINAL THOUGHTS ON TRANSMEDIA

How stories are told will continue to advance with technology. Storytelling will also evolve with the media consumption patterns of the fanbase. Media that can be accessed any time but on a constant drip feed – no matter the length or the source of that media – is the future. Storytellers will need to learn how to shape the content output and harness it to avoid, what I call, IP fatigue. Yes, there can be too much of a good thing. Even Bob Iger, during his second stint as CEO of Disney, bemoaned the oversaturation of sequels of Disney-owned IP in a televised interview in the fall of 2023.[26] Dwindling sales/gross receipts/ratings of a beloved franchise are inevitable. But the opportunity is extending the life of the franchise at the right pace. An IP creator should be like *Seinfeld*: One should never overstay their welcome. They should leave at the top of their game, so that consumer goodwill remains positive and enduring.

Not all franchises need to have transmedia. That's something a team will need to determine. Will their players appreciate the extension of the game's world outside of the gaming experience? If so, which media will the players gravitate to? How much should the team feed their playerbase so that the playerbase is excited to play their game?

Lastly, transmedia storytelling isn't a necessary component of the narrative of a game. However, it is strongly recommended to adopt if one's goal is to create an enduring franchise that feeds its customers wherever they're consuming media. It is likely that a gamer is on social media and digital platforms like Twitch, TikTok, and YouTube, either sharing their love of the game or following someone who does. Transforming that from a spectator experience into a story experience is a delicate one. Success depends heavily on how one wants to use the fiction of their game to penetrate these sacred areas. They might want to keep the spectator element completely free from the fiction. If not, transmedia storytelling through the "Fractured Story Experience" framework will be their best option.

NOTES

1 Chatfield, "Video Games Now Outperform Hollywood Movies" 2009.

2 Shieber, "Video Game Revenue Tops $43 Billion" 2019.

3 Entertainment Software Association, "U.S. Consumer Video Game Spending" 2023.

4 Ault, "Survey: YouTube Stars" 2014.

5 Shows that are created specifically for digital platforms like Hulu and Netflix are excluded from this category. Their content is closely aligned to the formats of cable and network shows.

6 Story, in this case, is one hero's journey that is either finite or persistent. The focus is on their life and how they react to actions by other characters or events in their world. I delve into another type of transmedia experience that is "less" pure but more common, under the section "Fractured Story Experience."

7 Platform, in this context, refers to a showcase of content, often technological, like apps, online games, social media sites, streaming services, or even an interactive toy or robot. It could also refer to a live experience, like theater, amusement park rides, or even alternate reality games.

8 Also known as the "anchor property," the tentpole project is the flagship media product that's supposed to attract the most fans for a single franchise within a specific segment of time within the life cycle of that franchise. For instance, a certain franchise launches a video game every three years. A specific segment of time could refer to *TBD Franchise Part III* that will launch by Year 9 of the life cycle of the franchise. Transmedia professionals and franchise planners will need to determine the media extensions to come out before and after *TBD Franchise Part III*'s launch to create greater awareness of it to drive sales. The tentpole project will receive the lion's share of a franchise's budget for its assigned segment of time.

9 Jenkins (2006, p. 113).

10 A major continuity issue between the second and third films centered on the change in appearance of the Oracle character. The game's fiction retro-actively explained the character's physical change as a result of an attack by Merovingian. In reality, actress Gloria Foster (who played Oracle) had passed away and was replaced by Mary Alice in *The Matrix Revolutions*.

11 Quick note: the Wachowskis wrote and directed both the live action films and the video games, with the exception of the MMO.

12 The MMO came out in 2005, but in the story chronology of the franchise, it actually takes places before the fiction of *The Matrix Revolutions*, which came out in 2003.

13 Jenkins (2006, p. 120).

14 Cavalli, "Halo Novel Becomes NYT Best Seller" 2007.

15 Video Game Sales Wiki, "Halo" n.d.

16 VGChartz, "Halo 3" n.d.
17 AppMagic, "Annual Revenue Generated by Pokémon GO Worldwide" 2024.
18 Rodriguez et al., "TikTok Parent ByteDance Battles Meta" 2023.
19 Gorman, "Obama Buys First Video Game Ads" 2008.
20 *Fifty Shades of Grey*, for instance, was originally an R-rated fan fiction exploration of the *Twilight* characters that was published as a novel in 2011 and then adapted into a film in 2015.
21 "Whales" typically refer to high-value customers who spend an inordinate amount of money on all the offerings of a single product, service, or brand. In video games, they will spend exponentially more money on microtransactions (console) or in-app purchases (mobile) than an average player will, and they will buy or consume most or all of the related media and merchandise that launch outside of the game.
22 Upon full disclosure, I was a writer for the latter two IPs as well as a narrative designer for the previously mentioned *Quantum Break*.
23 For further reference on the strategies behind tentpole releases in traditional entertainment, check out Anita Elberse's *Blockbusters: Hit-Making, Risk-taking, and the Big Business of Entertainment* (2013).
24 Box Office Mojo, "The X-Files" 1998.
25 IMDB, "The Office: The Accountants" 2007.
26 New York Times Events, "Bog Iger, Disney's C.E.O." 2023.
27 For additional visual representation of *The Matrix* story chronology, which includes the comics, check out Geoffrey Long's *Transmedia Storytelling: Business, Aesthetics and Production at the Jim Henson Company*, pp. 15–18.

REFERENCES

AppMagic. (2024, February 7). "Annual Revenue Generated by Pokémon GO Worldwide from 2016 to 2023 (in million U.S. dollars) [Graph]." In *Statista*. Retrieved on February 11, 2024 from www-statista-com.libproxy2.usc.edu/statistics/882474/pokemon-go-all-time-player-spending/

Ault, Susanne. (2014, August 5). "Survey: YouTube Stars More Popular than Mainstream Celebs Among U.S. Teens." Retrieved on February 10, 2024 from https://variety.com/2014/digital/news/survey-youtube-stars-more-popular-than-mainstream-celebs-among-u-s-teens-1201275245/

Box Office Mojo. (1998). "The X-Files." Retrieved on February 10, 2024 from www.boxofficemojo.com/movies/?id=x-filesfightthefuture.htm

Cavalli, Earnest. (2007, November 20). "Halo Novel Becomes NYT Best Seller, Just Like My Novel Jurassic Park." Retrieved on February 10, 2024 from www.destructoid.com/halo-novel-becomes-nyt-best-seller-just-like-my-novel-jurassic-park-55076.phtml

Chatfield, Tom. (2009, September 27). "Videogames Now Outperform Hollywood Movies." Retrieved on February 9, 2024 from www.theguardian.com/technol ogy/gamesblog/2009/sep/27/videogames-hollywood

Elberse, Anita. (2013). *Blockbusters: Hit-making, Risk-taking, and the Big Business of Entertainment*. New York: Henry Holt and Co.

Entertainment Software Association. (2023, January 17). "U.S. Consumer Video Game Spending Totaled $56.6 Billion in 2022." Retrieved on February 9, 2024 from www.theesa.com/news/u-s-consumer-video-game-spending-tota led-56-6-billion-in-2022/

Gorman, Steve. (2008, October 17). "Obama Buys First Video Game Campaigns Ads." Retrieved on February 10, 2024 from www.reuters.com/article/idUSTR E49EAGL/

IMDB. (2007). "The Office: The Accountants (Awards)." Retrieved on February 10, 2024 from www.imdb.com/title/tt0840149/awards/

Jenkins, Henry. (2006). *Convergence Culture*. New York and London: New York University Press, p. 113.

Long, Geoffrey. (2007, June). *Transmedia Storytelling: Business, Aesthetics and Production at the Jim Henson Company*. [Master of Science dissertation.] Massachusetts Institute of Technology, Cambridge, MA.

New York Times Events. (2023, November 30). *Bob Iger, Disney's C.E.O., on How the Movie Business Is Changing | DealBook Summit 2023*. YouTube. Retrieved on February 10, 2024 from www.youtube.com/watch?v=8pSxx1e5n34

Rodriguez, Salvador, Meghan Bobrowsy, and Jeff Horwitz. (2023, April 13). "TikTok Parent ByteDance Battles Meta for Virtual-Reality App Developers." Retrieved on February 10, 2024 from www.wsj.com/articles/tiktok-parent-bytedance-battles-meta-for-virtual-reality-app-developers-30ce091f

Shieber, Jonathan. (2019, January). "Video Game Revenue Tops $43 Billion in 2018, an 18% Jump from 2017." Retrieved on February 9, 2024 from https://techcrunch.com/2019/01/22/video-game-revenue-tops-43-bill ion-in-2018-an-18-jump-from-2017/

VGChartz. (n.d.) "Halo 3." Retrieved on February 10, 2024 from www.vgchartz. com/game/6964/halo-3/?region=All

Video Game Sales Wiki. (n.d.) "Halo." Retrieved on February 10, 2024 from https:// vgsales.fandom.com/wiki/Halo

CHAPTER 15

College and University Programs

LIST OF UNIVERSITIES FOR GAME DEVELOPMENT

If you're looking to pursue a degree in game development, there is a growing list of colleges and universities to choose from. In fact, you'll find some of the most prestigious institutions in engineering on that list. They understand that video games aren't some flimsy diversion; they are a lucrative business that requires as much programming and design savvy as traditional software does ... maybe even more so. These schools continue to develop robust design and engineering programs, either as an adjunct to a major or as a major itself, to train the next generation of innovators in entertainment and interactive technology.

The following list is not comprehensive by any means, but it should give you a broad view of the types of institutions out there, be they for-profit or non-profit, public or private. To qualify for inclusion on this list, the school must confer a Bachelor's, Master's, or certificate in game development or design *and* offer (or have offered) at least one course in game narrative. If a university offers a game writing course in a department such as English or Creative Writing but does not have a major in game development, that school will not be included here. Omission from this list also applies to schools that offer a game development program but have never offered a game writing class. University of Southern California, Rensselaer Polytechnic Institute, and Worcester Polytechnic Institute have

DOI: 10.1201/9781003438113-15

been pretty consistent in their offerings of narrative coursework for close to ten years (if not more so). For a school's program updates, check out the provided URLs.

I've included some of the following institutions mainly because I have worked directly with many of their alumni and can vouch for their high level of preparedness. For the other schools, I have included them based on the pedigree of their game writing faculty. And yes, as mentioned in the forward of this book, I have taught at three institutions on this list. Whether you interpret that as bias or not, they are still worth exploring; courses in game writing and narrative design remain scarce in institutions across the world.

There are plenty of alumni from other great schools doing great work. I recommend checking out those institutions at www.gamedesigning.org/category/schools/ for more information.

Not-for-profit, Private Colleges/Universities

- **ArtCenter College of Design**

  Entertainment Design (Game Design Track)

  Pasadena, CA

  www.artcenter.edu/academics/undergraduate-degrees/entertainment-design/tracks/game-design.html

  Offers: Bachelor of Science in Entertainment Design (Game Design Track)

- **Carnegie Mellon University**

  Entertainment Technology Center

  Pittsburgh, PA

  www.etc.cmu.edu

  Offers: Master of Entertainment Technology[1]

- **Champlain College**

  Division of Communication & Creative Media

  Burlington, VT

  www.champlain.edu/academics/undergraduate-academics/majors-and-programs/interactive-narrative-for-games-and-digital-media

  Offers: Bachelor of Science in Interactive Narrative for Games & Digital Media.[2]

- **New York University**

  Interactive Telecommunications Program (part of Tisch School of the Arts)

  New York, NY

  https://tisch.nyu.edu/itp

  Offers: Bachelor of Fine Arts in Interactive Media Arts; Master of Professional Studies; Master of Arts in Interactive Media Arts (1-year low residency)

- **Rensselaer Polytechnic Institute**

  Games and Simulation and Arts and Sciences

  Troy, NY

  www.hass.rpi.edu/pl/gaming

  Offers: Bachelor of Science in Games and Simulation Arts and Sciences; Master of Science in Critical Game Design (Co-Terminal Program); PhD in Critical Game Design; Master of Science in Critical Game Design (Co-Terminal Program)

- **Rochester Institute of Technology**

  Game Design, Development, and Arts

  Rochester, NY

  www.rit.edu/study/game-design-development-and-arts

  Offers: Bachelor of Fine Arts in 3D Digital Design (Game Arts Option); Bachelor of Science in Game Design and Development (also offers a Minor); Master of Science in Game Design and Development

- **University of Southern California**

  Interactive Media & Games Division (part of the School of Cinematic Arts)

  Los Angeles, CA

  cinema.usc.edu/interactive/index.cfm

  Offers: Bachelor of Fine Arts in Game Art; Bachelor of Fine Arts in Game Development and Interactive Design; Master of Arts (Cinematic Arts (Media Arts, Games and Health)); Master of Science in Game Design and Development; Master of Fine Arts in Interactive Media & Games; Master of Fine Arts (Master of Fine Arts, Interactive Media (Games and Health)); Minors: Game

Animation; Game Audio; Game Design; Game Entrepreneurism; Game Studies; Game User Research; Immersive Media

- **Worcester Polytechnic Institute**

Interactive Media & Game Development (IMGD)

Worcester, MA

www.wpi.edu/academics/departments/interactive-media-game-development

Offers: Bachelor of Arts in Interactive Media & Game Development; Bachelor of Science in Interactive Media & Game Development (minor also offered); Master of Science in Interactive Media & Game Development; Master of Fine Arts in Interactive Media & Game Design; PhD in Computational Media. Students may pursue an IMGD Writing Concentration

Not-for-profit, Public Colleges/Universities

- **George Mason University**

Computer Game Design Program

Fairfax, VA

https://catalog.gmu.edu/colleges-schools/visual-performing-arts/computer-game-design/#coursestext

Offers: Bachelor of Fine Arts in Computer Game Design; Minor in Computer Game Design; Minor in Sport and Computer Game Design

- **Michigan State University**

Games and Interactive Media (department of Media and Information in the College of Communication Arts and Sciences)

East Lansing, MI

gamedev.msu.edu

Offers: Bachelor of Arts in Games and Interactive Media; Minor in Game Design and Development; Certificate in Serious Game Design and Research (Graduate Certificate (GRC2))

- **University of California, Irvine**

Donald Bren School of Information & Computer Sciences (Department of Informatics)

Irvine, CA

https://www.ics.uci.edu/about/

Offers: Bachelor of Science in Game Design and Interactive Media

- **University of California, Santa Cruz**

  Jack Baskin School of Engineering (Department of Computational Media)

  Division of Arts (Performance, Play & Design Departments)

  Santa Cruz, CA

  https://admissions.sa.ucsc.edu/majors/artgamemedia

  Offers: Bachelor of Science in Computer Game Design (at Baskin School); Bachelor of Arts in Art & Design: Games & Playable Media (at Division of Arts)

- **University of Central Florida**

  Florida Interactive Entertainment Academy (FIEA)

  Orlando, FL

  https://fiea.ucf.edu/

  Offers: Master of Science in Interactive Entertainment (with tracks in Production/Design, Art, or Programming)

- **University of Utah**

  Utah Division of Games

  Salt Lake City, UT

  https://games.utah.edu/

  Offers: Bachelor of Science in Games; Minor in Games; Bachelor of Science in Computer Science, Entertainment Arts and Engineering Emphasis (in conjunction with School of Computing); Master of Entertainment Arts and Engineering; Dual Master's degrees in Entertainment Arts & Engineering (MEAE) and Business Administration (MBA) (in conjunction with The David Eccles School of Business)

- **University of Washington**

  Professional & Continuing Education

  Seattle, WA

  https://www.pce.uw.edu/certificates/game-design

  Offers: Certificate in Game Design

For Profit, Private Colleges/Universities

- **DigiPen Institute of Technology**

  Redmond, WA; Singapore; Bizkaia, Spain

  www.digipen.edu/about

  Offers: Bachelor of Arts in Game Design; Bachelor of Science in Computer Science and Game Design; Bachelor of Science in Computer Science in Real-Time Interactive Simulation

- **Full Sail University**

  Game School

  Orlando, FL

  www.fullsail.edu/area-of-study/games

  Offers: Bachelor of Science in Game Business & Esports; Bachelor of Science in Game Development; Bachelor of Science in Interactive Technology (by way of a game design concentration); Bachelor of Science in Simulation & Visualization; Master of Science in Game Design

- **University of Silicon Valley**

  Department of Game Design & Development

  San Jose, CA

  https://usv.edu/academics/game-design-development/

  Offers: Bachelor of Arts in Game Art; Bachelor of Arts in Game Design; Bachelor of Science in Game Engineering

NOTES

1 Undergraduate students can seek a Minor in Game Design through the university's Integrative Design, Arts, and Technology program. Visit www.ideate.cmu.edu for more details.

2 Enrollment for the major begins in the Fall of 2025.

Index